Vegan Tea Time

James Ross Spencer II
Copyright 2018

Table of Contents

Soups (82)

Salads (105)

Tea Parties (148)

Bio (208)

Acknowledgments

James Spencer would like to thank the following for their support in the creation of this beautiful vegan tea recipe book and for their commitment to upholding the beautiful traditions of English high tea as well as support for the vegan movement and elegant Victorian décor.

Artwork and Cover Design: A special thanks goes out to the elegant Yvonne S. Pratt from *Stone Gable Blog: American Farmhouse Living* for the beautiful cover photo featured on the cover of this book. Yvonne's website is dedicated to elegant vintage American style, delicious recipes and gracious living. I think Yvonne takes some of the most elegant photos for table and tea settings I have ever seen. I'm truly honored that she agreed for me to use one of her photos for the book jacket. James Spencer designed the book cover.

Photography: The photos of James Spencer were taken by photographer Jeanne Wathier at *Chez Wathier*, Santa Ana and at *Entertainment Consultants*, Newport Beach, California.

To my extended family: I would like to thank the following people who have loved me unconditionally, and supported my artistic visions, my vegan recipes and the creation of this book. All of you inspire me: Arlene Korte, Koop Kooper, Rheinhardt Arnold, Dr. Jane Battenberg, , Rev. Donna Baranyay, Dr. Denise Estrada, Aram Barsamian, Barbara Bertrand, Robert Talley, *Peet's Tea* (Belmont Shore), *Harney and Sons Teas, Whole Food's Market* (Long Beach), *Lazy Acres* (Long Beach), Dale Carter, Linda Carpenter, Beverly Terfloth, Heidi Kuyper, and Joe Casey. I would also like to thank the vegan members of my immediate and extended family.

The Vintage Vegans: I would like to thank my "Vintage Vegans" from all over the world that supported me in spreading vegan high tea hosting around the world after the publication of my 2015 book *The Vintage Vegan*. Since then I'm delighted to report that many tea rooms around the world have adopted vegan and gluten free options, even local Southern California chain tea/coffee houses like *Peet's* offer vegan and gluten free scones, pastries and muffins with delicious high quality loose leaf tea. I couldn't be happier. I have loved receiving your delicious vegan recipes, photos of your elegant tea parties, and new fads and trends on the Vintage Vegan scene. My new 2018 book *Vegan Tea Time* is an updated replacement for *The Vintage Vegan,* with additional new recipes and tea party ideas for your enjoyment. I have included with permission a few recipes that I loved from the fans, as well as some of my new creations. I would love to hear from you on which recipes and tea party menus you have liked the best so feel free to write me at: spencermusicschool@gmail.com or visit **jamesrspencer.com.**

How To Use This Book

Vegan Tea Time contains nearly 300 unique and healthy vegan gourmet recipes that are associated with English afternoon and high tea ceremonies. Recipes include tea sandwiches, canapés, scones, soups, salads, desserts and additional beverages. The majority of the recipes are of easy to moderate difficulty in preparation. Feel free to explore the recipes that appeal to you and to incorporate them not only for your personal tea functions but also in your daily living. Many of these recipes are excellent for brunches, lunches or dinners. As you explore recipes bring your subtle awareness to how certain flavors pair well with specific high grade loose leaf tea choices. This is the art of vegan tea hosting. For the best quality and variety of loose leaf teas there are many companies to choose from. I personally prefer *Harney and Sons*. For residence of Southern California I also feel that *Peet's* have some high quality loose leaf teas that are accessible to the general tea fan. I especially enjoy their *Snow Leopard White Peony, Winter Solstice,* and *Irish Black Currant.*

I have included several recipe options for gluten-free, no-oil and sugar-free versions so all recipes should be accessible to all diets or health restrictions. In addition I have included a plethora of raw and no bake recipes for those following raw plant-based diet. Many recipes can also be made quickly when one is on a time crunch. I have included flavors from all over the world as well as vegan twists on traditional English tea favorites.

As a proud British descendant from the royal family of Spencer, I have always been fascinated by the favorite flavors in tea and pastries of Queen Elizabeth and my distant family relatives at Althrop. I have included "Spencer" recipes that are nearly 2 and sometimes 3 hundred years old tweaked to vegan perfection.

Veganism is a plant-based diet consisting of consuming (preferably organic) vegetables, fruit, seeds, nuts, legumes (beans and lentils) and whole grains. Vegans never consume meat, dairy and eggs. Though vegans are allowed to eat processed "vegan" alternatives for dairy such vegan mayonnaise and vegan cheeses, many of these products contain processed low-grade oils and are not recommended as a daily practice. I myself prefer to consume avocadoes, olives and hemp naturally instead of using oils. Also it should be noted that cooking with oils ads unnecessary fats and can "cook" or "fry' out essential nutrients. I myself prefer raw or lightly steamed vegetable preparations. One can sauté veggies for example with vegetable broth instead of oil. Of course it is a matter of belief, habits and taste. Many vegans also avoid processed refined sugars. You will find that many of the dessert and scones recipes are sweetened with coconut sugar, stevia leaf, xylitol, maple syrup or raw honey. Some argue that honey is not vegan, but I personally use it in many of my recipes as a natural sweetener, and of course it can add dimension to various tea pairings. You will find the recipes in this book especially adaptable to your needs. In addition many vegans also avoid grains that may cause allergy sensitivity and proneness to inflammation. Many of the recipes actually taste better using almond, rice, spelt or coconut flour to refined white flour. Again, feel free to experiment. You may adapt these recipes to your level of health, and favorite flavors.

It is useful to have a food processor, blendtec or vitamix and a high-speed blender. However, these tools are not absolutely necessary. They are adaptable usually to whatever is available in your personalized kitchen. I have personally tried many of these recipes in variants: food processors, nutribullet, blendtec, etc. The recipes are indeed adaptable. I also adapt to the kitchen I'm working in. Alas my current kitchen at my beachfront condo is not as large as I usually like to work in, so using smaller units like a nutria-bullet over a large blender works fine. Feel free to adapt to your own personal needs

It should be noted that all recipes including in *Vegan Tea Time* are either completely original recipes by James Spencer, recipes shared by permission from James' *Vintage Vegan* meet up group and expanded on, or carnivorous recipes completely revamped to vegan healthier options. James has taken liberty with traditional recipes such as *Caesar Salad,* rearranging traditional ingredients such as anchovy paste to vegan alternatives. Most vegan patrons report they really do not taste much of a difference. Your carnivore friends will truly be surprised how luxurious, rich, and glorious vegan preparation is. These recipes are elegant, sophisticated, surprising, and fun to prepare. You might even win over many meat eaters to a healthier vegan lifestyle (also saving them most likely years of disease, obesity, heart disease, diabetes and other disorders linked to heavy meat and dairy consumption). So you can feel good about sharing these recipes made with love with your family and friends.

Tea may be served anytime but there are specific times during the day where tea is most common in British culture. **Afternoon Tea** was served in England around 3-5 pm to the upper aristocratic classes. In England in the Victorian and Edwardian era, dinner was most often served quite late around 8 or 9 pm. *Afternoon Tea* was a light service of usually tea, finger sandwiches, scones and occasionally a small dessert that served to tie people over till formal dinnertime.

The working classes took *High Tea* as a larger meal often served around 6 pm. This was because many workers had to be available to serve in the aristocratic houses to prepare for aristocratic formal gatherings.

Many business working classes also worked into the evening hours. Contrary to popular belief *high tea* did not refer originally to the "high" upper classes but to the height of the table that tea was served on. A "high" table meant dinner table. *High Tea* was a heartier meal of sandwiches, soup, salad, a meat entrée and often a dessert. *Low Tea*, on the other hand refers to tea taken by aristocrats usually in lavish libraries, living rooms, salons or verandas/solariums on "low" tables or coffee tables.

At the end of the book James Spencer offer forty theme suggestions for tea parties as well as sample menu with recommended tea pairings. In addition James offer suggestions for flower arrangements, decorations, and suggested music. The menus offer several suggestions and do not feel you have to serve them all. Tea hosts often like to offer guests options such as a decaf or green tea alternative, soup or salad and a variety of tea sandwiches and canapés. Utilize all or just a few of the suggested menu items or create your own unique menus from the wonderfully diverse recipes in this book.

Mr. Spencer rarely serves all the food suggested. He likes to serve usually 2 or 3 tea sandwiches: One traditional sandwich (cucumber or watercress on white), one savory (herb or curry sandwich on wheat) and one fruit and vegan cheese usually on black bread. I will often serve a soup or a salad but rarely both unless I'm hosting high tea. I don't always serve a dessert unless I am throwing an evening gathering. Scones are usually the only sweet. Of course it is up to you and the needs of your guests. Nowadays it should be noted that *High Tea* might refer to any elegant tea gathering. I prefer light to heavy rich food preparation. I also believe most tearooms serve way too much food. I usually serve a couple of finger sandwiches, soup or salad, and scones with a delicious couple of tea pairings. When I'm just having a few friends over for afternoon tea, I might just make one pot, and either a couple of tea sandwiches or some hot baked scones with preserves or vegan lemon curd.

You might notice that though some tea themes have ethnic imagery such as: *Chinese New Year Tea Luncheon* or *Indian Yogi Tea and Kirtan*. I also include traditional English cuisine and only hints at ethnic cuisine. It is more traditional to do tea hosting this way from the traditional English tradition. Feel free to add your own tweaks and flavors to the recipes. You will find that many recipes are versatile as to flour, sweeteners and spices used. I prefer coconut sugar or maple syrup (B grade) to refined white sugar. I also prefer coconut, almond or spelt flour to unrefined wheat flour. I usually substitute cheap GMO laced soy products with organic unsweetened almond milk, coconut milk or rice milk. I also try to avoid cooking with oils that may go rancid quickly or just add unwanted calories. You will find many recipes in this book that may be made with no oils or fillers. Many of the recipes are no-bake and raw, making them super easy and super nutritious!

Some thoughts: In hosting a tea gathering take the time to create a beautiful and elegant mood with flowers, elegant tea pots and cups, china, silver and other touches. Background lighting such as dimmer switches, candles and tea lights can enhance the mood promoting intimate conversation and a relaxed atmosphere. Music choice is also essentially important. Tea time is about self-love, intimacy and sharing so take the time create a cozy environment.

As a concert pianist of jazz and classical repertoire, my albums are internationally recognized, streamed on digital radio stations and featured in podcast radio shows such as: *The Cocktail Nation, Penthouse Radio, The Drive In Lounge, The Vintage Lounge, Cool Jazz Connection, The Cocktail Piano Hour* and *The Martini Hour*. You can find my current available digital albums from my website jamesrspencer.com.

Feel free to be extravagant and eccentric. Anyone who knows me knows my passion for *Alice in Wonderland, Gothic Victorian, Steampunk, Edwardian England. Art Deco 1920s-1930s* and *Murder Parties*. Feel free to dream, and explore fantastic and outrageous tea hosting. Have fun. My belief is: *Tea Gatherings are a time of ritual purification from the stresses of everyday life and a time of deep sharing and intimacy. Teatime is an opportunity to practice elegance, manners, courtesy and sympathy for fellow humans and an opportunity to explore the health benefits of veganism while protecting and nurturing Mother Earth. Let it be your daily spiritual practice.*

James Spencer cannot remember a time when tea was not part of his daily lifestyle. As the oldest of six raised in Huntington Beach, California James was a highly intuitive, creative and musical child. Both parents are highly musical.

James showed extraordinary musical talent from an early age, and by age 6 Mr. Spencer was already concertizing performing Mozart, Beethoven and Chopin. One of James' fondest childhood memories was reading novels with his mother at bedtime. Little Jimmy had a magical nautical themed *Pirates of the Caribbean* bedroom equipped with a mirror in the shape of a ship's steering wheel, a treasure chest of toys and windows that were similar to a ship's galley. Jimmy's favorite childhood story was *Alice in Wonderland*. His mother would read this usually sipping a hot cup of *Apricot Ceylon, Earl Grey* or *English Breakfast* and nibbling on some ginger snaps. Little Jimmy was first introduced to the magical world of tea parties through the story of Alice and the Mad Hatter. Jimmy also had a stuffed Cheshire Cat (He still collects *Alice and Wonderland memorabilia* today). As a child Jimmy began imagining tea parties for his mom (The Queen), Cheshire Cat and the other *Wonderland* characters.

James grew up in an elegant Georgian style home. His parents had traveled to plantation houses in the South to recreate the feel of an antebellum mansion. The living room is especially theatrical with Victorian furniture in smoke blues with dusty rose and champagne accents. Over the fireplace is a portrait of his mother reminiscent of the heroine Violetta from Giuseppe Verdi's opera *La Traviata*. As an English descendant of the aristocratic Spencer family, James was brought up with British manners, protocol and an interest in the Victorian era, English literature and history. By age 8 James was partaking of afternoon tea and developed a love like his mother for dark chocolate and gingersnaps.

James also had an interest like his mother in classic cinema especially suspense and film noir as well as horror and Gothic themes. Around age 8 or 9 James became fascinated with the *Universal* Horror villains especially: Dracula, The Phantom of the Opera and The Wolfman. If James received high marks in school and was diligent in his music studies he was allowed to stay up to watch television shows like: *Night Gallery, Twilight Zone* or *Elvira Mistress of the Dark*. An evening ritual developed of making tea, served usually on his Grandmother's burgundy china setting, with some chocolate or snaps and staying up late with mom to watch horror. Tea instantly became linked with feeling loved, cozy and a "special time".

In high school, James became involved performing in a noted *New Romantics* band called *In Common Hours*. The band toured throughout the Southland often opening up for celebrated *New Wave* or *New Romantics* bands of the time. *Goth* music was all the rage and bands like *The Cure, Siouxsie, Visage, Eurhythmics* and *Clan of Xymox* influences James' interest in *Gothic Victorian* fashion, Gothic literature and style. James Spencer had an honors English teacher, Linda Carpenter who introduced him to not only English literature but also history and his first high tea ceremony.

In James' sophomore year of high school, he developed a natural aptitude for psychic awareness and he began studying astrology, tarot, numerology, tea leaves fortune telling and psychic development. His first high tea experience was with his three best friends: Jennifer, a feisty, opinionated and independent red-headed exchange student from Sweden; Sher an artistic and progressive Bohemian; and Kari, a talented dancer. An afternoon excursion to the historical *McCharles House* in Orange, California proved a prophetic and mystical trip. The house had a private and haunted attic room decorated *Victorian* in rich mauve and sage tones. Dressed in *Victorian* regalia, James shared his first "theatrical" high tea with his best friends. The experience would shape his love of the tea tradition and his need to explore other tearooms as well as stimulated in James an interest in the history of tea.

While James was pursuing a Master of Music degree at *California State University, Fullerton*, James began performing as a jazz artist throughout the Southland in resorts and hotels often having the opportunity to partake in mediocre to excellent afternoon teas. James became a vegetarian in his early high school years after a difficult childhood plagued with severe asthma, allergies and neurasthenia (a nerve inflammation condition causing painful nerve pain and occasional bouts of panic attacks and anxiety). James became introduced to Jeanne, a holistic doctor of acupuncture, Chinese herbology and medical Qi Gong. Jeanne instantly became like an older sister to Jim. Jeanne is a direct descendant of the composer Franz Liszt and Jeanne shares James' love of classical music, Victorian décor and literature. Jeanne introduced Jim to veganism, yoga, tai chi, and transcendental meditation. Through Jeanne, James began attending yogi vegan dinners and retreats where he became introduced to chai tea, and Indian and Ayurvedic tea practices. This furthered James' tea education as he often attended tea-blending workshops, workshops on the health benefits of tea as well as traditional tea ceremonies.

While in college James became close with a high school friend named Anita, who was an active vegan, animal rights activist and a member of *Green Peace*. Through Anita, James was made aware of the horrors of the meat industry visiting slaughter houses as well as animal labs where animals had been tortured and abused. This further James awareness of the health challenges linked with dairy and animal consumption. Alas the movement was new to James and James would swing back in forth between veganism and vegetarianism. At the time there were many famous musicians that were beginning the Vegan Rights movement. Morrissey and the band *The Smiths* had released the album *Meat is Murder*. Many of James' politically aware friends were becoming vegan and this seemed the natural progression for him. With in about a three-year period James completely healed up through veganism a lifetime of childhood asthma, allergies, skin issues and irritable bowel syndrome.

After university, James became a college professor of music as well as opening up a successful music school of his own. During his late twenties and thirties James had the opportunity to travel throughout the Southern United States partaking of tea in Southern mansions and five star resorts. James fell in love with Savannah having the opportunity to perform jazz there during the filming of the movie: *Midnight in the Garden of Good and Evil*. James developed a deep love for the South. James' father is originally from Key West, Florida, so many fond memories of childhood were of eating his grandma Spencer's southern cuisine like key lime pie or pineapple upside down cake with a tall glass of iced Sweetened Southern tea. Many of the recipes in this book are inspired by Key West or Georgian flavors as well as the exotic Cuban cuisine James grew up with. Other recipes are inspired by his father's own recipes.

Though James mother did not cook, James' father is an excellent and intuitive cook who has prepared delicious Cuban dishes like black beans and rice and fried platanos, or the Spanish cuisine of James' mother's heritage such as paella or flan. James and several of his siblings developed a talent for cooking and baking.

In addition to James exposure to Southern tea luncheons and cuisine, he had the opportunity to travel to experience regional teas and cuisines. James enjoyed afternoon tea at the Victoria's *Fairmont Empress* and other tearooms. After his excursions, James began to study in detail the history of British tea and how traditional cuisine developed. James also studied the variants between Scottish and Irish afternoon tea traditions.

After a severe car accident in 2001, James consulted a local known clinical hypnotherapist, Dr. Jane who helped him to recover from pain and nerve issues through the modalities of hypnotherapy, EFT, NLP, and body talk. James work with Jane inspired him to pursue a degree in clinical hypnotherapy. Upon acceptance, James began studies in clinical hypnotherapy at *Hypnosis Motivation Institute* located in Tarzana, California. Within the program James was required to take extensive courses in nutrition as well as courses in such modalities as: Eriksonian and Kappasian Hypnosis, Time-Line Therapy, Cognitive Therapy, Neuro-linguistic programming, Emotional Freedom Technique, Handwriting Analysis and Reiki. His studies specifically in nutrition would come in handy. Upon graduation in 2006 with the school's top honors, James began taking a few clients out of his home office and incorporated 'nutritional' consults to singers specifically suffering from asthma, allergies, and throat issues. His nutritional consults often-included recommendations towards a vegan plant-based lifestyle. James also received hypnotherapy clients complaining of diabetes, obesity, skin conditions, allergies, and other disorders. James found that his clients who adopted a plant-based diet, tended to show improvement quicker than those who didn't make any dietary changes. Unbeknownst to James this background in nutrition would be helpful in the creation of this book. James also decided in his mid thirties to choose alternative health care such as acupuncture, Chinese herbs, massage and nutritional awareness over traditional Western pharmaceutical. This led James to attend lectures in veganism, herbology and nutrition.

In 2002 James relocated to the beachside area of Bluff Park in Long Beach, California. Amongst the classic California Spanish mansions, Craftsman homes and art deco, James settled into a beachfront condo four-plex a block from the ocean. James began to look for local tearooms to partake in high tea. After a few mediocre trial and errors, James was introduced to *The Vintage Tea Leaf* owned by tea mistress *Beverly Terfloth*. Beverly offered superior tea blends, and the room became a favorite "replenishing" spot for afternoon tea or luncheons. James was also introduced to a local tearoom chain called *Peet's*. *Peet's* serves loose leaf organic tea, and daily baked scones. This was a far cry from the vulgar local coffee joints serving burnt bean, corn syrup, and high sugar multi-venti fat-ass caramel frappuccino macchiattos for $5.00. *Peet's* has a refined atmosphere with classical music or cool jazz programming and even offers loose leaf tea in glass teapots with a timer. The staff is super friendly. *Peet's* quickly became James' morning hangout, meeting new neighbors, friends and other vegan tea enthusiasts.

One afternoon, James decided to try a tearoom in the area that was recommended by a local friend. Attending with his good friend Sabrina, James ordered the high tea luncheon. James noticed that the food was not only extremely rich with heavy sauces, refined sugars and gooey over-frosted desserts but also the place did not look completely clean and sanitary. Only after about a half hour, James began to feel ill and developed a severe incident of food poisoning. Obviously this infuriated James and it propelled him to look into other tearooms as well as talk to many tea enthusiasts. Here is a partial list of the some of the comments presented to James over the course of writing this book:

- " I used to love to visit tearooms, but I find the food too heavy and rich. I always feel horrible after eating and though I love tea, the risk of getting sick is not worth it. I have visited several places that do not offer any vegetarian or vegan alternatives. It is highly frustrating and I feel alone. I wish more restaurants, bars and tearooms would offer at least a few vegan options."
- "Why would I want to pay the high prices of $50.00 or more for finger sandwiches I could make healthier at home? I once went to tea room that tried to pass off Campbell's Cream of Mushroom soup with a little sherry as an "original recipe."
- "I have to refrain from eating at tearooms as I'm vegan and gluten intolerant."
- "What is with the frilly pink girly décor in tearooms? As a man I feel totally out of place. I also prefer simple scones and tea to all that sugary cupcake over-frosted junk. Most tearooms do not allow me to just order tea and scones."
- "I don't trust the cleanliness and sanitation of our local tearoom. I once went there and saw a few desserts sitting out for nearly an hour on a display table in 100 degree weather. Several of my friends have not felt well after eating in tearooms."

Outraged that as a vegan James felt he was being "penalized" for making healthier dietary choices, he decided to research if there were others who felt like him. He started to connect first with friends from around the world but most notably his friends in the Southern states of Georgia, Louisiana and Texas as well as friends he met from London and Dublin in his travels or over social media. Many friends stated that they were vegans that loved the English tradition of afternoon tea, as well as the *Victorian* and *Edwardian* periods. He also discovered other vegans who enjoyed tea in yoga and meditation classes. He noticed vegans emerging from the *Gothic Victorian*, *Steampunk* and *Vintage Retro* communities.

Researching vegan groups online, James discovered that there were indeed vegans who were enthusiastic about tea hosting that were sharing recipes or putting up simple preparation videos on YouTube, websites and recipe blogs. He noticed that many of these vegans were irritated that there was not one book on the market yet to address vegan tea hosting and it was hard to locate other vegans that felt the same way. Were there only a few of us?

James decided to talk to a few close friends. His dear friend Arlene is a seventy-year-old herbalist and psychic that he met at a local coffee house. As they began to hang out, they began to exchange vegan recipes. Arlene shares James' love of classic cinema and classical movie. Mr. Spencer started to have a few little dinner gatherings of 2-4 people. They began to exchange more recipes and this led to Mr. Spencer starting a group called *The Vintage Vegan*.

The Vintage Vegan group began to grow and this led James to consider writing a vegan preparation book for tea hosting. James also became interesting in participating more with the eccentrics who had elaborate themed tea parties. Jim's first experience was a *Victorian* era murder party in a beachside mansion in Long Beach. Jim had dressed like a *Victorian* lord and each guest was asked to stay in character to see who would be the murderer in a plot that was developing. The atmosphere was exciting. An evening gathering with fine *Victorian* china, candles, and elegant cuisine was presented accompanied by a classical harpist. The host was gracious enough to include some vegan options and Jim was able to dine on a lovely salad and scones. The evening was so gratifying he felt he had been on a mini vacation.

As a *Gothic Victorian* James decided to co-host an Anne Rice Vampire themed tea. His friend Camille and Cecilia went all out. Coffee tables were actual coffins, and James was able to entertain on the fortepiano with selections of Chopin and Schubert. James was surprised to find that many in the Goth scene were actually politically and economically aware college students or self-employed artists. Many were indeed vegan and interested in *The Vintage Vegan* book idea.

Cecilia stated a theme James found enlightening: "*Goths* enjoy vegan tea because it combines the sensual theatricality and romance of the *Gothic Victorian* period with English traditions and delicious and healthy cuisine. It is one of the few places where I feel I can be myself and engage with other intelligent and interesting people that would rather read Edgar Allan Poe, or attend an opera then listen to most of the junk on the radio and waste their lives away twittering or playing Candy Crush on facebook. Vegan teas allow people to engage. It is intimate, sensual and at times erotic, but never dirty or banal. Vegan teas make me feel like a Queen. Call me an old-fashioned romantic, buy I so prefer the quiet reflection of tea with friends to noisy pickup and annoying sports bars with beer-guzzling obnoxious frat boys."

James indeed felt the same way and decided to immerse himself in other tea party "scenes". His next stop was to visit downtown Orange, in Orange County for a *Steampunk* themed tea luncheon. For those unfamiliar with *Steampunk:* it is a movement based on the steam industrial movement of the late *Victorian* period. It pulls imagery from *Victorian* science fiction such as the works of Jules Verne and H. G. Wells. *Steampunk* fans often dress in sci fi inspired *Victorian* regalia that are often quite elaborate. Men might wear opera slacks, tight corseted brocade vests, ascots and top hats, or leather fetish adventurers or steam engineer pants. Often watches, and accessories are made out of copper and other metals with wheels and motors. One might wear aviator goggles or other costumes that suggest the industrial age and advancements in transportation (aviation, hot air balloons, and steam trains). Women often wear corsets, petticoats and elaborate bonnets and parasols. A fun and festive group, again James found that most *Steampunk* enthusiasts were independent actors and artisans, Bohemians or the intellectual college nerd type that let their inhibitions free in such colorful gatherings. All the guests were elegant, cultured and again many were vegan. A trend?

James began working on his recipes and decided the *Vintage Vegan* would contain: finger sandwiches, canapés, scones, soups, salads and desserts. Within a short time James' *Vintage Vegan* contacts grew to well over one hundred. Many began calling James "The Tea Master" and would email him tea questions, many of which will be answered in the upcoming question and answer session. James decided to have all members vote on favorite recipes, what they liked and didn't like as well as how to create elegant and appropriate presentations of cuisine for high tea and afternoon tea ceremonies. Little by little this book began to take shape.

James welcomes all comments, questions, sharing of pictures and recipes. You may follow James at: **jamesrspencer.com** At this website you will find his store to purchase his albums, books. His blogs will have information about upcoming book signings, workshops, concert tours and more. If you are interested in private music and acting coaching, artist development and management services or Skype lessons you may also find that information presented there.

You may email James directly at: **spencermusicschool@gmail.com**

⤳Veganism and Vegan Tea Hosting Questions⤳

In preparing this book James received literally hundreds of delightful and thought-provoking questions concerning veganism and vegan tea hosting. Many people are new to veganism and want to explore vegan lifestyle and where to begin. Others had questions on tea preparation and tea history in general. Mr. Spencer greatly appreciates all the amazing fan mail, and support for the vegan movement. He is here to support you on your journey with veganism and vegan tea hosting. He may be reached directly at: **spencermusicschool@gmail.com.** Fee free to pose questions, share your recipes, photos of tea gatherings or suggestions. Tea is a beautiful opportunity to share healthy recipes and to spread the love.

Question: "Mr. Spencer: I am not sure what is meant by the term *vegan?* Does that mean you eat vegetables and fruit? May a vegan eat eggs or dairy?" (*Martha W. – Santa Monica, CA*)

Answer: "Thanks for the question Martha. *Vegan* means plant-based diet that includes: vegetables, fruit, legumes (beans and lentils), nuts, seeds, and grains. There are indeed many degrees of veganism. Many "newbie" vegans will eat processed vegan cheese, vegan sour cream, and vegan cream cheese. I do not however recommend them in your daily diet as they have cheap "man made" oils and fillers. Vegans who have practiced the lifestyle for years usually try to eat only organic plant-based and avoid all oils as well as GMO cheap soy products all together. I myself prefer almond and coconut milk to soymilk. Each person is different. I myself also have sensitivity to certain grains, therefore I prefer sweet potato as a daily carb over eating refined white bread. If you are considering making the shift to veganism I highly recommend the excellent documentaries: *Forks Over Knives* and *Vegucated.* Both movies should be easily found for purchase on Amazon, or look for them at Netflix.

My father suffered from several health issues. After changing to a vegan lifestyle, he dropped nearly 80 lbs, and at 85 looks and feels better than he did at 60. Veganism can definitely transform your life. I feel so blessed that my jovial father looks so amazing for his age. He is happy and inspired to try new recipes. His unique culinary skills inspired many of the recipes in this book. I'm forever thankful that both of my parents are in such great health. My parents inspire me and it is lovely to be able to share regular vegan meals with them. It is a highlight of my week. My beautiful parents remind me that radiant health through veganism and compassion for the planet is available to us at any age.

Question: "Jimmy, my children are gluten intolerant, and I am myself very sensitive to food allergens, especially during times when the Santa Ana winds are blowing hard. May I still use the recipes in this book?" (*Doris-Ann L. —Santa Ana, California*)

Answer: "Doris, thanks for your question. Absolutely! I myself include for all recipes gluten-free alternatives (that I also prefer.). All the recipes can be made with gluten-free alternatives as well as soy product substitutes. The recipes are completely adaptable. I also include sweetener alternatives such as maple syrup, coconut sugar and honey."

Question: "Mr. Spencer: How much food should I serve for an afternoon tea? Also is it ok to use teabags which seems easier?" (*Lorna Tierney—Seal Beach, California*)

Answer: "Great question Lorna: For an afternoon tea I would serve 2-3 variants of tea sandwiches: one traditional like cucumber or watercress, one berry with cream cheese, and one savory sandwiches. Try to have sandwiches that utilize various breads: white, wheat, whole grain, black and pumpernickel. Think elegant display and variety. I choose usually to serve two types of scones: usually a berry or lemon, and a chocolate or seasonal dessert scone. You may serve soup or salad. I often offer two choices. You may serve both soup and salad if guest or hungry or you are serving very late afternoon that might take the place of dinner. I usually do not serve a dessert unless tea is served 5 pm or after. Usually fresh fruit ambrosia, tarts or vegan cheesecakes are good choices. I also believe presentation is key. Consider your table settings, lighting and china. You might want to invest in a tiered-tea service. Garnishes and little touches also make a difference. This book will offer several great suggestions.

As for tea bag –Absolutely Never! I'm sorry but as a tea master I find teabags just tacky. Tea bags are often in bleached cheap papers and have staples both destroy the delicate oils and scents of tea making for a bland brew. Use loose-leaf tea. There are many delicious blends to choose from. Most teapots come with mesh strainers or better yet silk tea socks. Loose-leaf is not all that expensive in comparison. You may of course purchase loose leaf tea at local teashops or online at Amazon. A few of my favorite companies include: *Harney and Sons, Tevanna* and *The Metropolitan Tea Company*. As for what teas to serve your guest, look at my theme menus for a few suggestions. I usually like to include four display teapots. I serve a traditional English black tea, a fruit or scented black tea, a green or white tea and a decaf or herbal. This way all your guests are happy. Also consider serving tea in Asian cast iron teapots or heat resistant glass (to display the beautiful colors of your tea). I personally prefer these to porcelain and ceramic teapots that my chip or leak leads and paints. Consider having beautiful dishes for fresh lemon slices, and coconut sugar cubes."

Question: " What type of tea pot should I serve my tea in: porcelain, ceramic, glass, cast iron, or silver?" (John Garland—San Francisco, CA)

Answer: "Thanks John: The answer of course is a matter of taste but here are my thoughts for what they are worth. I myself prefer cast iron as it is both decorative, sturdy and holds the heat of the water. I also prefer heat resistance glass teapots as they preserve the delicate flavors and oils the very best. Also glass displays the colors of your teas. Just be sure to get a heat resistant higher end glass teapot. I made the mistake of burning myself when a glass teapot cracked and broke spilling scalding hot tea in my lap. Ouch. I love the look of fine Victorian porcelain but only usual for special occasions as china is delicate and chips easily. I hate to find pieces of ceramics, or powder from porcelains floating in my teacup. I think yikes, I'm probably digesting leads, and paints. Silver is also a good choice but silver is a pain to maintain and keep polished."

Question: "Is it ok to also serve other beverages besides tea at afternoon teas that I plan to host?" (Jenny Higgins—Bixby Knolls, California)

Answer: "Of course it is fine to serve other beverages but I do not know why when there are so many teas to choose from: *Ceylon, Assam, Cougou, Ooolong, Darjeerling, sencha, white, rooibos* and many more. I do enjoy serving ice cold *Old-Fashioned Lemonade* or an occasional cocktail, chilled champagne or wine, or cider, hot chocolate and vegan eggnog depending on the occasion. I personally do not care for coffee, and would probably not serve it."

Question: "I live in rather small studio apartment and vegan tea hosting seems rather elegant and fancy. I'm not sure what I could do to host a tea in my home. What might be appropriate and not too expensive? Any suggestions, Jim?" (*David G.—Hollywood, CA*)

Answer: " Great question David: Tea is about sharing and intimacy. Simple decorating is fine. Just put a few cut flowers in a vase on your coffee table. Places like *Target, Bed Bath and Beyond* or even *Big Lots* should have inexpensive glass teacups, teapots, and servers. You'll find the recipes are often rather simple to prepare in this book. You can make soups quickly with just a blender. Remember you can create a quiet and elegant atmosphere just by having a tidy house, and lighting some tea lights. I purchase 300 tea lights at *Big Lots* for about $6.00. Have some quiet music on the stereo. Simple teas with just dark chocolate or scones can be elegant. Choose times of days where your home environment is quiet. I also suggest talking with local tearooms and teashops for ideas or purchasing loose-leaf teas. Plants, bamboo, table fountains, dimmer switches, incense or a fireplace can also transform your home to that of a quiet tea sanctuary. Dress casual smart: Meaning if you are the typical tee-shirt and jeans type of guy, consider at least wearing a button down dress shirt and slacks that are comfortable."

Question: "Mr. Spencer, I get totally confused with water temperatures for tea brewing. When do I need to bring water to a boil, and when do I not." (Masako Onishi—Lakewood, California)

Answer: Here is a simple chart that should help:

> *White* and *Green Teas*: Just below boiling temperature (175-185F)
> *Oolong*: Medium boiling temperature (185-190F)
> *Black, Red* and *Herbals:* Full boiling temperature (206-212F)

Question: "What are tea steep times?" (Julie Jones—Westchester, NY)

Answer: Check out the chart below for steep times.

> *White:* 7-8 minutes
> *Chinese Green*: 3 minutes
> *Japanese Green:* 2-3 minutes
> *Black:* 3-4 minutes
> *Darjeerling:* 3 minutes
> *Oolong:* 2-3 minutes
> *Herbal:* 5-7 minutes
> *Tisanes:* 7-8 minutes

Questions: "What is meant by breakfast tea and what are the differences between: *English, Scottish, Irish* and *Canadian Breakfast* blends? Are there indeed differences?" (Scott Randolph—Victorian, B. C.)

Answer: *Breakfast teas* are black tea blends intended to accompany a hearty, rich traditional morning breakfast. Think of the typical British breakfast of eggs, bacon, sausage, and English muffins with jam. Therefore breakfast blends are stronger and more robust then teas that are served for afternoon gatherings or evening. Breakfast teas have the highest caffeine count and were traditionally served with whole milk (but not cream). Of course vegans may take their breakfast teas with almond milk. I prefer unsweetened vanilla almond milk. Let me now present regional **breakfast teas**:

> *English Breakfast:* According to tea historian Frank Sanchez of *Upton Tea Imports* the first British tea imports came in from China in the early 1600s. Over time tea blenders incorporated exotic teas from India and Sri Lanka as well as later Africa and Indonesia. The first teas every used in *English Breakfast* were Chinese *Cougou* tea.

Sanchez states: "Then, during the Opium Wars, China imposed an embargo on tea. Around the same time, the *British East India Company* started producing tea in Assam, India. For a while the old stocks of Chinese tea were dwindling and the new stocks of India teas started to arrive in London in interesting blends. Jump ahead to the end of the 19th century and tea was beginning to be mass-produced in Ceylon (Sri Lanka). You started to have a stronger and stronger Ceylon component in *English Breakfast* blends. Most modern *English Breakfast* blends are a mix of Chinese *Cougou* and *Ceylon*."

Irish Breakfast tea has a stronger *Assam* Indian component, which gives the tea is more robust, malty flavor and rich reddish color. "My theory is that tea must have been growing in popularity in Ireland around the time that the *British East India Company* was producing rich *Assam* teas," says Sanchez. Again an easy way to tell *English* from *Irish Breakfast* is Irish has a reddish color and a slightly malty taste.

Scottish Breakfast tea tends to be the heartiest of the bunch, possibly due to Scotland's softer water. "Back in the day, teas were blended specifically for the water conditions in the areas in which they were marketed and consumed," Sanchez says. "It's conjecture, but perhaps the water in Scotland demanded a stronger tea." *Scottish Breakfast* has the strongest caffeine count of any tea. *Scottish Breakfast* combines *Cougou, Assam, Ceylon* and even black tealeaves from Bali.

Canadian Breakfast: Canadian Breakfast combines blacks that would be featured *English and Irish Breakfast* with touches of maple overtones. I adore *Canadian Breakfast* as it goes so very well with Autumn flavors of maple, pumpkin, pecans and cinnamon apples. I first tasted *Canadian Breakfast* at the beautiful *Chateau Frontenac* in Québec.

Question: "Why is Russian tea considered a masculine or "men's" tea? What are the differences between English and Russian black tea blends? Why do many English natives look down on Russian tea? What am I missing?" (Ursula Tesli—San Diego, CA)

Answer: "Great question: *Russian Caravan*, a traditional tea of the Soviet Union has a very smoky taste and is quite robust. *Russian Caravan* is a blending of Chinese *Oolong, Keemun* and *Lapsung*. The teas are smoke-dried in leather satchels that give the tealeaves a smoky, full-bodied flavor with a strong copper color. *Russian Caravan* is not for all tea drinkers, some people including myself fee it tastes like tires. The smoky feel is way overpowering to the tea in my opinion. The *Russian Tea* blends are the "campfire" blends of tea. English and myself feel they lack the elegance and refinement of English equivalents.

Question: "What is meant by first and second flush? Why are flush terms connected specifically with *Darjeerling* teas? Where is the *Darjeeling* region? (Maxmillian Reinhardt—Anaheim, California)

Answer: "Tea flush refers to tea growing seasons (certain seasons) in the region of *Darjeeling* located in Northern India."

> *First Flush:* Mid March-May (Spring)
> *Second Flush:* June to Mid August (Summer)
> *Third Flush:* October and November (Autumn)

However there were also two minor flushes as well:

> *In-Between Flush* for two weeks in-between the first and second flushes
> *Rain-Monsoon Flush* between the second and third flushes during the month of September

It should be noted that the time periods are not fixed and it depends on the weather patterns in *Darjeeling*. Excess rainfall earlier than expected can reduce the timeline of second flush while increasing the rain flush by a few weeks.

What kind of flavors may I expect from each *Darjeeling* tea flush?

Darjeeling First Flush: The color of the tea is light and clear with a bright liquor. The leaves have a light floral scent, with a lively character.

Darjeeling Second Flush: The tea has a dark color and stronger flavor then the first flush. The tealeaves have a purplish bloom and the tea has a fruity taste generally. To explain further the tea has amber-copper hues and taste similar to muscatel grapes due to this tea plant reacting to small insects that suck juices from the stems.

Darjeeling Third Flush: The tea color is dark or coppery and the texture full-bodied bit has a lighter flavor. Autumn *Darjeeling* has a delicate as well as a sparkling character.

Which flush is the most expensive and why?

Generally speaking, first flush teas are considered more expensive due to its bright liquor and lively character. First flush teas are produced in less quantity and hence the demand outstrips the supply. However, it should be noted that *Darjeeling* tea connoisseurs generally have a specific preference for either first or second flush and do not mind paying premium prices for the best cup of tea.

What makes *Darjeeling Second Flush* tea so unique? How does it get its signature muscatel flavor?

Darjeeling Second Flush is so unique because it clearly brings the unique muscatel flavor *Darjeeling* is known for, as no other tea in the world is able to do. The unique muscatel flavor is caused due to the combination of unique weather, topography, and plant types. Scientists from *Tocklai Experimental Station* (TES) of the *Tea Research Association* (TRA) in Upper Assam and Japan's *Kyoto University* molecular mechanism experts have identified that genes in the plants that only express themselves after being infested by the insects—that leads to the creation of the unique flavor and the tarpins (geraniol and lunalook) enrich the natural flavors of the leaves. I myself prefer the second flush to first. *Darjeeling Second Flush* has the fine subtle flavors of an elegant wine. I locally purchase *Peet's* loose leave *Darjeeling* blend.

Is there anything else you'd like to share about the seasonality of *Darjeeling* tea?

The seasonality of *Darjeeling* tea i.e., the various flushes bring out different flavor from the tea that is picked from the same plants during different times of the year. Though no season/flushes are the same, hence during first flush you can get golden color liquor and that same leaves would give dark brown liquor during the second flush. Such tastes can satisfy the pallets of various tea drinkers effectively.

Question: "I do not speak Japanese and I feel totally confused between all the varieties of green teas. Can you help me understand the teas, Jim?" (Drew Coolidge—Boston, Mass.)

Answer: Japanese Tea History

The world "cha" in Japanese means "tea".

Ryokucha (green tea): Gyokuro, Sencha, Bancha

Various grades of green tea are cultivated, differing on the timing of harvest and on the amount of sunlight the tealeaves are subjected to. The highest grade is *gyokuro,* which is picked during the first round of harvest and shaded from the sun for some time before harvest. Next is *sencha,* which is also picked during the first round of harvest but whose leaves are not protected from the sun. Finally, *bancha* is a lower grade of green tea whose leaves are obtained from the later rounds of harvesting.

Matcha (powdered green tea)

Only the highest quality leaves are used for *matcha,* which are dried and milled into a fine powder that is then mixed with hot water. *Matcha* is the form of green tea that used for the tea ceremony. *Matcha* is now known the world over for its amazing health benefits including: fat burning and cancer-fighting properties, and boost to the immune system. *Matcha* has nearly 137 times the antioxidant properties of green tea. One cup of *matcha* is equivalent to 10 cups of the nutritional content in traditional green tea. *Matcha* is a natural detoxifier, and is rich in vitamins, chlorophyll and fiber. It has been noted by psychologists and hypnotherapists to be a healthy safe aid in memory concentration, mood enhancement and emotional well-being. *Matcha* also contains vitamin C, selenium, chromium, zinc and magnesium. It aids in the prevention of disease as well as an effective agent in helping to lower cholesterol and blood sugar levels.

Konacha (residual green tea)

Konacha consists of tea dust, tea buds and small tea leaves remaining after processing *Gyokuro* or *Sencha.* Although considered a low grade of tea, *Konacha* is thought to complement certain foods well, such as sushi. It is often provided for self-service at inexpensive sushi restaurants.

Hojicha (roasted green tea)

Hojicha is processed by roasting the tealeaves, which gives the leaves their characteristic reddish-brown color. The heat from the roasting also triggers chemical changes in the leaves causing *hojicha* tea to have a sweet, slightly caramel like aroma.

Genmaicha (Green tea and roasted brown rice)

Genmai is unpolished brown rice. The roasted rice is mixed with the tealeaves. The tea has a light toasty flavor and a yellow color. It is often served as an alternative to *sencha. Genmaicha* is also known for its probiotic qualities aiding digestion.

Jasmine Green

Green tea is often mixed with jasmine flower to create a lovely scented tea. Sometimes jasmine is added to black or oolong teas as well. Jasmine has a natural calmative effect on the nervous system.

Question: "I have been hearing about the health benefits of white and green tea. Is this just hype?"

Answer:

Green Tea Benefits:

The *University of Maryland Medical Center* reports that green tea may help stop the growth of cancer cells in many varieties of the disease, including breast, esophageal, prostate and stomach. UMMC notes that green tea has also shown positive results in preventing atherosclerosis and high cholesterol, both of which can lead to heart disease. It also may promote thermogenesis, a fat-burning process that contributes to successful weight loss. A report published in the "Journal of Indian Society of Periodontology" in 2012 found that green tea may even promote good dental health by reducing inflammation and bacteria associated with gum disease. *The Chopra Institute* in Encinitas published a study in 2013 on the health benefits of green tea and specifically matcha on its ability to help reverse disease, aid energy levels and promote gentle detoxification and weight loss.

White Tea Benefits:

When it comes to cancer prevention, white tea may have an advantage over green. Researchers at the *Linus Pauling Institute* in 2000 tested four kinds of white tea on rats to assess their benefits for colon cancer protection. Because of white tea's higher content of some polyphenols, the scientists found it was better than green at mitigating harm done to DNA -- a type of cell damage that can be a precursor to cancer. However, the researchers cautioned that additional studies would be needed to confirm the same benefits in humans. University of California Irvine published a study in 2010 that silver needles of white tea mixed with white peony had the anti-inflammatory properties useful to those suffering from fibromyalgia and other inflammatory disorders. The study stated that in test groups for patients with arthritis, those partaking in 1 to 2 cups of white tea daily over a two-week period showed noticeable improvements in their symptoms.

Tea Drinking Considerations:

Both green tea and white tea have less caffeine than black tea or coffee. White tea contains the least, with 30 to 55 milligrams per cup, compared to 35 to 70 for green tea. A study published in *Molecular Nutrition and Food Research* in 2007 found that adding lemon or soy or rice milk to green tea significantly boosted the body's absorption of its antioxidants. *The National Cancer Institute* advises that hot brewed tea has greater concentrations of polyphenols than iced or bottled varieties. Talk to your doctor before adding green or white tea to your diet because they may interfere with some medications. Chinese herbal doctors and acupuncturists are also a good source of to consult if your are concerned about adding white or green tea to your diet

Question: "What is *rooibos* and what is all the recent craze concerning it?"

Answer:

Rooibos is African for "red bush" It is a plant that grows in Africa. Its leaves are used to make a delicious robust red herbal tea with no caffeine. This is a great tea for those concerned about caffeine as it has Vitamin C and acts as a tonic for the nervous system. *Rooibos* is often paired with citrus and spices, for a hot winter tea, or with tropical fruit like mango and passion fruit to serve over ice.

There are also some lovely African herbal teas with similarities.

Honeybush: *Honeybush* is a plant in the same family as *rooibos*. It produces a rich amber tea that taste like honey.

Green Rooibos is made from leaves that are not fully ripe. Its taste is milder to red *rooibos*.

Question: "I am a man who has always preferred tea to coffee. I am often teased by my peers for visiting tearooms. Some tearooms I have visited are indeed geared towards women and I feel a bit out of place sipping tea amongst all the pink decor. I don't want to be the only guy in an all girl tearoom. HELP!"

Answer: "I hear you. It is sad that in the US especially there are all these stupid stereotypes that if a man prefers tea to coffee he must some how be effeminate. Actually in Europe especially England and Ireland, working men take tea daily. Think of all those macho men who worked in coal mills all-day or slaving away in sweat shops. There only rejuvenation was sometimes sitting with friends smoking a cigar with a hearty cup of tea. On face book I created a page entitled *The Gentlemen's Tea Room* where men can gather to discuss tea, share recipes are talk about the men's tea movement. I posted several photos of famous actors who enjoyed tea over coffee. They include: James Dean, Cary Grant, Jude Law and many others.

I often get asked what can I do when local tearooms seem so "girly"? Well not all tearooms are. I myself had to search and attend several tearooms till I found one I felt comfortable with. There are however coffee and teashops that cater to the work crowd. I myself love *Peet's Tea and Coffee* that is a Southern California chain. They offer very hearty men's teas and I go there at least 4 times a week, to meet my guy friends, play a game of chess or to just flirt and meet new people. *Peet's* serves *Russian Caravan*, as well as other hearty "men's teas" My favorite is *Phoenix Mountain Oolong.* I also love their *Black Currant Ceylon.*

However if you get teased for attending a high room, tell the guys they are the stupid ones. You have it all figured out. Girls attend tearooms, and you have the choice of whom you flirt with no other guys around. I have met many gorgeous women over high tea. I have also met life long friends at tearooms.

Men, we need to bond together and keep this tradition alive. There are groups on facebook and other places where you can meet other guys who enjoy tea.

Also men don't rule out game nights and *Super Bowl* parties serving tea, hearty sandwiches, scones and desserts. Last game night they were all devoured in minutes LOL. Men indeed like scones. We might just prefer black currant, and dark chocolate to let's say pink lemon scones.

Another place where active men get together for tea is at yoga and tai chi studios. After a rigorous workout I often have a cup of *Tulsi* (holy basil tea) or *Chai Masala* with the guys. I think a much healthier choice then ruining your gym workout with guzzling a bunch of beer at a bar.

Often church, temple and spiritual groups have a coffee/tea hour. I usually enjoy a cup of *English Breakfast* at my local church with my friends. I often bring scones so I don't have to eat those cheap vulgar sugary donuts.

Join the community at: *The Gentlemen's Tea Room* on facebook:

https://www.facebook.com/pages/The-Gentlemens-Tea-Room/1652043998347704?ref=hl

Question: "I read that you are an expert psychic and read tea leaves? I think this would be fun to learn and I would like to read tea leaves at my Halloween tea this autumn. Is it easy to learn? Can you recommend a good book?"

Answer: Tea reading is indeed a fun art. You can take classes most likely at your local New Age or occult shop. Here are some books I like that should help you get started:

Reading Tea Leaves by Highland Seer
Tea-Cup Reading and Fortune by Highland Seer
Your Fortune In A Tea Cup by Timon Forst
The Cup of Destiny by Jane Lyle

Question: "I'm concerned about throwing an all vegan tea. Many of my friends are heavy meat eaters or might expect at least some meat dishes. However killing an animal and serving pork grosses me out. What should I do Jim?"

Answer: Don't compromise your morals and your choice to be vegan—EVER. There are so many hearty recipes in this book that everyone should be satisfied. I find the *Reuben* sandwich with its hearty bbq flavor works well. There are so many choices. I found that vegans lead by example. If you look at most vegans compared to people on the average American diet of fast food, heavy dairy and meat consumption as well as processed foods, veganism speaks for itself. This is about YOU! What do you want? Do you want to feel healthier or weighed down? Also it is ok to when you go to traditional tearooms to avoid the foods that are not vegan. I often just eat a salad, enjoy the tea and munch on a scone. You will find that others will start changing slowly around you as you lead by example. It took years to change members of my family to veganism but the wait was worth it. I feel so thankful to have parents that look and feel great and are in radiant health.

Tea Sandwiches

AALT (Avocado, Alfalfa, Lettuce and Tomato)

This delicious sandwich recipe has a slightly French Country flavor with the addition of Dijon and tarragon herb.

Ingredients:

- 1 loaf of gluten-free whole grain bread
- 2 large ripe tomatoes
- 1 carton of alfalfa sprouts
- 1 bag of herb greens (washed)
- 1 jar of capers (drained)
- 2 large ripe avocadoes
- 1 jar of *Grey Poupon*
- Sea Salt and Black Pepper (To taste)
- Tarragon (fresh)
- Balsamic vinegar

Directions:

In a small glass bowl mix 4 tablespoons of *Grey Poupon* with 1 Tablespoon of Balsamic vinegar, and capers. Add a small handful of fresh tarragon and just a dash of sea salt and pepper to taste. You should have a thick creamy mustard. If dressing is too watery add a little more *Grey Poupon* to thicken it up.

Slice your tomatoes thin and blotch excess moisture out using a few cloth towels. Cut your avocado into slim slices. Cut thin strips of herb greens (sandwich size) and also blot out excess moisture with paper towels.

Take a slice of grain bread. Layer your dijon/caper spread onto the slice. Then lay down your herb greens, then tomato, and then avocado and a sprinkling of alfalfa sprouts. Spread Dijon on another slice of bread and top it to create your sandwich. Slice off the crust and cut into attractive triangle wedges, finger rectangles, or you may use cookie cutters to create interesting displays. These finger sandwiches have a fresh *French Country* feel. I often garnish with fresh tarragon and serve with pickles and black olives. These sandwiches are slightly savory. Some people like to add a little vegan mayo for a creamier sandwich. Feel free to explore and tweak this recipe.

~≈⊱ Apple-Cashew ⊰≈~

One of my favorite fall sandwiches is the Apple-Cashew that combines the flavors of creamy cashew butter, and cinnamon apple butter with fresh apples. Black Arkansas apples are my favorite if you can find them in season. They are deliciously juicy.

Ingredients:

- 4 Arkansas red apples (or apple of choice, stay within the red variety)
- Apple butter (I prefer one prepared with cinnamon and spices)
- Creamy cashew butter (You may substitute almond or peanut butter)
- Ground Cinnamon
- Maple syrup (preferably Grade B)
- 10 slices of gluten-free dark grain bread
- Coconut oil (for grilling)

Directions:

Wash and scrub apples. Peel, core, and thinly slice them. Dry with paper towels.

On a slice of bread, spread apple butter, put a layer of thin apple slices, sprinkle with cinnamon and drizzle just a little maple syrup B. On another slice of bread spread cashew butter. Place together into sandwich. Grill both sides with just a drop of coconut oil. Grill till toasted. Cut off crusts and cut into 4 triangles. Serve on a platter with slices of apples sprinkled with a dash of cinnamon. This is a perfect tea sandwich for autumn and winter gatherings. It goes well with chai tea or holiday tea blends. I often sprinkle a little ground nutmeg on the top of the sandwiches.

~≈⊱ Artichoke ⊰≈~

This delicious artichoke tea sandwich is a staple of tea luncheons in the South. I have been eating this sandwich for years and tweaked the recipe to a vegan variety. Enjoy!

Ingredients:

- 2 (14oz) can of artichoke hearts in water (drained and finely chopped)
- 1 cup of vegan mayo
- 1 tsp rosemary
- 1 tsp garlic powder
- 1 tsp dried parsley
- ½ tsp cayenne pepper
- Sea salt and lemon ground pepper to taste
- 10 slices of white bread
- 10 slices of black bread

Directions:

In a medium glass bowl, stir together the artichokes, mayo, rosemary, garlic powder, dried parsley, and cayenne and season with salt and lemon pepper.

Divide mixture evenly between 10 white slices sandwich bread; top each with remaining black bread slices, and cut off crusts. Slice each sandwich square diagonally to make 2 triangles then cut again. 4 triangles per sandwich. The black and white sandwiches are theatrical for tea hostings.

Transfer to a platter and wrap in plastic wrap. Refrigerate for at least 1 hour. Serve on a tea tray, garnish with fresh parsley and on a bed of herb greens.

Basil-Tomato Grilled Cheese Panini

This is an Italian Panini style grilled sandwich with the flavors of tomato and sweet basil. I like to serve this sandwich preferably in the fall and winter.

Ingredients:

- 8 slices of gluten-free multi grain bread
- 8 slices of almond cheese (mozzarella flavor is best)
- 2 large tomatoes, sliced
- 2 tbsp of minced fresh sweet basil
- 2 tsp balsamic vinegar
- Sea salt and ground pepper to taste
- ¼ cup of virgin olive oil
- 3 Tbsp of vegan parmesan cheese
- ¼ tsp garlic powder
- Black olives and fresh sweet basil leaves (garnish)

Directions:

On four slices of bread layer 1 slice of mozzarella cheese then tomato (be sure to use a paper towel to get out excess moisture) then another cheese slice); sprinkle with the sweet basil, Balsamic vinegar, salt and pepper. Top with remaining bread slice.

In a small glass bowl, combine the oil, almond cheese and garlic powder; brush over the outsides of each sandwich.

In a small skillet over medium heat, toast sandwiches until golden on both sides and cheese has melted. Cut crust off and cut into triangles. Put on a display platter and garnish with some fresh basil leaves and black olives.

Cucumber

Cucumber sandwiches are the most-served traditional sandwiches for afternoon tea. They are light and refreshing. One should consider serving this sandwich at any tea gathering. I like the added taste of fresh dill.

Ingredients:

- 1 loaf of gluten free white bread
- 1 carton of vegan cream cheese
- An organic English cucumber
- Dill (fresh) or dried
- Fresh mint or parsley for garnish, dill or sweet pickles

Tools:

- Knife, favorite cookie cutters, paper towels, peeler

Directions:

Cucumber sandwiches are a traditional English afternoon tea favorite. They are delicious, and very simple to make as long as you follow the directions carefully.

Peel the skin off your cucumber. Cut cucumber into super thin slices and lay on a paper towel. Dab the paper towel against the cucumber to soak up excess moisture. If you don't do this tea sandwiches will get soggy. Take a bread slice and layer it with cream cheese, then layer thin slices of cucumber. Once covered, sprinkle with a dash of fresh dill. Top with another piece of bread. Either cut off crust and slice into small triangles or rectangle strips to make cucumber finger sandwiches or use cookie cutters to turn your sandwiches into creative shapes. Explore using heart shaped cookie cutters or flower designs. Layer your sandwiches attractively on a platter or on a tier of a 3-tiered service. Feel free to sprinkle a little more dill on top of the sandwiches and garnish with flower petals, fresh mint leaves or fresh parsley.

Cucumber sandwiches should not only taste fresh and delicious but should also have a beautiful display. Look online for display ideas. Cucumber sandwiches are adaptable to any tea party theme. I have used flower cutters and garnished with a black olive in the middle to look like flowers. I have cut them into hearts, diamonds, clubs and spades to give the display a card game casino effect. I also sometimes garnish a plate of cucumber sandwiches with pickles, or black olives. Again feel free to get creative.

Curried Tofu Salad

This is my vegan equivalent to the traditional English Empire curried chicken salad sandwich recipe. This sandwich is absolutely delicious and filling. It may be served as an appetizer or as an entrée sandwich. This sandwich goes best complimented with a cup of spicy Masala Chai.

Ingredients:

- 1 lb of extra firm sprouted tofu
- 1/3 cup golden juicy raisins
- 1 tsp yellow mustard seeds

- ¼ cup apple cider vinegar
- 2 Tbsp roasted pepitas (pumpkin seeds)
- 1 scallion (chopped finely)
- 1 Tbsp chopped parsley
- ½ cup vegan mayo
- 2 Tbsp curry powder
- ¼ cup sliced cashews
- ¾ tsp of sea salt
- Pinch of turmeric and ground black pepper
- Strips of herb greens
- 1 loaf of dark gluten-free multi grain bread

Directions:

Place the mustard seeds and golden raisins a small heat resistant glass bowl. Bring the apple cider vinegar to a boil and pour it over them. Let them soak for at least 20 minutes (longer is even better).

Rinse and drain the tofu and gently press it between towels to rid of excess moisture. Place the tofu in a large bowl and crumble it using your hands or a fork. Add the raisins and mustard seeds (along with any excess vinegar), pumpkin seeds, cashews, scallions, and parsley.

In a separate bowl, stir together the mayo, curry powder, salt, and pepper and turmeric to taste. Add this to the tofu mixture and stir until combined. Taste and adjust your seasonings if desired.

On a piece of bread, add strips of herb greens. Then spread a generous layer of curried tofu topping with bread to make your sandwich. Cut off crust and cut into triangles.

This sandwich idea is great for English Empire or Indian Tea luncheons. The sandwich goes well with a cup of *Masala chai*, or a 5 star *Darjeerling*.

Figgy Cheese

This is a fall and winter tea sandwich favorite of mine that is perfect for Halloween and Autumn Harvest or Christmas Holiday teas.

Ingredients:

- 1 loaf of your favorite dark bread. Try pumpernickel, Bavarian black bread, or any dark gluten-free variety.
- 1 jar of fig preserves
- 1 tub of vegan cream cheese (Try Tofutti Better)
- Garnish: black mission figs and dried black currents

This is such a simple recipe that will make for an excellent sweet tea sandwich addition to any function. Simply spread 1 generous layer of cream cheese on a slice of dark bread. Then spread on a layer of fig preserves. Put a top layer of bread. Cut the crust off your sandwiches and cut into triangles, finger rectangles or use cookie cutters. Since this is a fall favorite I often use leaf shape cookie cutters. After layering the sandwiches attractively on a platter, I garnish with some delicious black mission figs and sprinkle a few black currants around the sandwiches. Your guests will love this simple sandwich.

Galician Apricot

This is a most simple recipe and a surprising one to consider when you are working against the clock and do not have much time. It is elegant but takes less then 5 minutes to prepare. You can make quickly as many as you need. Great to consider when hosting larger parties and timing is critical.

Ingredients:

- 1 loaf of already thinly sliced black bread (Try Bavarian pumpernickel or schwartzbrot)
- 1 jar of creamy cashew butter (or substitute almond butter)
- 1 jar of apricot preserves
- Spanish dried apricots and dried cranberries (Garnish)
- Optional (cookie cutters)

Directions:

Simply spread a generous amount of cashew butter onto a slice of black bread, and then spread an equal amount of apricot preserves onto another slice. Put together to make your sandwich. Yes it's that simple.

Ideas for display: I cut off the crust and slice into large rectangles to make finger sandwiches. I cut the dried apricots into very small pieces. I layer on the top of the sandwich apricots/cranberries alternating. The effect is the sandwiches look like stain-glassed mosaics. You can get as creative as you like using black currants, dried cherries, dried blueberries etc to make other colorful designs. My guests love the artsy display: perfect for gallery exhibition teas. Children love them too as it is similar to the traditional peanut butter and jelly sandwich. The blending of dried apricots, black currants, and dried berries is used quite a bit in Galician (Northern Spanish) recipes. It is simple but oh so stylish!

Georgian Harvest

This new tea sandwich invention of mine has the flavors of my beloved Georgia in the fall. I adore autumn that is my favorite time of year. Serve this sandwich for Halloween, autumn and Thanksgiving tea luncheons. I often use pumpkin or fall cookie cutters to add extra drama.

Ingredients:

- 1 loaf of already thinly sliced black pumpernickel
- 1/3 cup of orange marmalade
- 1 container of vegan cream cheese about 8 oz
- 2/3 cup of dried cranberries
- ½ cup of toasted or candied pecans
- Arugula
- Slice of vegan turkey lunch meat (Try Tofurky slices)

Directions:

Simply mix marmalade, cream cheese, cranberries and pecans together in a bowl, stirring till fully mixed. Layer on slices of bread. Put down Arugula leaf and 1 slice of vegan turkey. Put sandwich together and cut off crust and cut into quarter triangles. Or use cookie cutters. Display attractively. I sometimes throw a few pecans on the plate and a slice of orange (dabbed to get out excess moisture)

Greek

This is a simple take on Greek Salad and a more exotic version of a traditional cucumber sandwich.

Ingredients:

- 1 loaf of a dark bread of choice (try Schwartzbrot, pumpernickel, dark wheat, or gluten free multi grain)
- 1 cucumber (peeled and thinly sliced, dab with paper towels to get out excess moisture)
- 1 tomato (thinly sliced dabbed with paper towels to get rid of excess moisture)
- Black olive tapenade spread
- Thin slices of vegan white cheese
- Fresh basil leaves

Directions

Simply spread black olive spread generous on a slice of bread, then put a think layer of tomato, then basil leaf, then cucumber, then black olive spread on another piece of bread and put together into a sandwich. Cut off crust and cut into quarter triangles. Or you may use cookie cutters to make your favorite shapes. Display attractively and garnish with a few basil leaves cut into strips and some kalamata black olives.

King Charles (Black Bean-Guacamole and Mango Wraps)

I created this simple swirl wrap that is great for summer tea parties. Truly delicious.
It combines the Key West Cuban flavors of black beans with tropical mango. A simple recipe that is sure to please.

Ingredients:

- 1 jar of black bean dip/spread
- 1 jar or container of fresh mango or tropical salsa
- 1 container of spicy guacamole
- Grilled caramelized onions
- 1 container of vegan sour cream
- Fresh cilantro
- Juice of 1 key lime
- A pinch of cayenne pepper
- 1 pinch of cumin
- A pinch of chili powder
- 1 jar of marinated red peppers

- 2 packages of tortillas (I prefer 1 package of green spinach tortilla, and 1 red corn package). The colors of red and green make for a pleasing display.)

Directions:

In a small bowl, mix the sour cream with about ¼ cup of chopped cilantro, limejuice and seasoning. Mix well.

Assembly:

Take your spinach tortilla and spread generously with black bean dip, and then a layer of guacamole, and then a layer of mango salsa. Lay down the red tortilla directly on top (note: buy tortillas of the same size). Over the top of the red tortilla layer with vegan sour cream, grilled red peppers and grilled onions on top. Carefully roll the tortilla tightly into a pinwheel. Carefully cut into about 4 slices. You may use toothpicks to hold together. I serve them on a tray with slices of avocado and mango. Garnish with fresh cilantro.

Lady Anne's Lemon-Dill

This creamy cool lemon twist on the traditional English cucumber sandwich is a refreshing change. I always serve this sandwich for springtime teas like Mother's Day, Easter, or Baby Showers.

Ingredients:

- 8 oz container of vegan cream cheese
- 4 Tbsp of freshly chopped dill
- Zest and juice of two lemons
- Sea salt and ground lemon pepper to taste
- 12 slices of gluten-free white bread
- 1 English seedless cucumber (peeled and thinly sliced) Remember to pat dry with towels to get out excess moisture)

Directions:

Mix your vegan cream cheese, dill, and lemon zest/juice in a bowl to thoroughly mix. Season with a dash of sea salt and ground lemon pepper.

On your slices of white, spread your lemon-dill cream cheese. Layer on a slice thin cucumber then top with another slice of bread and spread. Either cut off crusts and cut into quarter triangles. Or you may use cookie cutters to make creative patterns. I often cut these sandwiches into flower shapes. I use 1 fresh blueberry for the center of the flower. I garnish with thin patted dry lemon slices and some fresh dill, fresh mint leaves or parsley. For added flair serve on a yellow plate.

~Lady Caroline's Strawberry Patch~

For all those who love the taste of fresh juicy strawberries. It is easy to make and children especially love them. I always make this sandwich for Valentine's Day and Alice and Wonderland themed teas. I also use heart cookie cutters for added display! This is a fun and lovely sandwich.

Ingredients:

- 1 loaf of gluten free white bread (about 10 to 12 slices)
- 8 oz of vegan cream cheese
- ¼ cup of Strawberry Preserves (I prefer Knott's)
- 1 lb of fresh Strawberries (thoroughly washed and sliced into super thin slices) Note: Please pat dry strawberries with paper towels to get out excess moisture, or sandwiches may become soggy.
- Fresh sweet basil leaves (cut into very thin strips)
- A pinch of ground orange rind and nutmeg

Directions:

Warm cream cheese to soften and mix with strawberry preserves to super smooth and creamy (no lumps). Mix in just a small pinch of orange rind and ground nutmeg (this is optional-I sometimes add this for a slight variety in the Autumn and Winter months).

Simply layer your slices of white bread with strawberry cream cheese then place a thin layer of strawberries and a few tiny strips of basil. Put your sandwich together. Either cut off crust and cut into triangles or better yet use heart shaped cookie cutters. Display your heart shaped strawberry sandwiches on a platter. Use thin strips of basil shavings for garnish. I often put 1 thin heart slice of strawberry in the center of my heart sandwiches. The Queen of Hearts loves this little touch.

~Lady Dolores Aimee's Ginger-Carrot~

With a regal Spanish twist, this Galician tea sandwich recipe is perfect for fall time teas. The ginger flavor is warming to people who get cold easily and goes perfectly with a cup of tea.

Ingredients:

- 4 grated carrots
- 4 Tbsp of room temperature vegan cream cheese
- 4 Tbsp of vegan mayo of choice
- 8 tsp of vegan butter (I prefer *Earth Balance*)
- 2 tsp of sweet ginger paste
- Sea salt and pepper to taste
- 1 loaf (10-12 slices) of favorite gluten-free multi grain bread
- Fresh bean sprouts

Directions:

In a medium glass bowl, combine carrots, vegan cream cheese, mayo, and ginger paste; add salt and pepper.

Spread one side of each piece of bread lightly with vegan butter. Top the buttered side of 2 slices of bread with carrot/ginger mixture (about 1.5-inch thick). Top with bean sprouts and top with the remaining bread slices, buttered side down.

Carefully cut the crusts from the sandwiches. Cut the sandwiches in half diagonally and then cut in half again. If you wish, decorative shapes can be made with cookie cutters. Garnish serving platter with curly carrot shavings and fresh parsley.

Lady Emily's Raspberry-Rose

In honor of the Victorian novels of Emily Bronte, I have created this romantic and enchanting tea sandwich. This sandwich also reminds me of visiting Knott's Berry Farm in Buena Park, California. Berries are a big staple in my home. This raspberry-rose sandwich is whimsical and surprisingly delicate in its blending of flavors. I often make this sandwich for romantic teas for two, Valentine's Day or Alice and Wonderland themed teas. I often cut these sandwiches into heart shapes and garnish a platter with fresh pink and red rose petals and fresh raspberries.

Ingredients:

- 1 loaf of gluten free multi grain bread (you may also use any wheat bread variety)
- 8 oz of vegan cream cheese
- ¼ cup of raspberry preserves (I like Knott's brand)
- ¼ cup of fresh red raspberries (washed and patted dry with paper towel to get rid of excess moisture)
- ½ tsp of raw honey
- 2 Tbsp of edible rose water (or jasmine water)

Directions:

Simply bring vegan cheese to room temperature. Mix in a bowl cream cheese, raspberry preserves, fresh raspberries, honey and rose water. Mix until super creamy and blended well. Take a piece of bread and generously spread on your raspberry-rose cream cheese. Top with another piece of bread. Cut off crusts and cut into quarters. Or better yet use heart shaped cookie cutters. Display heart shaped sandwiches on a bed of pink, red and white rose petals and a few fresh raspberries for garnish. I sometimes top each sandwich with a thin heart shaped strawberry for added effect. This sandwich is pure love! Enjoy with a vintage rose tea.

Lady Mary's Blueberry Patch

Anyone who is blueberry crazy like me will love this elegant tea sandwich. Blueberries are a favorite fruit. I created this lovely blueberry patch tea sandwich for all those who requested it. For a truly blueberry splash serve with a cup of blueberry vanilla Ceylon tea in cobalt blue glass tea cups or blue flower porcelain china. This is also such a simple recipe when you need to make a lot of tea sandwiches quickly. You can serve them in triangles, finger rectangles or use your favorite cookie cutters to get various shapes. I often cut these sandwiches in the early spring into flower shapes and use a blueberry or heart shaped strawberry slice for the center of the flower. Young children especially love this magical presentation. I often include this sandwich in my Alice in Wonderland themed tea parties. Jimmy, and the Mad Hatter also love this sandwich.

Ingredients:

- 8 oz of vegan cream cheese
- Juice from one tangerine
- Zest of one tangerine
- ¼ cup of powdered sugar
- 1/2 cup of blueberries with extra for garnish
- Edible flowers for garnish
- 1 loaf of gluten-free white bread

Simply mix all ingredients until smooth and creamy.

Add in ½ a cup of fresh (rinsed) blueberries. Fold into cream cheese mixture until fully mixed.

Spread berries/cream generously onto bread and make sandwiches. Use knife to cut off crust, and cut into triangles. Serve on a platter garnished with fresh berries, and edible flowers. Blueberries, Blackberries and Raspberries make for colorful garnish.

Or better yet: Use flower cookie cutters. Cut sandwiches into flowers. Place on a platter. Use one raspberry, 1 blueberry or 1 sliced strawberry heart for the center of the flowers. Serve the flowered tea sandwiches for spring and summer teas, or an *Alice and Wonderland* tea party. You'll find Mary conversing with the White Rabbit.

Lebanese Cucumber

This delicious and exotic tea sandwich is a Middle Eastern twist on traditional English cucumber sandwiches. It is simple to make.

Ingredients:

- Radishes (peeled and cut into paper thin slices) Pat dry with paper towels to get out moisture
- 1 English Cucumber (peeled and cut into thin slices) Pat dry with paper towels to get out moisture
- 1 tomato (thin slice) Pat dry with paper towels
- Baba ganoush (Lebanese eggplant Tahini spread) You should be able to find this at *Trader Joe's* or *Whole Foods*. You may also use any form of hummus.
- 1 loaf of dark multi grain gluten-free bread

Assembly:

Simply put a generous layer of Baba ganoush (or hummus) on a slice of bread. Then a thin layer of tomato, then cucumber then radish. Layer another piece of bread with baba ganoush or hummus spread. Put sandwich together. Cut off crust, cut into four triangles. Display on a platter with some dill pickles and black olives.

Martinique Banana Toast

Back in my mid 20s I had the pleasure of performing jazz piano for a few weeks in the Caribbean. Martinique cuisine is known for it's fantastic blending of exotic island flavors and traditional French cooking. As a vegan, I became friends with a native cook named Marcel. Marcel tweaked a traditional French Toast recipe and together we came up with this unbelievably amazing banana French Toast sandwich. This sandwich is reminiscent of the famous Monte Cristo, but has some unusual twists. If you love banana bread, you'll especially love this exotic and simple recipe. I serve the Martinique for brunch teas especially in the spring and summer season.

Ingredients:

- 1 large ripe banana (1/2 a cup mashed)
- 1 ¼ cups of unsweetened vanilla almond milk
- ½ Tbsp of ground flaxseed
- ¼ tsp of ground cinnamon
- ¼ tsp of ground nutmeg
- Loaf of hearty gluten-free wheat bread
- Optional: ½ tsp vanilla extract

Filling:

- Sliced thin bananas
- Chopped pecans (may be candied which I prefer)
- Maple Syrup (Grade B is best)

Toothpicks to hold together.

Serve with sprinkled powder sugar and serve with orange marmalade or lemon curd.

Directions:

Mash banana in a large bowl.

Add almond milk, flaxseed, cinnamon spice and stir. If your batter seems extremely lumpy, add a bit more almond milk to thin it out. It should be pourable. (Vanilla extract is optional.)

Let batter rest for approximately 5 minutes while you preheat your skillet to medium heat.

Once your surface is hot, coat generously with vegan butter or coconut oil (I use Earth Balance because I like the flavor-though I do not use margarine in my regular diet.)

Dip your slices of bread into the batter and let it rest for 5-10 seconds on each side, using your fingers to make sure the bread is fully submerged. Transfer quickly to the skillet.
Cook for 3-4 minutes on each side or until evenly golden brown. Flip carefully using a sturdy spatula, as the banana mixture can be a bit sticky if you're not careful. If your French toast appears to be burning or browning too quickly turn down your grill.

You may need to make up more batter as needed to create as many French toast as needed. After several slices of French Toast are completed, lightly pat dry with paper towel.

Meanwhile in a bowl, mix banana slices with chopped pecan and just enough Maple Syrup to cover the mixture. Scoop onto French Toast and put another piece of toast on top. Cut off crust (optional), and cut into four triangles. Feel free to use decorative toothpicks to keep together. Lie onto a serving platter and sprinkle with powder sugar. In the center of the platter, put a small dish with a spoon of Orange Marmalade. This is pure heaven. It reminds me of leisure days at Club Med.

Matcha-Gotcha Mango

This exotic tea sandwiches pairs well with Japanese teas like sencha, or white needle tea. It also pairs well with tropical ice tea for summer luncheons. It is an unexpected sandwich to serve and always makes a great impression on tea guests.

Ingredients:

- 2 cups of coconut, rice or almond flour (Coconut works best)
- 1 Tbsp of baking powder
- ½ cup of light vegetable oil (Safflower works well)
- ¼ cup of soymilk
- 1 Tbsp of matcha powder (I use *Vitacost* brand from *Mother's Market*)
- 1.5 cups of chopped mango
- ½ cup of coconut sugar
- ¼ tsp of ginger powder

Directions:

Preheat oven to 450F.

Combine coconut flour, baking powder and matcha powder in a medium glass bowl

Gradually add the oil to dry ingredients. Mix well with your hands.

Now, add the milk so that the dough forms into a ball. Knead the ball of dough a few times and then roll it out with a rolling pin

Using the rim of a medium size cup, cut out circles in the dough. I was able to get about 9 round scones from one batch.

Pour some sugar onto a platter and dip both sides of each scone in it. Then place them on an ungreased baking sheet. Bake for 12-15 minutes.

Meanwhile, prepare your filling by combining the mango, 1/2 cup sugar, and ginger in a skillet.

Bring to a boil on med. high heat, stirring occasionally. After a couple minutes, and once the mixture begins to thicken, lower heat and continue to cook for a few minutes. Then set aside.

Once your scones have cooled down, you can assemble your sandwiches. Because this recipe only makes about four sandwich style scones., you might need to double or even quadruple the recipe depending on how many sandwiches you need.

Serve these sandwiches on a platter and garnish with some tropical fruit cubes like mango, passion fruit and melon. They are exotic and go great with white and green teas.

⚜ Monsieur Poire-Bleu ⚜

This unusual sandwich was created quite by accident but has a lovely blend of pears and the flavor of bleu cheese: quite unexpected and unusual for those more adventurous tea patrons.

Ingredients:

- 1 can of pears (drained and patted dry). Then cut into small squares.
- Vegan blue cheese dressing (Look for this at *Whole Foods*)
- 1 Tbsp of nutritional yeast
- Herb greens
- 1 loaf of thinly sliced pumpernickel

Directions:

In a bowel mix vegan blue cheese dressing with nutritional yeast to thicken up. Feel free to add any favorite herbs for seasoning. I often add just a dash of Herbs de Provence (Thyme, Sage and Rosemary); however feel free to experiment with a little Dill or Tarragon. Also just a dash of sea salt and pepper work great.

Then spread your layer of dressing onto bread. Layer some herb greens then a layer of pear cubes. Then top with another slice of bread layered with dressing. Cut off crust and cut into 4 triangles.

Serve on a platter on a bed of herb greens and feel free to add slices of golden pear to your plate. Garnish with fresh parsley.

⚜ Monte Cristo ⚜

Monte Cristo sandwiches were a childhood favorite. I would have this sandwich for brunch every time I visited the Disneyland Resort at their Blue Bayou Restaurant located in the Pirates of the Caribbean ride. This sandwich always brought up the feeling of Caribbean pirate adventures. Later in my life I tweaked this traditional New Orleans sandwich recipe to a completely guilt free vegan equivalent. This sandwich is perfect as a brunch entrée, or can be cut into sweet tea sandwiches for a surprise on the menu. This sandwich is also perfect for "Southern" themed tea parties. I served it for Mardi Gras tea brunch, and children's "Treasure Island" pirate brunches. (I still am partial to pirates growing up a child in Key West, Florida: Thus I still love to dress up and get out my skull and crossbow boots from my youth.) This sandwich goes especially well with Pirate Rum ice tea in the summer. Your guest will love this! I leave many options to personalize your sandwich and tweak it to your own Pirate Monte Cristo creation. Bon Appétit!

Ingredients:

- 2/3 cup of filtered water
- 1 vegan egg replacer
- 2/3 cups of coconut flour
- 1 ¾ Tbsp of baking powder
- ½ tsp sea salt
- 4 or more slices of soft sandwich bread. Try gluten-free white, Sourdough, or a multi grain. Or for an ultra sweet breakfast sandwich: you may use cinnamon raisin bread or Hawaiian sweet bread.

- 4 slices of vegan turkey (there are so many vegan luncheon meats to choose from – I never liked the taste of ham, thus I double up with vegan Tofurky. Nut loaf slices also work just fine. Be creative to your own personal likes. Do not worry about being perfect. Explore various flavors.)
- 4 slices Mozzarella *Daiya* cheese or thin almond cheese slices or vegan sliced cheese of choice (this recipe works best though with a white cheese such as Mozzarella, Jack, Swiss etc)
- Your favorite berry preserves: Traditional is Raspberry, but I prefer Knott's Boysenberry. For creative Southern twists try: Huckleberry, Marionberry, Blackberry or Razzleberry preserves. Vegan butter or light oil for grilling
- Powdered sugar
- Decorative toothpicks

Directions:

Heat the oil in a skillet to 350F.

Mix the water, vegan egg beater, flour, baking powder and salt and set aside.

Put the sandwiches together like so: bread, 2 slices vegan turkey, 1 slice cheese slice, 2 slices vegan turkey, 1 slice a cheese, bread. Cut each sandwich into quarters. Dip each quarter sandwich into the batter and completely coat. Fry the sandwiches on both sides in the oil until lightly browned and cheese has melted, and then set on a paper towel covered plate to cool. Dab both sides of sandwiches to get excess moisture out.

It is optional but you may put decorative toothpicks back into the sandwich to hold them together and for display.

Lightly dust the tops of the sandwiches with the powdered sugar.

Set attractively on a display platter and in the center of the platter place a decorative small bowl with a spoon of your favorite raspberry or boysenberry preserves.

Peruvian Chocolate-Avocado

This is always an unexpected tea sandwich that adds something a little exotic to the table. This is a simple grilled sandwich recipe that is sure to please.

Ingredients:

- 4 slices of bread of choice (try gluten-free multi grain, whole dark wheat, or even black or pumpernickel)
- 1 avocado (ripe)
- 1 large banana (ripe)
- 1/3 cup of dark chocolate chips or dark cacao chips
- ¼ cup of coconut flakes (may be toasted)
- ¼ tsp of cayenne pepper (adds as spicy Peruvian kicker)
- 1 Tbsp of light oil or vegan butter for grilling.

This recipe will make 8 tea sandwiches. Double the recipe for 16.

Garnish ideas: Slices of fried sweet bananas, coconut meat sliced into cubes, pieces of dark chocolate.

Directions:

Cut the Avocado into two remove the seed and scoop out the pulp of the fruit and place it in a bowl. Mash well with a fork. You can also make it a pulp in a mixer grinder. Blend in cayenne pepper and coconut flakes.

Slice the bananas into thin roundels and keep aside.
Apply the mashed avocado on one side of all the bread slices.

Arrange the thin banana slices on top of the avocado mash. Sprinkle the chocolate chips on the banana slices and close with the other bread slice with the avocado facing down and press slightly together but firm.

Place the sandwich on a hot pan and drizzle either butter or oil around the sandwich and cook till golden brown and crisp. Place an object that's heavy on top of the sandwich so that that they could stick together. I placed my rolling board on it.

Very gently flip to the other side and let it cook for a few seconds till it becomes golden brown and crisp too.

Cut the sandwich into 4 triangles and cut off crust.

Place on an attractive platter with fried bananas, and pieces of chocolate.

Pumpkin Harvest

Ingredients:

- 1 loaf of Bavarian black bread or pumpernickel
- 1 jar of pumpkin butter (try to find a spicy variety that taste like pumpkin pie filling)
- 1 jar of creamy cashew butter (you may substitute pecan butter if you can find it.)
- 1 black Arkansas apple (if you can not find, use a dark juicy red apple)
- Dried orange cranberries.

Directions:

Using a peeler peel your juicy red apple. Then peel off thin shaving strips of apple. Blot apple strips with a paper towel to get out all moisture. Set aside for now.

On a piece of pumpernickel bread generously spread a layer of cashew or pecan butter. Then lay thin shaving slices of apple over the top and sprinkle with a few dried cranberries. On another piece of bread spread a generous layer of cashew or pecan butter. Put the sandwich together and then cut off crust and cut into triangles. You may also use holiday cookie cutters to create a more festive display. I love to cut these fun sandwiches into pumpkin shapes. Feel free to garnish your sandwich tray with attractive black Arkansas apple slices and sprinkle a few more cranberries around. This is a great sandwich idea of autumn, Halloween and Thanksgiving themed tea luncheons.

Vegan Reuben Sandwiches are by far my very favorite. This is a great tea sandwich to serve if you need something a little heartier. This sandwich could be served with soup or salad for a complete tea luncheon experience. I use fancy toothpicks to hold this sandwich together. Though it's usually customary to cut off the crust for tea sandwiches, I serve this sandwich more like a club, leaving the crust on. Absolute heaven!

Ingredients:

- 1 loaf of rye bread (I prefer Jewish, or dark rye)
- 1 large jar of sauerkraut (also for added gourmet taste try sauerkraut with caraway seeds. I usually buy Eden brand)
- 1 package of fakin' bacon (or bbq flavored tempeh)
- Sliced vegan cheese of your choice (Cheddar, Swiss etc) (I prefer Swiss)
- 2 ripe avocados
- Vegan 1000 Island dressing (try Annie's or Organicville)
- 1 bottle of vegan mayo
- Fancy toothpicks. (Party stores have toothpicks with international flags, or festive colors.)
- 1 jar of dill pickles sliced
- Black olives and small sweet pickles (garnish)
- Vegan butter

Directions:

On a slice of rye bread, spread a generous coating of 1000 Island dressing. Then layer strips of fakin' bacon (or bbq tempeh). Then layer slice of dill pickle (optional)…and be sure to pat dry before adding to sandwich to get out excess moisture. Then put a slice of your favorite flavored vegan cheese. I prefer almond cheese slices or vegan cheddar for a heartier feel. Then put on your thin slices of avocado. Put a generous amount of sauerkraut that has also been patted dry with paper towel to get out excess moisture. Caraway sauerkraut is especially awesome.

On another slice of rye bread, spread vegan mayonnaise. Top the sandwich. Be cautious when transferring to a skillet with just a dash of melted vegan butter enough to grill your sandwich till golden toasty and vegan cheese has melted. Transfer grilled Reuben to a plate and pat dry with paper towel to get rid of excess moisture.

Cut Sandwiches into 2 triangles. It is your choice if you'd like to cut off the crust or leave on. You of course may cut into 4 triangles for smaller tea sandwiches. This sandwich is so delicious and versatile. Serve as many as needed arranged beautifully on a platter. Put your fancy toothpicks to hold your sandwiches together. Garnish plate with sweet or dill pickle slices, and black olives.

I once had a Civil War themed tea, where guests came as Yankees or Confederates. I made Yankee themed sandwiches like Reuben' and Waldorf Salad Sandwiches originally served in NYC, as well as Southern style sandwiches. Depending on the region I used Confederate flag or Union Jack Toothpicks. Everyone thought it was hysterical and clever. While guest mingled I had board games of Stratego available to play. The party was a huge success.

Roasted Bell Peppers and Pesto

Pesto and roasted peppers are a lovely combination for simple tea sandwiches, the peppers and pesto also add color.

Ingredients:

Loaf of bread of choice (choose whole grain, gluten free, or dark bread varieties, I esp like black olive bread for this recipe)
Thinly sliced assorted color bell peppers (green, red, orange, yellow) roasted and marinated (You can get them already marinated in a jar to save time or roast and marinate yourself. I prefer marinating in Balsamic vinegar, or red wine vinegar.
Green pesto (I prefer vegan variety made with walnuts, or pinenuts)

Directions:

Simply spread pesto on slices of bread, top with thing roasted peppers (you might want to pat peppers dry to take out oil) and then put together. Cut sandwich into four triangles and cut off crust or use cookie cutters to make your favorite shapes. Garnish with a sprinkle of walnuts or pine nuts or black olives.

Sir James' (Nutella, Cream Cheese and Preserves)

One day I was looking for a quick dessert tea sandwich I could serve instead of a full dessert. I was having a light afternoon gentlemen's tea and I wanted to combine my some of my favorite flavors in a display that would be more masculine. I have always loved dark berries especially boysenberries, blackberries, black currants and cherries. I also am wild about hazelnut and chocolate. Voila! I created the Sir James. Both King James and I have an attraction to all things mystical, and this dark dessert sandwich is perfect for serving the Knight's of the Realm, or any Warlock or Witch Coven. It is sinfully delicious! I often serve this sandwich for mystery murder teas and at Halloween or Gentlemen's gatherings. Enjoy!

Ingredients:

- 1 loaf of thinly already sliced Bavarian Schwartzbrot (black bread), pumpernickel, or black squaw bread. (Black bread is not only used in this recipe for flavor but also for the dark masculine and mystical presentation)
- 1 8 oz vegan cream cheese
- 1 jar of Nutella (hazelnut/chocolate spread)
- 1 jar of dark berry preserves: Suggestions: *Knott's Boysenberry Preserves*, Blackberry Preserves, Dark Cherry Preserves, Cassis/Black Currant Jam or Preserves.
- Fresh Mint leaves (garnish)
- Fresh berries (garnish). Choose boysenberries, blackberries, and dark cherries. Or garnish (dried fruit): Dried blueberries, dried cherries, and black currants.
- *Earth Balance* vegan butter (For grilling)
- Optional (Powdered Sugar)
- Optional broken pieces of dark chocolate

Directions:

Simply spread 1 layer of Nutella generously on 1 slice of bread. Then 1 layer of your favorite preserves (Boysenberry is best). On another slice of bread spread vegan cream cheese. Put your sandwich together. Lightly grill with just a touch of vegan butter on both sides until nutella has a warmed chocolate filling consistency.

Take sandwiches and cut crusts off. Cut into 4 triangles. Or you may use cookie cutters for favorite shapes. I often like to use Clubs and Spades, as they are perfect with the black bread. Serve decoratively on a platter. You may sprinkle the top of the grilled Sir James with a little powdered sugar. I serve this garnish with fresh mint leaves, fresh dark berries, and broken pieces of the darkest chocolate (at least 70% cacao). Every one loves this simple creation! This dessert tea sandwich is perfect with a cup of black currant Ceylon, my favorite *Metropolitan* boysenberry tea or any chocolate dessert tea.

Smoked Portobello Mushroom and Horseradish

Ingredients:

3 Tbsp. olive oil
1/2 medium sweet onion, sliced
2 medium portobello mushroom caps, sliced
Dash liquid smoke
Salt and pepper, to taste
4 slices of bread (use dark bread)
Horseradish sauce
1 roasted red pepper, sliced (jarred or prepared at home)

- Heat 1 tablespoon of the olive oil in a skillet over medium heat. Add the onions and cook for about 15 minutes, until lightly caramelized. Remove the onions from the pan and set aside.
- Add another tablespoon of oil to the pan. Add the mushrooms and cook over medium heat for about 3 minutes. Add a dash of liquid smoke and cook for 1 more minute. Season with salt and pepper and remove from the heat.
- Heat a panini press according to the manufacturer's instructions until hot, or heat a panini pan over moderate heat.
- Brush the slices of bread on 1 side with the remaining 1 tablespoon of oil and then lay, oiled side down, on a work surface. Divide the horseradish sauce among the 4 slices and top with the onions, mushrooms, and roasted red peppers. Put 2 of the slices together and then the other 2 together, making 2 sandwiches.
- Put the sandwiches on the press and close. Cook until browned, about 4 to 6 minutes. If using a panini pan, place the weight on top of the sandwiches and cook for 2 to 3 minutes on each side.

Cut sandwiches into four triangles/cut of crust. Serve on a tray with garnishes of parsley, pickle or black olives.

Sweet Onion and Hummus

This sweet onion and hummus sandwich is a savory surprise for tea sandwich and pairs best with masculine rich black tea blends. I often serve this for Gentlemen's teas.

Ingredients:

Loaf of a dark bread of choice (Schwartzbrot, Pumpernickel are good choices)
1 small sweet onion
1 tablespoon of coconut oil
Herbes de Provence
Favorite Hummus spread (Trader Joe's has all types of hummus to play with you can mix flavors. I think red pepper hummus or black olive hummus works well with the sweet onion.

Directions:

Simply cut your sweet onion into thin slices and pull out to create small rings. Sautee them in a skillet with a bout a tablespoon of coconut and a dash of herbes de Provence until caramelized and golden brown. Cool and then pat off the excess oil with paper napkins (this is important so your sandwiches will not be soggy.

Spread a think coat of hummus on to slices of bread, and place onion on one. Make sandwiches. Cut them into triangles and cut off the crust, or use your favorite cookie cutters. I often serve these on a platter or tiered tea tray service garnished with a little fresh parsley and black olives and maybe if Im' feeling slightly eccentric some small cocktail onions.

Tahini Goddess

This Asian inspired sandwich is lovely for springtime and summer and pairs well with white and green tea blends. It is a light but savory sandwich.

Ingredients:

- 1 lb of extra firm sprouted tofu
- ¼ cup of white miso paste
- ½ cup of tahini butter (sesame)
- 1 Tbsp of fresh lemon juice
- 2 Tbsp of minced scallions
- 3 Tbsp of minced carrots
- 1 tsp of crushed and minced garlic
- 3 Tbsp of unsalted sunflower seeds.
- 1 loaf of gluten-free whole grain or wheat bread
- Lemon slices and edible flowers for garnish

Directions:

Simply drain sprouted tofu and pat dry with paper towels. Cover in paper towel for at least 30 minute to dry out excess moisture.

Crumble tofu with your hands into a medium bowl. Mix in tahini butter, miso paste, lemon juice and other ingredients. Once mixed cover and chill in the fridge for at least 45 minutes.

Spread generously on slice of bread and top to make sandwiches. Either cut into triangles cutting off crust or you may use your favorite cookie cutters to make interesting shapes. I serve these usually in triangles on a tiered tea tray with slices of fresh lemon (that have been patted dry to get rid of excess juice) and edible flower petals. This is a simple but effective spring sandwich.

Tarragon-Herb

This is a hearty "meatless" chicken sandwich with French Country flavors. Great for a finger sandwich or sandwich entrée.

Ingredients:

1 package Trader Joe's Chickenless strips or 1 1/2 cups of grilled seitan, firm tofu or tempeh
1 1/2 cups celery chopped thinly
2 tsp black pepper
1 tsp salt
1 Tbsp paprika
1 small orange, diced
1/2 cup green cabbage, shredded
2 Tbsp Tarragon, chopped
4 Tbsp Vegan mayo, heaping
1 Tbsp olive oil 1 lemon, juiced or 2 Tbsp apple cider vinegar
1 tsp lemon zest
1/4 cup flat parsley, chopped
3-4 Tbsp sunflower seeds, roasted/salted
2 scallions, chopped thinly
Optional: 3 Tbsp nutritional yeast *(natural thickener)*
Optional: 1 tsp cayenne
*Add more Vegenaise if you want a richer creamier chickenless salad

Bread: Use any rye or multi grain bread. (I like Jewish or dark rye)
Greens: Use herb greens.

Directions:

Sauté, grill, bake or chicken-less strips or seitan/tofu/tempeh. Chop into small cubes. Place into medium sized bowl-set in fridge to cool while you prep the other ingredients.

Clean and chop celery (finely)

Finely chop tarragon leaves.

Shred and chop green cabbage. Dice orange. Zest and squeeze lemon.

Add to a medium glass bowl: Protein: chickenless cubes or seitan/tofu/tempeh cubes.

Add olive oil. Stir oil into cubes.

Add celery, orange, lemon juice, lemon zest, salt, pepper, paprika, cabbage, parsley, sunflower seeds, parsley and scallions. Mix well. Fold in veganaise and tarragon.

Add optional nutritional yeast gradually and fold into salad. Add optional cayenne and more black pepper to top of salad.

Press salad firmly into bowl, cover and place in the fridge for a half hour to chill. Chill overnight if you have time.

Serve! Add to sandwiches with fresh herb greens Cut off crust and cut into triangles or finger rectangles. Garnish with fresh tarragon and orange slices.

Tofu "Eggless"

This is a great vegan alternative to traditional English egg salad. I like to serve this sandwich for spring, Mother's Day and Easter teas.

Ingredients:

- 1 loaf of gluten-free whole grain bread or any dark bread favorite: Try pumpernickel, dark rye, black olive bread, or dark wheat.

Tofu "Eggless"

- 16 oz tub of extra firm sprouted tofu (well-drained) You might want to dab the cube of tofu with paper towels to get out the excess moisture.
- 1 large stalk of celery (finely diced)
- 1 green onion (scallion) (finely chopped)
- 1 red pepper (very finely chopped)
- 1 small can of chopped black olives (drained) Use a paper towel to get out excess moisture or sandwiches can become soggy.
- 1/3 a cup of vegan mayo (your choice)
- 1 to 2 tsp of yellow mustard (I personally like mustard and often use 3 tsp)
- 1 or 2 tsp of high quality curry powder
- 2 or 3 Tbsp of nutritional yeast or yellow pea protein powder (makes creamy)
- A pinch of ground turmeric
- Sea Salt and Ground Pepper to taste

Directions:

Slice the tofu into six slabs crosswise and blot well with a paper towel to get out any excess moisture. Place slices of tofu in a large mixing or salad bowel, and mash down with a large fork or you may use a potato masher. Add the diced celery, red pepper, olives and scallions. In another small bowel combine veganaise, mustard, curry powder, turmeric and nutritional yeast and mix well. Pour the veganaise mixture over the tofu/veggie mixture. Stir well to combine. Add a little more veganaise if you prefer a creamier consistency. Season to your liking. Cover and chill for at least 45 minutes.

In the meantime take your bread out. When tofu salad is chilled, spread generously on one side of a piece of bread to a bout a 1 inch height. Top with another piece of bread. You may either cut of the crust and cut into triangle or rectangle finger sandwiches, or use cookie cutters to create various tea sandwich shapes. Serve elegantly on a platter or tea tiered service. Garnish with parsley, mint leaves, kalamata black olives, pickles are flower petals. Get creative. Tofu sandwiches are a great and healthier substitute to traditional springtime egg salad sandwiches. They are a perfect tea sandwich companion to Easter, Mother's and Father's Day tea luncheons or any springtime and summer afternoon tea. Note some people add curry powder for a kick.

Unicorn Bites

These campy fun tea sandwiches are great for children's party or gay pride events. They are crazy and unusual.

Ingredients:

3 or 4 rainbow swirl bagels
fresh banana sliced thin
Your favorite peanut butter or cashew butter
Your favorite fruit preserves (I prefer berries: Strawberry, Bosyenberry, Blackberry)
Garnish: Fruit slices

Simply spread thin coats of peanut or cashew butter on sides of sliced bagels. On top of one bagel at banana slices, on the other spread preserves. Put the sandwiches together, cut bagel sandwich into manageable bits. You can use decorative toothpicks and garnish with outrageous cut fruit. I sometimes create a kaleidoscope of fresh fruit strips on a plate and place the sandwiches in the middle. Kids love them.

Waldorf Astoria

This is a beautiful vegan recipe tweak of the famous New Yorker Waldorf Salad. This is a heartier sandwich recipe and thus can be served as a main sandwich entrée as well as smaller finger sandwiches. I made my own personal tweaks to add additional flavor. Waldorf Astoria Sandwiches are a lunch staple in my home This sandwich is great anytime of year but it especially lovely for spring and summer season.

Ingredients:

- 1 loaf of gluten-free multi grain bread
- 1 bunch of green seedless grapes (washed thoroughly and cut in half)
- Several Green Granny Apples or New Yorker Jazz Apples peeled, cored (no seeds), and cut into small bite size bits. Use 1 to 2 cups depending on how many sandwiches you plan to make.
- 1 -2 stalks of celery (washed and cut into thin sliced bits)
- ½ cup of candied pecans (the traditional recipe calls for chopped walnuts which is perfectly fine if you prefer a less sweet variety)
- About ¼ a cup of black raisin or for a twist try black currants.
- 1-2 carrots (washed, peeled and cut into small bits)
- 1 tub of extra firm sprouted tofu
- Vegan mayo of choice
- Dill (free is best)

Directions:

In a large salad bowl, drop in the firm tofu (after blotting dry with paper towels to get out all excess moisture). Use a fork or a potato masher to mash to tofu down into a crumbled "egg salad" consistency. Toss in celery, carrots, grapes, raisins, pecans or walnuts. I just intuitive look at the balance of ingredients for the sandwiches I'm making. Now slowly mix in vegan mayo. I start with about ¼ of cup. The trick is to use just enough vegan mayo to cover all ingredients but you don't want your salad to overly saturated in mayo that will make for a runny and soggy sandwich. As you blend your ingredients, sprinkle some dill. I tend to be generous with dill, as I love the mix of flavors of dill and chilled veggies and grapes.

Cover your salad bowl with plastic wrap and chill your Waldorf Salad for at least 30 minutes. You may of course use an airtight Pyrex bowl for chilling.

Simply spread a very generous layer of the salad on a piece of bread, and top with another piece of bread to make your sandwiches. You may cut in twos (triangles) and cut off crusts for a sandwich entrée. Or you may cut into fours (triangles) for tea sandwiches. I often use toothpicks to hold the sandwich together when I'm making a hearty entrée. Lay attractively on a platter or tea tiered server. I garnish with flower petals, fresh dill and often whatever green grapes or apple slices are left over.

Vegan Cheese and Dill Pickle

This is a simple tea sandwich that adds a Jewish deli tinge to your tea.

Ingredients:

Loaf of Jewish rye bread
Mykonos Vegan Cream Cheese Spread (I pick this up at Trader Joes)
Thin sliced Deli dill pickle

Simply spread a thin layer of cream cheese on two slices of bread (preferably deli rye) and top with thin slices of dill pickle (be sure to pat dry excess water before assembly). Put sandwich together and cut into four squares no crust or use your favorite cookie cutters. Garnish with pickle and black olives.

Watercress

A Victorian tea tradition, these simple sandwiches are served at English tea luncheons and afternoon tea around the world.

Ingredients:

- 16 thin slices of gluten-free white bread
- 2 bunches of watercress
- Vegan butter
- Sea salt and ground lemon pepper to taste
- Fresh dill or parsley (garnish)

Directions:

Simply butter 16 slices of bread generously. Clip the stalk end off watercress and wrap leafs in paper towels to get out excess moisture. Lay slice of watercress on buttered bread; lightly sprinkle a pinch of sea salt, a dash of lemon pepper. Then top with the other bread. After making your sandwiches, cut off crusts and cut into triangles. You may also use your favorite cookie cutters to make shapes. I usually sprinkle the tops of the sandwiches with a dash of fresh dill, and serve garnished with fresh parsley, or edible flowers.

~~~~ Beet-Nectarine ~~~~

This raw canapé is especially colorful with the burgundy of the beet against the bright orange of the nectarine.

Arugula Cheese Ingredients:

- 2 cups of organic un-salted and un-roasted cashews soaked overnight, drained, rinsed and dried.
- 1/3 to ½ cup water
- 1 lemon (juice)
- 1 Tbsp nutritional yeast
- 1 clove of garlic (minced finely)
- 2 cups of fresh organic arugula leaves
- A pinch of Himalayan sea salt and ground pepper to taste

Directions for cheese: In a high speed blender blend cashews and water till thick and smooth. Start with 1/3 a cup of water and add rest if needed.

Add the lemon juice, garlic and nutritional yeast. Blend till smooth. Add arugula and process until creamy and smooth. After creamy, stir in a few bits of arugula. Season to taste.

Beets:

2 medium red beets, sliced about 1/8th inch
3 nectarines (no skin, small wedges). You may use 1 can of nectarines already wedged and drained. (Consider using paper towels to dry out excess juice).
½ cup finely chopped pecans.
Fresh cracked lemon pepper.

Assembly:

1. Place beets on a serving platter
2. Top with arugula cheese, sprinkle with pecans, and add 1 nectarine wedge to the top. Sprinkle a little cracked lemon pepper on the top. Place plastic wrap over the top of the platter. Chill 30- 45 minutes before serving.

~~~~ Bavarian Apricot Flower ~~~~

The Bavarian flower canapé is especially whimsical and attractive. This is a great choice for spring and Alice and Wonderland themed teas. This canapé is also especially fun to decorate for children and adults.

Ingredients:

- 12 thin slices of Bavarian pumpernickel bread (when I buy this already in a square package it comes already sliced thin for tea sandwiches). Slices should be ¼ to ½ inch.

- Creamy preferably unsalted cashew butter. (Creamy almond butter works too)
- Apricot preserves
- Dried Cranberries, Dried Raisins, Dried Blueberries (or dried cherries)
- Your favorite cookie cutters (I like to use floral for this recipe)

This is such a simple recipe anyone can prepare. It creates a beautiful presentation as well.

Take your bread-cut into flower shape with your cookie cutter (You of course may make canapés in any shape with any cookie cutter you like). Once bread is cut. Layer first with cashew butter, then apricot preserves. I garnish each flower canapé with 1 raisin, 1 dried cranberry and 1 dried blueberry or cherry. They are colorful and festive. You can play with design. Several friends cut them into squares or other triangle shapes and create modern art patterns with the dried fruit.

Black Lentil

This delicious and slightly spicy Middle Eastern canapé resembles caviar.

Ingredients:

- 2 cups of cooked baby black lentils
- 2 Tbsp extra virgin olive oil
- 1 Tbsp Balsamic vinegar
- Sea salt and cracked black pepper
- ½ cup roasted red bell peppers (jarred is fine)
- ½ cup roasted red pepper hummus (or any hummus or baba ganoush)
- 6 slices of gluten-free multi grain bread
- Dash of turmeric

Directions:

Combine cooked lentils, olive oil and Balsamic vinegar in a bowl. Add salt and pepper to taste and a dash of turmeric. Toss to combine

Dry the roasted peppers well with a paper towel. Make sure all excess moisture is out. Slice into thin julienne strips and set aside.

Heat oven to 300F. Lay all 6 slices of bread on a cookie sheet. Toast bread for about 5 -7 minutes.

Spread a thick layer of hummus over each piece of toast, then cut off crusts and cut each slice of bread into 4 equal size triangles.

Scoop the lentils onto one half of the triangle toast. (Half or your triangle will be black. Lay julienne slice of pepper down the middle of the triangle and cut off excess. Arrange attractively on a platter with other tea canapés.. Garnish with gourmet olives around the canapés.

Dijon Potatoes

A great and savory addition to any brunch menu, these Dijon potatoes melt in your mouth.

Ingredients:

- 2 Tbsp extra virgin olive oil
- 1 Tbsp Grey Poupon
- 1 clove garlic (minced)
- ¼ tsp thyme
- 1/2 tsp rosemary
- Sea salt and ground pepper to taste
- 5 red potatoes, cut into 1 inch pieces

Directions:

Preheat oven to 375 degrees F. Grease a roasting pan.

Stir olive oil, Dijon mustard, garlic, thyme, rosemary, salt, and pepper together in a bowl; add potatoes and toss to coat. Transfer potatoes to prepared roasting pan.

Roast in preheated oven, turning occasionally, until tender in the middle, 40 to 45 minutes. Serve these savory potatoes hot and garnish with fresh herbs like rosemary and thyme. Perfect for a tea brunch.

Edwardian Cucumber

A more creative and expressive version of the traditional English cucumber sandwich, I serve this canapé for the arts/music crowd. It is artwork on a platter.

Ingredients:

- Gluten-free white bread or Gluten-free multi-grain bread
- Organic Cucumber (preferably English)
- Fresh Dill
- Fresh Parsley and Mint leafs
- Vegan Cream Cheese or Vegan Butter

Tools:

- Peeler
- Paper towels
- Cookie Cutters (hearts, diamonds, clubs, spades, flowers etc. (optional)

Directions:

1. Shave long strips of cucumber with a peeler and save strips with no skin. Pat with a paper towel and wrap to get out extra moisture (this will help you canapés from getting soggy).
2. Spread 12 bread slices with cream cheese or butter.

3. Lay cucumber strips over the bread creating pretty striped patterns. Try diagonally. Hint: If you line end of cucumber strip with crust you should have cucumber left over for another canapé.
4. Cut of the crusts. Either cut in to triangles or use cookie cutters to make festive canapé shapes. Present about 1 dozen canapés on an elegant platter. Sprinkle a light dash of fresh dill on top, and garnish each canapé with a tiny mint or parsley leaf in the center. Serve immediately.

Fall Fig

The fig canapé is perfect in flavor and aesthetics to Fall teas.

Ingredients:

- 12 slices of Bavarian pumpernickel (The package I use already comes thinly sliced for tea sandwiches.
- Vegan cream cheese of choice
- Fig preserves
- Crushed walnuts and pecans (for garnish)
- You might like to use cookie cutters with fall shapes like leaves, maple leaves. Cutters should be small enough for tea canapés. Or you may choose to cut of crust of break, and then cut in strips, or triangle shapes.

Instructions: Simply cut shapes out of bread slices or cut off crust and put into triangles. Spread cream cheese on bread. Then a layer of fig preserves. Garnish with crush walnuts and pecans. Feel free to get creative with the presentation. I sometimes cut up little pieces of black mission figs to add as a garnish as well.

Fried Green Tomatoes with Red Pepper Aioli

I'm originally from the South and one of my favorite appetizers is the delicious Fried Green Tomatoes. This recipe is a nice twist when you want to avoid gluten or tea sandwiches. They make elegant appetizers that bring to mind the beautiful antebellum homes of areas like Savannah and Charleston.

Ingredients:

3 small green tomatoes
1/2 cup yellow cornmeal
1 tsp. salt
1 tsp. herbes de provence (optional, I like mind savory)
1/4 tsp. ground black pepper
1 tsp. Cajun seasoning
3 Tbsp. olive oil for frying

Dressing: Red pepper aioli or black olive tapenade (I usually just buy some already made to save time)
Fresh basil leaves (washed and dry
Bread choices: Hearty baguette, deli hamburger buns, black olive loaf

Directions:

•Cut each tomato into 3 thick slices.
•In a medium bowl, combine the cornmeal, salt, pepper, and Cajun seasoning.
•Dredge both sides of each tomato slice in the cornmeal mixture.
•Heat the oil in a large sauté pan and fry the tomato slices over medium-high heat until golden brown on both sides.
•Set aside on paper towels to drain.

On bread of choice spread a little red pepper aioli or black olive tapenade, lay the tomato and basil. Cut in fours. Place on a tray. I usually garnish with some decorative green tomato slices, black olives or basil leaves.

Mushroom and Caramelized Onion Polenta Bites

The pairing of mushrooms, caramelized mushrooms and polenta is both festive and tasty.

Polenta: Get a tube of pre-cooked sun-dried tomato polenta. It is vegan and gluten-free.

Shredded Vegan Cheese: Look for a mozzarella

Caramelized Onion Ingredients:

- 2 large sweet onions peeled and chopped
- 1 Tbsp of Balsamic vinegar
- 1 Tbsp brown sugar
- Pinch of sea salt

Sautéed Mushrooms

- 1 small box of sliced Crimini mushrooms (washed)
- 1 tsp of rosemary
- 3 Tbsp of red wine
- 2 tsp of extra virgin olive oil
- 1 large clove of garlic minced
- Pinch of sea salt

Directions:

1. Cut Polenta from the tube into ½ inch slices. You can experiment with shapes by keeping some round, or cutting into bite size squares, circles or triangles. Go for basic geometric shapes. After cutting: Place polenta gently onto a baking cookie tray. Be sure they don't touch.
2. To make the caramelized onions, heat a large frying pan over a medium low heat and add the olive oil before adding the onions and reduce the heat to low. Cook for 10 minutes before adding the balsamic and brown sugar. Cook for a further 10 minutes until caramelized. Set aside.
3. For the mushrooms, heat a large frying pan over a medium heat and add the olive oil. Add the mushrooms and season with salt and pepper. Cook for 10 minutes before adding the garlic

and cook for 2 minutes before adding the rose or red wine and rosemary. Simmer for a further 10 minutes, or until the wine has all but evaporated. Set aside.

4. Take a small spoon and put a little caramelized onion onto each polenta bite, try to get them in the middle of the bite.

5. Then take a small spoon and put a little mushrooms on top of the onions.

6. Take a few tiny vegan cheese shreds and lay them across the polenta bites in interesting striped patterns. Heat an oven to 350F.

7. Once oven is pre-heated, take your baking sheet and place in the oven for just about 5 -10 minutes. Only till the cheese melts. Use a spatula to carefully scoop the bites onto a tray for a dazzling artwork display of festive canapés. You might garnish your plate with some parsley. (For a luncheon or dinner: I often lay a few grilled and marinated asparagus tips against the polenta bites. Think masterpieces of edible art. The green asparagus against the golden polenta is elegant and festive.

Pesto Baguette Bites

A little taste of Genoa with these lovely pesto bites.

Ingredients:

- ½ cup of roasted pine nuts
- 8 sun dried tomatoes halves drained and finely chopped
- 2 garlic cloves minced
- ½ cup of vegan parmesan cheese
- ¼ cup of extra virgin olive oil
- 1/3 cup of fresh parsley minced
- 1 Tbsp of basil minced
- Fresh ground pepper
- Slices of white vegan cheese
- 1 long baguette, sliced diagonally ¼ thick (about 45 to 50 slices)

Directions:

Preheat the oven to 350°. Spread the pine nuts on a baking sheet and toast for about 8 minutes, shaking the pan occasionally, until golden. Transfer the nuts to a cutting board surface and coarsely chop them.

In a bowl, combine the sun-dried tomatoes with the garlic, vegan cheese , olive oil, parsley, basil and pepper. Lay thin slices of cheese on each baguette slice. Top each with 1/2 teaspoon of the pesto, sprinkle with the pine nuts. Put back into oven for 2 -3 minutes till baguette is warm and cheese melts. Serve hot.

Stuffed Fiesta Mushroom

This is a great canapé for mushroom lovers. A great simple source of protein to serve with other finger sandwiches.

Ingredients:

- 10 mushrooms Crimini or white. (remove stems and hollow out.) Be sure to wash and clean thoroughly.
- 8 Cherry Tomatoes (quartered)
- ½ cup of sweet corn (drained)
- ½ cup cooked kidney beans (drained)
- 2 Tbsp fresh cilantro
- 3 garlic cloves (crushed)
- 1 tsp cumin
- ¼ tsp sea salt
- ½ tsp paprika
- Lime juice
- Hot sauce

Instructions:

1. Clean mushrooms and remove stems.
2. Carefully hollow out mushrooms with a small spoon, and dice what has been hollowed out. (Stems will not be used in this recipe).
3. Combined diced mushrooms, with quarter tomatoes, corn, beans, cilantro, garlic, cumin, salt and paprika. Toss until mixed.
4. Fill mixture into mushrooms drizzling with a dash of limejuice.
5. Place stuffed mushrooms on a foil pan and grill covered on med-high heat for 6-8 minutes until mushrooms are tender. Or if using an oven. Heat oven to 435F. Place stuffed mushrooms in a deep roasting pan. Cover roasting pan with tin foil and roast in oven middle rack for 12-15 minutes. Serve on a platter hot. You may add a drop of 2 to each mushroom of hot sauce for a spicy kicker. Or have a bottle available so guests can choose to add it.

Sweet Potato-Avocado

This canapé is a festive fall favorite. I love the bright sweet potato orange against the avocado green.

Ingredients:

- 2 medium sweet potatoes, scrubbed thoroughly and sliced into ¼ inch thick pieces
- ½ tsp cumin
- ½ tsp paprika
- Sea salt to taste
- 1 ½ tsp olive oil
- 1 large avocado
- ¼ cup fresh lime juice
- ½ tsp sea salt
- 5 cherry tomatoes sliced into 1/8 inch thick pieces

- ½ cup bean sprouts

Directions:

Preheat oven to 400 degrees Fahrenheit.
Add the sliced sweet potatoes, cumin, paprika, olive oil, and sea salt to a bowl. Toss to coat.

Line a baking sheet with parchment paper and spread the sweet potato slices out into a single layer. Bake for 15 minutes or until tender.

Scoop the flesh of the avocado into a medium bowl. Add the limejuice and ½ teaspoon sea salt and mash together with the back of a fork.

Spread the sweet potato slices out of a serving platter or tray. Top each slice with a dollop of smashed avocado, one tomato slice, and a sprinkling of bean sprouts. Garnish with a lime slice
Serve and enjoy!

Scones

Aloha

The Aloha scone is a pleasant surprise from traditional English scones. It combines the Hawaiian taste of coconut and pineapple.

Ingredients:

- 4 cups of coconut flour
- 1 ½ cups of shredded coconut (may be toasted)
- ¼ cup of dried pineapple
- 2 Tbsp of coconut sugar
- 2 tsp baking powder
- ¼ tsp seal salt
- ½ cup virgin coconut oil
- 1 tsp vanilla
- 1 ½ cups of coconut milk

Instructions:

Preheat the oven to 400F.

In a large mixing bowl, mix the dry ingredients (flour, coconut, sugar, baking powder and salt).

Use your hands or a spoon to mix in the virgin coconut oil.

Add the vanilla extract and then slowly mix in the coconut milk or other milk substitute, working the dough as little as possible, until you have dough that just barely sticks together.

Turn the dough out on a heavily floured cutting board.

Knead the dough slightly. When it is done, it should be easy to handle and smooth.

Gently pat the dough to two 1.5–inch thick discs.

Cut each disc into 6 pieces.

Transfer the scones to a parchment-lined baking sheet.

(Optional) For lighter, fluffier scones, place the baking sheet into the freezer for about five minutes immediately before baking.

Bake the scones in a preheated 400-degree oven for 15-20 minutes or until lightly golden. (Optional: Turn pan halfway through baking.)

Cool on the baking sheet.

Serve with a tall glass of tropical mango or passion fruit ice tea.

Apple Harvest

These cinnamon apple scones are a great treat for the fall and winter months.

Ingredients:

¼ cup + 1 tablespoon coconut / palm sugar, divided
2 cups almond flour
2 tsp baking powder
½ tsp baking soda
¼ tsp salt
1 tsp ground cinnamon
⅓ cup solid or softened coconut oil
1 apple, peeled and shredded (about 1 cup of apple shreds)
½ cup unsweetened vanilla almond milk

Directions:

Preheat your oven to 425°F and line a baking sheet with a silicone mat or parchment paper.

Place the ¼ cup coconut / palm sugar in your spice or coffee grinder and give it a quick pulse to powder it; this should take more than 10 or 15 seconds. You can skip this step if using brown sugar.

Pour the powdered coconut sugar (or brown sugar) into a large bowl. Whisk in the flour, baking powder, baking soda, salt, and cinnamon until everything is well combined. Add the coconut oil (or other fat) and using a fork or pastry blender, cut it in until the mixture resembles coarse crumbs.

Stir in the apple and almond milk beverage, until the mixture starts to come together. It should be a little crumbly, but fairly easy to handle (not sticky) and easy to form into two balls. If it is too wet, add a little flour, too dry, sprinkle in some more milk alternative.

Take those two balls of dough, and gently flatten them into two disks that are about an inch to an inch and a half high on a baking sheet. Sprinkle the scones with the remaining tablespoon of sugar (the stuff you left coarse) or even a little more if desired.

Cut or score the disks into 4 or 6 triangles (like a pizza), and bake for 15 to 20 minutes, or until the scones begin to take on a nice golden brown hue on the tops and edges. I like to keep the scones touching as they bake for a pull-apart effect and tender middle.

Serve hot with a cup of tea. Chai, Rooibos or Ceylon are good choices

Apricot

Apricot is a delicious traditional scone flavor and especially wonderful serveed with apricot preserves or lemon curd.

Ingredients:

2 cups spelt flour
1/4 cup coconut sugar
1 1/2 Tbsp aluminum-free baking powder (I used Rumford brand)

1 Tbsp Ener-G egg replacer (powder only)
1/2 tsp salt
10 Tbsp vegan margarine (I use Earth Balance, chilled and cubed)
1/2 cup dried apricot (diced)
3/4 cups vanilla almond milk (or other non-dairy milk + a little extra for brushing on top of scones)
Coconut sugar (for sprinkling on top of scones.)

Directions:

In a mixing bowl combine flour, coconut sugar, baking powder, egg replacer and salt. Then add your cubed vegan margarine and work it into your dry ingredients with your hands until crumbly.

Add your dried apricots and fold them in.

Slowly gently mix in your almond milk with your hands until dough starts to form.

Turn your dough out onto a lightly floured surface and roll out into a ¾ inch thick square. Cut the square into four squares. Then cut each square diagonally to create 8 triangle scones.

Line two baking sheets with parchment paper and put four scones on each sheet. Place baking sheets in the fridge for 30 minutes.

About 10 min before dough is done chilling set oven to 400F.
 Then pull your scones out of the fridge and dust them with a light coat of almond milk and sprinkle with a little more coconut sugar.

Bake scones at 400F for 15 mins. Serve warm with your favorite lemon curd or apricot preserves.

Asian Pear

Due to the health benefits I often drink white or green Japanese teas and decided to come up with a Japanese flavored inspired scone that would pair well with sencha, jasmine green or white tea. I have always enjoyed the taste of pears and thought I wonder if anyone has ever created an Asian Pear scone? I looked online but could not find any pear scone recipes. I thought ah a challenge! Like wouldn't you think Pear would be a delicious choice for a scone? I started to try recipes. I have to say my first batch was not that great. After tweaking the recipe a few times I came up this delightful light scone. Serve it with a cup of jasmine green or sencha.

Ingredients:

- 2 cups of coconut flour
- 3 tsp baking powder
- 1 Tbsp of coconut sugar
- ¼ tsp ground cardamon
- ¼ cup of Earth Balance margarine (I try not to use vegan butter when I can, but this recipe does indeed work best with Earth Balance, which is a staple of many vegan/vegetarian homes)
- 2 large Asian pears (peeled and diced)
- 3 Tbsp candied ginger
- 1 Tbsp vanilla extract
- ¾ cup of thick unsweetened coconut milk (or almond milk)
- 2 Tbsp of coconut sugar for topping

Directions:

Preheat oven to 400F. In a large bowl, combine the flour, baking powder, and sugar. Cut in the margarine and blend it into the flour so that it resembles oats. Spoon in pears and ginger. Add the vanilla to the milk and pour into flour mixture. Use a large spoon to combine and then knead the mixture 4 or 5 times with your hands until it comes together.

Place dough onto parchment paper and pat into a round shape. Cut into 8 triangles, like a pie and place parchment paper and scones onto a cookie sheet. Brush with remaining tablespoon of milk and sprinkle with the coconut sugar. Bake for 15-20 minutes, or until the tops of the scones are golden. Serve warm with your favorite preserves.

*Please note that if you do choose to make these with unsalted butter instead of Earth Balance, please throw in 1/4 teaspoon of salt. I find most vegan margarines too salty and got rid of the salt for this version.

Autumn Carrot

This scone is my healthier equivalent to carrot cake. This is sure to please especially in the fall. Try serving this with a spicy cup of Masala chai. Yum!

Ingredients:

- 2 ¼ cups of spelt flour
- 1 Tbsp baking powder
- 1 tsp baking soda
- 1 tsp ground cinnamon
- 1 tsp ground nutmeg
- ½ cup coconut oil
- ½ cup shredded carrot (preferably organic)
- ¼ cup of chopped walnuts
- ¼ cup of unsweetened vanilla almond milk
- ¼ cup of maple syrup (Grade B)

Directions:

Preheat oven to 375. Lightly grease cookie sheet.
Whisk flour, baking powder, baking soda, and cinnamon/nutmeg together.

Cut in coconut oil until there are no big chunks remaining.

Stir in carrots, almond milk, and pure maple syrup. .
Sprinkle some flour on your countertop and place dough on top of that, shaping it into a circle about 1.5 inches thick.

Using a pizza cutter, cut into eighths. Transfer slices to prepared baking sheet.

Bake for 27-30 minutes.

Let cool and drizzle with icing if desired (1 cup powdered sugar, 1 Tablespoon water) Enjoy! Serve with your favorite cup of tea. I recommend chai.

Banana Nut

This scone taste like Grandma's banana nut bread: a perfect holiday seasonal favorite.

Ingredients:

- 1 cup of raw pecans
- 2 cups almond flour
- 1 Tbsp baking soda
- 1 tsp cinnamon
- 1/2 tsp nutmeg
- ½ tsp ground ginger
- ½ tsp salt
- 1/3 cup coconut oil
- ¾ cup mashed ripe bananas (about 2 medium size)
- ¼ cup of unsweetened vanilla almond milk
- 2 Tbsp maple syrup
- ½ tsp vanilla extract

Maple glaze

- 1 cup powdered sugar
- 1/8 tsp fine grain sea salt
- 1 Tbsp coconut oil
- ½ tsp vanilla
- ¼ cup maple syrup

Instructions:

Preheat oven to 425F. Place the nuts in a single layer on a rimmed baking sheet lined with parchment paper. Toast the nuts in the oven until fragrant, about 3 minutes. Chop the nuts into very fine pieces.

In a medium mixing bowl, combine the flour, ¾ of the chopped nuts, baking powder, cinnamon, nutmeg, ginger and salt in a bowl and whisk together.

Use a pastry cutter to cut the coconut oil or butter into the dry ingredients. If you don't have a pastry cutter, use a fork to cut the coconut oil into the flour, or use a knife to cut the butter into tiny pieces and mix it into the flour.

In a liquid measuring cup, measure ¾ cup mashed banana. Add almond milk until you have a total of 1-cup liquid. Pour in the maple syrup and vanilla extract, and mix well.

Pour the banana mixture into the dry mixture and combine with a big spoon. At first it will seem like there isn't enough liquid to wet the dough, but keep mixing until you have thoroughly incorporated the wet and dry ingredients. If you must, use your hands to knead the last of the flour into the dough.

On a flat surface (like a cutting board), form dough into a circle that's about an inch deep all around. Use a chef's knife to cut the circle into 8 even slices.

Separate slices and place on the baking sheet covered with parchment paper. Bake for 15 minutes to 17 or until lightly golden brown.

While the scones are baking, whisk together the glaze ingredients in a small bowl until smooth and creamy. (If you're using coconut oil and it solidifies on contact with cold syrup, gently warm the glaze in the microwave or on the stove, then mix again.) Let the scones cool for a few minutes, and then drizzle the glaze generously over the scones. While the glaze is wet, sprinkle it with the remaining chopped nuts.

Serve hot with a cup of tea. Try Canadian Breakfast.

Carnival Apple

Ingredients for Scones:

- 1 Tbsp ground flax seed
- 1 medium black Arkansas apple (any apple will do)
- 1 Tbsp of maple syrup (I prefer Grade B)
- 2.5 cups of almond flour (or whole wheat flour)
- 1 Tbsp baking powder
- 3 tsp of ground cinnamon
- ½ cup unsweetened vanilla almond milk
- ½ cup of unsweetened apple sauce
- ¼ cup coconut oil
- ¼ cup coconut sugar
- 1 tsp vanilla extract

Directions:

As with nearly all my baking recipes, we'll replace the egg with ground flax. To make, stir together 1 tbsp flax with 2 tbsp water in a small bowl and set aside for 20 minutes until it forms a gel.

Dice one red apple and add to a small skillet with 1 tsp of cinnamon, 1 Tbsp of maple syrup, and 2-3 Tbsp of water. Let these simmer into little bite-sized cinnamon apples while preparing the scone batter.

In a large bowl, sift together the dry ingredients (flour, baking powder, salt, and the other 2 tsp of cinnamon). Next, combine the almond milk, applesauce, coconut oil, sugar, vanilla, and our "flax egg" in a saucepan and warm just until the coconut oil and sugar are dissolved.

Carefully pour the wet mixture into the dry ingredients and use a wooden spoon to gently combine. Also at this time, drain those cinnamon apple bits and add them into the batter as well. Be careful not to over-mix, as that will develop too much gluten and result in rubbery scones. This will be very thick, but you should be able to form it into one solid ball of dough. If not, add 1-2 tsp of almond milk and try again. (This should NOT be sticky).

Lightly-flour a surface on your counter and roll the dough out until it's about 1/2 inch thick. Then, use a sharp knife to cut these into triangles or any other shape you want. Dust the tops with cinnamon, then add to a parchment-lined baking tray for about 15 minutes, or until the tops just start to brown.

Remove from the oven and allow to cool before icing.

Caramel Icing Ingredients:

- 10 large dates (no seed)
- 2 Tbsp creamy smooth almond or cashew butter
- 2 Tbsp maple syrup (B)
- 1 Tbsp unsweetened vanilla almond milk
- 1 tsp vanilla extract
- ¼ tsp salt

Directions:

This vegan no-bake caramel icing is modified from a recipe I found online. I modified it with maple syrup instead of powdered sugar. This icing in my opinion is more flavorful. I am crazy about maple syrup in Autumn cooking.

To make, simple combine all the above ingredients in a food processor or blender (don't forget to pit the dates!) and blend until totally smooth. If it needs to be slightly thinner to spread as icing, add a teaspoon of non-dairy milk at a time until just right. You can make this ahead of time and store (refrigerated) in a sealed container for up to 5 days.

Glace your apple scones with the caramel icing. Serve with your favorite cup of tea.

——⇜❧Cherry Almond❧⇝——

My dear friend Arlene knows how much I adore cherries so she came up with this delicious cherry-almond scone that is healthy and guilt free. Here's her fabulous recipe.

Ingredients:

- 1 cup of almond flour
- 1 cup of spelt flour (the mixing of the two flours adds for a unique texture and flavor I really like)
- ¼ cup of coconut sugar
- 2 tsp baking powder
- ½ tsp baking soda
- ½ tsp seal salt
- ¼ cup of nonhydrogenated margarine (cold)
- ½ cup of unsweetened vanilla almond milk
- ¾ cups of drained thawed out (dark cherries)
- 1 tsp of almond extract
- ¼ cup of sliced almonds

Directions:

Preheat the oven to 400F. Line a baking sheet with parchment paper and spray with nonstick spray. Set aside.

Sift together the flours, sugar, baking powder, baking soda, and salt. Add the margarine and cut into the flour mixture using a pastry cutter or your fingers, until the mixture resembles a coarse, crumbly dough.

Add the almond milk, cherries, almond slices and almond extract. Mix well with a wooden spoon or your hands until the mixture comes together to form dough. You may need to add an extra Tbsp of almond milk if the mixture is too dry.

Turn the dough out onto a lightly floured work surface. Divide the dough in half and form each half into a flat round, about 3/4 inch thick. Cut each round into six equal wedges.

Arrange the scones on the baking sheet. Brush the tops with a bit of almond milk and sprinkle with coconut sugar and top with a few more almond slices. Bake for 15 to 20 minutes, until the edges and bottom are golden. Serve warm or cover with dishtowel until ready to serve. Serve with cherry or other favorite preserves.

⤛⋆Chunky Monkey⋆⤜

One of my favorite childhood desserts were frozen bananas dipped in chocolate. One summer a friend of mine asked if there was a scone recipe that would combine the flavors of bananas and chocolate together. I came up with the Chunky Monkey Scone. Enjoy!

Ingredients:

- ½ cup of coconut flour
- 1 cup gluten free oat flour
- ¼ cup unsweetened cocoa powder
- 1/8 tsp fine sea salt
- 1 tsp baking soda
- 4 ounces ripe banana (about 1 cup)
- 3 oz of unsweetened coconut milk
- 4 to 5 drops of stevia drops
- 1 tsp vanilla extract
- 2 oz vegan chocolate chips (I prefer dark)
- Powdered sugar

Directions:

Pre heat oven to 350° with the rack in the middle. In a medium bowl whisk together flours, baking soda, cocoa powder, salt and add one ounce of the chocolate. Mix coconut milk, banana, vanilla, and stevia in a blender or food processor. Add wet to the dry ingredients and form dough. Press together with your fingers until you can knead into dough ball. Taste dough, add more sweetener if needed. Press dough into a 1/2 inch thick flattened disk. Cut into 8 equal pieces. Top with remaining one ounce of chocolate. Bake for about 10-12 minutes. Let cool on baking sheet and transfer to rack. Dust with powdered sugar and if you want more chocolate drizzle with some melted chocolate! Serve with a dessert tea. Try a chocolate dessert tea.

᚛Cranberry-Orange᚜

This is another holiday favorite scone combining the flavors of orange and cranberry. There is an optional recipe I have included for a frosting if you are having these for dessert. I like to serve these with orange marmalade and a cup of spicy tea like chai. Perfect for Thanksgiving or Christmas.

Ingredients:

2 cups all-almond or spelt flour
1/3 cup coconut sugar
1 Tbsp baking powder
1/2 teaspoon salt
Zest from 1 orange (at least 1 teaspoon)
1 1/4 cups cold canned coconut milk
1 cup dried or fresh cranberries (may use orange flavored cranberries for a more tangy scone)

Directions:

Preheat oven to 425 F. Lightly grease or line a baking sheet with parchment paper.

In a mixing bowl, combine flour, sugar, baking powder and salt. Pour in coconut milk. Gently mix just until everything's combined, don't over mix. Dough will be thick. Gently add in cranberries.

Transfer dough onto a floured surface and shape into a disc about 10 inches in diameter and about 3/4 inches in thickness. Using a sharp knife or pizza cutter, cut into 8 or 12 wedges. Place onto prepared baking sheet 2 inches apart.

Bake for 15-20 minutes at 350F or until golden brown. Serve immediately or store them in an airtight container after they have completely cooled. Enjoy! Serve with orange marmalade.

Optional glaze: orange juice, coconut milk and powdered sugar (mix small amounts of each until you reach frosting consistency. Drizzle on scones when hot. Delicious.

᚛Dried Very Berry᚜

A very berry winter seasonal scone.

Ingredients:

- 4 cups of almond flour or spelt flour
- ¼ cup of dried cherries
- ¼ cup of dried blueberries
- ¼ cup of dried black currants
- ¼ cup of dried raisins
- ¼ cup of dried cranberries
- ¼ cup dried goji berries
- 2 tbsp coconut sugar and extra for sprinkling
- 2 tsp baking soda
- ¼ tsp sea salt
- 1/8 tsp of orange zest
- ½ cup of virgin coconut oil

- 1 tsp of vanilla extract
- 1.5 cups of vanilla unsweetened almond milk

Directions:

Preheat the oven to 400F.

In a large mixing bowl, mix the dry ingredients (flour, dried berries, sugar, baking powder, salt and citrus zest).

Use your hands or a spoon to mix in the virgin coconut oil.

Add the vanilla extract and then slowly mix in the almond milk or other milk substitute, working the dough as little as possible, until you have dough that just barely sticks together.

Turn the dough out on a heavily floured cutting board.

Knead the dough slightly. When it is done, it should be easy to handle and smooth.

Gently pat the dough to two 1.5–inch thick discs.

Cut each disc into 6 pieces

Transfer the scones to a parchment-lined baking sheet.

Optional) For lighter, fluffier scones, place the baking sheet into the freezer for about five minutes immediately before baking.

Sprinkle the scones with extra sugar and then bake in preheated 400-degree oven for 15-20 minutes or until lightly golden. (Optional: Turn pan halfway through baking.)

Cool on the baking sheet.

Serve hot with tea and lemon curd or preserves.

⇜⇝ Fraises Lavande ⇜⇝

One day I was asked to create a new scone for a French Country tea luncheon. I was up for the challenge. I talked briefly with a dear friend named Louise who lives in Dordogne. Louise was a noted actress in the 1980s on one of my favorite horror television shows entitled Friday The 13th. She mentioned strawberries were in season, and then I thought about the lovely aroma of lavender from the Provence region. Lavender has always been a favorite color and fragrance I like. Voila Strawberry-Lavender French style scones. I like to serve these with either lemon curd or strawberry preserves.

Ingredients:

- 3 cups of gluten free all purpose flour
- ½ cup of coconut sugar
- 2 ½ tsp of baking powder
- 1 Tbsp of fresh dried lavender flowers
- ¼ tsp of salt
- ½ cup virgin coconut oil (cut into chunks)
- 1 cup of full fat organic canned coconut milk
- 1 Tbsp of pure vanilla extract
- 2 cups of fresh strawberries washed and cut into thin slices

- Coconut milk for topping/coconut sugar (sprinkling)

Directions:

Preheat oven to 425F with the rack set at the middle position. Line a cookie sheet with parchment. In a large bowl, combine the flour, sugar, baking powder, and salt. Cut in the coconut oil with a pastry blender or 2 knives until the mixture starts to clump into pea-sized pieces. In a small bowl, stir the vanilla into the coconut milk. Add the coconut milk to the dough, and stir a few times, but do not over mix. The dough should hold together when squeezed, but still be clumpy. Fold in strawberries and lavender until evenly distributed. Place dough on a floured work surface, and shape into a 4-inch wide log. Use a bench scraper to cut into triangles. There should be about 8. Place scones on the prepared cookie sheet, reshaping slightly if necessary. Brush the tops lightly with the coconut milk (only if they seem dry, you want the sugar to stick), and sprinkle with coconut sugar. Bake for about 20 minutes or until golden brown (after about 15 minutes you may need to reshape with 2 bench scrapers if the scones are spreading, then place back in the oven). Cool on a wire rack. Serve hot (use cloth napkins to keep warm). Serve with strawberry preserves or lemon curd and a cup of tea. Try a lavender Earl Grey for a real perfect pairing.

⤛⋙ French Vanilla ⋘⤜

These lovely scones are reminiscent of the ones I had at a local French style tearoom. I loved the vanilla taste with a cup of Earl Grey. A little taste of Paris.

Ingredients:

- 1 ¾ cups of coconut flour
- ½ tsp of vanilla bean powder
- 2 tsp baking powder
- ½ tsp baking soda
- ¼ tsp table salt
- 4 Tbsp of chilled cubed vegan butter
- ¾ tsp of vanilla extract
- ¾ cup of unsweetened vanilla almond milk

Directions:

Pre-heat oven to 400F. Sift dry ingredients together in a large bowl.

Chop in the chilled butter with a fork and knife, dough should be a little chunky and textured.

Add in the vanilla and milk, stir with a spoon to incorporate. Use your hands to really mix everything together well. If it is really dry add a Tbsp or more of milk.

In a well-floured cast iron skillet or lined baking pan shape bread into a flat circle.

Using a sharp knives slice the dough into 6 triangles. Bake the triangles about 2 inches apart for 17-20 minutes.

Let cool before eating. I serve these with lemon curd or favorite preserves (strawberry, boysenberry or apricot).

Grandma Sarah's Scottish

Scottish style scones almost always use oats as a base. You'll find other similar recipes with raisins, berry or buttered shortbread style varieties.

- 2 cups of rolled oats
- ¼ cup of coconut sugar
- 1 ½ cups of plain whole meal flour
- 4 tsp baking powder
- ½ tsp cinnamon
- ½ tsp nutmeg (optional)
- ½ tsp salt
- ½ cup dried currants
- 1/3 cup of vanilla unsweetened almond milk
- 1/3 cup of unsweetened oat milk
- 1 tbsp of tapioca starch (arrowroot powder will work too)
- 4 oz of butter (for vegan version.. non dairy margarine) melted

Directions:

Preheat the oven to 350F.

Combine the flour, oats, coconut sugar, baking powder, tapioca starch, black currants, cinnamon and salt in a large bowl.

Make a well in the middle and add the melted Nuttelex and milks. Mix to create a soft dough.

Turn out onto a floured benchtop and knead briefly until the dough is a smooth ball. Flatten slightly into a thick disk about 8-10 inches diameter. Score the top into eight wedges.

Bake for 20-25 minutes, or until a knife comes out clean when inserted. Cut into wedges and serve warm with lemon curd, vegan butter, or your favorite preserves (try black currant) (and a cup of tea preferably).

Irish Soda Bread

This traditional Irish soda bread scone recipe has been tweaked to a vegan equivalent. As an English –Scotsman I was not as familiar with subtle Irish variants to scones and other English recipes until my Irish friends Terry and Patrick filled me in. I learned that applesauce was often used as a sweetener especially in the Depression years of the early 20th century. Sometimes the scones would have caraway seeds, black currants or raisings thrown in. This recipe is close to a few traditional Irish scones I have tried. Enjoy this with Irish Breakfast or Black Currant tea.

Ingredients:

½ cup non-dairy milk (I use almond milk)
½ Tbsp apple cider vinegar
2 cups spelt flour, plus more for sprinkling
1½ tsp baking powder
¾ tsp baking soda

½ tsp fine grain sea salt
2 Tbsp unrefined coconut oil, solid
2 Tbsp unsweetened applesauce
1 cup currants, soaked in hot water for 5 minutes and drained
2 tsp caraway seeds, lightly toasted
1½ tsp freshly grated orange zest

Directions:

Pre-heat the oven to 375F. Line a baking sheet with parchment paper, lightly dust with flour, and set it aside.

In a small bowl, whisk together the non-dairy milk and apple cider vinegar to make vegan buttermilk. Allow to sit for 5 minutes.

In a large bowl, mix together the flour, baking powder, baking soda and sea salt. Add the coconut oil, using your hands to pinch it into the flour (pea sized or smaller pieces is ideal). Stir in the vegan buttermilk and applesauce until a sticky, thick dough forms. Fold in the currants, caraway seeds, and orange zest.

Transfer the dough to your prepared baking sheet, dust it with a little more flour, and form it into an 8-inch round. Cut into 8 parts. Bake for 20-25 minutes, until golden. A toothpick inserted in the center should come out clean. Allow the scones to cool slightly and enjoy with some marmalade, lemon curd, black currant or berry preserves.

⮞ Krazy Boysenberry ⮜

*A Southern California amusement park, **Knott's Berry Farm** started as a berry farm in Buena Park, California. Originally a farm owned by Walter and Cordelia Knott, they created the most delicious hybrid berry—Boysenberry (a cross between a black berry and a raspberry). Knott's boysenberry pie was my favorite dessert as a boy and to this day. As a child Knott's had a ride called "Knott's boysenberry tales". The ride followed stuffed animals of a Country Fair that gets robbed by the evil pie thief with a total addictions to boysenberry pies (LOL sounds like me). The creators of the animated ride pumped boysenberry aroma through the ride. The scent was intoxicating and afterwards I would have to get some boysenberry pie, boysenberry punch, boysenberry funnel cake, and boysenberry sorbet. Do I like boysenberries? Yes LOL. Nobody has created that I know of a boysenberry scone recipe so here it is.*

Ingredients:

- 1 ½ tsp of egg beater replacer   Try Ener-G
- 2 Tbsp water
- 2 ½ cups of spelt flour
- ½ cup of coconut sugar
- 4 tsp baking powder
- ½ tsp salt
- ¾ cup of Earth Balance butter
- 1 cup of fresh boysenberries (I know they are hard to find, so if you can't find go with fresh blackberries)
- ½ cup of unsweetened vanilla almond milk

Directions:

In food processor or by hand whip the egg replacer powder with the water until frothy, set aside.

In a large bowl combine the flour, sugar, baking powder and salt. Add the butter and with a fork or pastry knife combine to make crumbly. Add the milk and berries.

Bake in preheated 425F oven for 12-15 minutes in a round pan, use some non-stick surface spray. Cut like a pie into slices. Makes 9-10 scones.

Serve with *Knott's* boysenberry or blackberry preserves and a cup of tea.

Lady Fabienne's Raspberry and White Chocolate

This delicious raspberry white chocolate scone has a French twist. This is a great feminine scone for Alice themed teas, Valentine's Day or spring gatherings.

Ingredients:

For the Scones

1½ cup all-purpose flour
1 cup white whole wheat or all-purpose flour
3 Tbsp sugar
1 Tbsp baking powder
¼ tsp salt
⅓ cup vegan butter, cold and cut into pieces
½ cup vanilla almond milk
1 tsp vanilla extract
⅓ cup fresh raspberries
⅓ cup white chocolate chips

For Frosting Drizzle

½ cup confectioner's sugar
3-4 fresh raspberries, depending on size

Instructions

Preheat oven to 375. Line a cookie sheet with parchment paper.

In a medium bowl, whisk together flours, sugar, baking powder, and salt. Cut butter into flour mixture using a pastry blender or fork until mixture resembles fine crumbs.

In a small bowl, whisk together milk, and vanilla extract. Add wet ingredients to dry ingredients and stir until just combined. Don't worry if the mixture appears too dry. The raspberries will add moisture.

Fold in raspberries and white chocolate chips until combined. Dough will be sticky. If using all wheat flour, you may need to add an extra splash of milk.

Turn dough out onto a well-floured surface. Knead dough gently until a shaggy ball forms. You may need to add more flour as you knead. Pat dough into a circle about 1 inch thick.

Cut into 8 pieces and place pieces onto prepared cookie sheet.

Bake for 16-20 minutes or until scones are just starting to turn golden brown on the edges.

Remove to a wire rack to cool.

In a small bowl, mash 3 raspberries into the confectioner's sugar. Allow to sit for a minute for juices to form a bit. If mixture is still too thick, mash additional berries as needed to reach desired consistency.

Drizzle frosting glaze over scones. Allow glaze to harden before serving.

Lady Nicole's Butterscotch

This rich butterscotch scone is rich and satisfying. It is an unexpected flavor pairing of butterscotch with sweet potato and spices.

Ingredients:

2 cups spelt flour
1 1/2 tsp baking powder
1/2 tsp sea salt
1/4 tsp ground cinnamon
1/4 tsp ground nutmeg
1/2 tsp ground ginger
6 Tbsp unsalted vegan butter
1/3 cup sweet potato purée
1/3 cup soymilk
1/3 cup brown sugar
1 tsp vanilla extract
1/4 cup butterscotch chips (or caramel chips)

Directions:

Heat oven to 425° F and line a baking sheet with parchment paper.

Cut the butter into small pieces, put the pieces into a small bowl, and set it in the freezer.

Whisk together the flour, baking powder, salt, cinnamon, nutmeg, and ginger in a medium-sized bowl. Set the bowl into the freezer.

In another small bowl, whisk together the sweet potato purée, soymilk, brown sugar, and vanilla. Set this bowl in the freezer and remove the butter and the bowl with the flour mixture.

Cut the butter into the flour mixture until the mixture looks like coarse crumbs, and you still have small pieces of butter visible.

Stir in the sweet potato mixture -- it will look very dry and crumbly, don't freak out -- and then stir in the butterscotch chips.

Knead just long enough until the dough comes together -- too long and the dough will get sticky. I like to do this right in the bowl, but you can also dump it out onto a counter.

Form the dough into a circle, about 1 inch thick, and then slice it into 8 wedges. Put the scones on the baking sheet, and bake for about 15 minutes or until the scones are light brown on the bottom. This goes amazingly well with a caramel rooibos tea.

Lemon Ginger

This lemon ginger scone is a spicier winter scone.

Ingredients:

- ½ cup of unsweetened almond milk
- 1 Tbsp lemon juice
- ¼ cup of white granulated sugar plus more for sprinkling (you may use coconut or xylitol sugar)
- 1 tsp baking soda
- 1/8 tsp ground ginger
- 1/8 tsp salt
- ½ cup dairy free butter
- ½ cup chopped candied ginger
- 3 tbsp of lemon peel

Directions:

Preheat the oven to 350 F. Lightly grease a large baking sheet and set aside.

In a measuring cup or small bowl, whisk together the almond milk and lemon juice. Set aside.

In a large mixing bowl, sift together the flour, baking powder, baking soda, ground ginger, and salt. Using a pastry cutter, knife or your fingers, cut in the dairy-free soy margarine until the mixture resembles fine crumbs. Stir in the candied ginger and lemon peel (if using) until evenly distributed throughout.

Add the soy-lemon mixture, stirring until the mixture just holds together. Turn out the dough onto a lightly floured surface and knead the dough into a soft ball. Place on the baking sheet and flatten the ball into a circle about 8-9 inches in diameter. Using a sharp knife, cut 8-10 equal wedges into the dough, but not quite all the way through. Top each wedge with a piece of candied ginger and sprinkle lightly with sugar.

Bake for 20-25, or until golden brown. Let scones cool on a wire cooling rack before serving. Serve hot with tea and lemon curd.

Lemon Poppyseed

This Lemon poppyseed scone is perfect for spring and summer. I'm always reminded of the Wicked Witch from The West who put Dorothy and her friends to sleep with her devious poison poppies. This scone recipe is indeed wickedly delicious.

Ingredients:

- 3 cups of almond flour
- 1 cup of coconut sugar (plus more for sprinkling)
- 1 Tbsp of baking soda
- 1 Tbsp of grated lemon zest
- ½ tsp of sea salt
- ¾ cups of dairy free butter
- ¼ cup poppy seeds
- 2 Tbsp lemon juice
- 1/3 cup of chilled coconut milk

Directions:

Preheat the oven to 375 F. Line a large cookie sheet with parchment paper and set aside.

Sift together the flour, sugar, baking powder, lemon zest and salt in a medium sized bowl. Cut in the dairy-free soy margarine using a pastry cutter or your fingers until the mixture resembles a coarse meal. Mix in the poppy seeds until evenly distributed. Gradually add the lemon juice and coconut milk, mixing until the dough just barely holds together, adding more if needed.

To make wedge scones: Press the dough into two discs, cut each of the discs into six wedges, placing the wedges on the sheet as you work. To make drop scones: simply shape the scones into 12 mounds and place on the prepared sheet.

Lightly sprinkle the scones with sugar, and bake for 16 to 20 minutes, or until golden brown. Serve with lemon curd and cup of tea.

Mary Anne Blueberry-Lemon

The unexpected duality of blueberry and lemon is like fraternal twins. This is an excellent scone to serve for summer teas and especially the 4th of July. It pairs well with Old-Fashioned lemonade or flavored Ceylon teas.

Dry Ingredients:

- 2 cups of spelt flour
- 2 tsp baking powder
- 1 tsp lemon zest
- ½ tsp baking soda
- ¼ tsp salt

Wet Ingredients:

- 1/3 cup of raw honey
- 1 cup of unsweetened almond milk
- 1 Tbsp of lemon juice
- 1 Tbsp of vegan egg replacer powder
- ¼ cup vegan margarine
- 1 cup of fresh blueberries

Directions:

Combine dry ingredients thoroughly in a large mixing bowl.

In a separate bowl combine the wet ingredients.

Pouring the wet into the dry ingredients, mix until everything is just moistened.

Fold in blueberries. Note: Yes, you can use frozen blueberries easily, but if you are using frozen blueberries, do not let them thaw prior to adding them or your dough will be blue. Still tasty, just blue. However blue dough makes for interesting scones.

Drop by the spoonful onto a preheated pizza/cookie sheet or just bake on normal baking sheets.

Bake at 400F for about 15 minutes until lightly browned.

While they bake, combine the powdered sugar, zest and juice so you can pour it over the scones while they're still hot. Makes 12 small or 9 huge scones.

Serve hot with lemon curd or blueberry preserves.

⟶Pumpkin Harvest⟵

This recipe is by far my favorite for fall. I have always loved the taste of pumpkin. It was early October, and as I looked out the window of a tearoom I saw beautiful fall colors. The flavors of Canadian maple and pecans with pumpkin are totally satisfying. I worked hard to create a healthy version that matches the beautiful flavors of the traditional Canadian scones. If you follow this recipe carefully, you should have an amazing tasting scone that will be perfect for Harvest Fall teas, Halloween or Thanksgiving.

- 1 cup of raw pecans
- 2 cups of whole wheat flour or gluten- fee equivalent (spelt or better yet almond flour works great)
- 1 Tbsp baking powder
- ¼ cup of brown sugar (packed) —Brown sugar is imperative to give you that Canadian scone taste
- 1 tsp cinnamon
- ½ tsp ground ginger
- ½ tsp nutmeg
- ¼ tsp of cloves or allspice

- ½ tsp salt
- 1/3 cup of solid coconut oil
- ¾ cup of pumpkin puree
- ¼ cup of unsweetened almond milk (this works perfectly esp. if you decide on using almond flour)
- ½ tsp of vanilla extract

Maple Glaze

- 1 cup powdered sugar
- 1/8 tsp of fine grain sea salt
- 1 Tbsp melted coconut butter
- ½ tsp vanilla extract
- ¼ cup of maple syrup (B if you can find)

Directions:

Preheat oven to 425F. Place the nuts in a single layer on a rimmed baking sheet lined with parchment paper. Toast the nuts in the oven until fragrant, about 3 minutes. Chop the nuts into very fine pieces.

In a medium-mixing bowl, combine the flour, ¾ths of the chopped nuts, baking powder, sugar, spices and salt in a bowl and whisk together.

Use a pastry cutter to cut the coconut oil or butter into the dry ingredients. If you don't have a pastry cutter, use a fork to cut the coconut oil into the flour, or use a knife to cut the butter into tiny pieces and mix it into the flour.

Stir in pumpkin puree, milk and vanilla extract. At first it will seem like there isn't enough liquid to wet the dough, but keep mixing until you have thoroughly incorporated the wet and dry ingredients. If you must, use your hands to knead the last of the flour into the dough.

Form dough into a circle that's about an inch deep all around. Use a chef's knife to cut the circle into 8 even slices.

Separate slices and place on the baking sheet covered with parchment paper. Bake for 15 to 17 minutes or until lightly golden brown.

While the scones are baking, whisk together the glaze ingredients in a small bowl until smooth and creamy. Drizzle the glaze generously over the scones (I preferred mine with a solid layer across the top). While the glaze is wet, sprinkle it with the remaining chopped nuts. Enjoy with a hot cup of tea such as Canadian Breakfast (Black tea with a slight maple flavor), Masala Chai, or any other favorite tea.

⇒⊶Razzle Dazzle Raspberry⊷⇐

I was experimenting one night and came up with this jazzy raspberry scone recipe that is sure to please at your next 1920s tea party. I serve these scones with raspberry preserves.

Ingredients:

- 2 cups of spelt flour
- 1 Tbsp of baking powder
- ½ tsp salt

- 1/3 cup of melted coconut oil, plus a little more for brushing
- 1/3 cup of maple syrup (grade B)
- 1 Tbsp vanilla extract
- 1 cup of fresh or thawed raspberries

Directions:

Preheat oven to 350°F.

Mix together dry ingredients in a medium bowl. Add coconut oil, maple syrup, and vanilla and stir until you have a thick batter. Add warm water and continue mixing. Gently fold in the raspberries until they're mixed evenly throughout the batter.

Line a baking sheet with parchment paper, and drop a dollop of batter for each scone-to-be. Leave room between each for them to spread, just like when making cookies. Brush the top of each with coconut oil.

Bake for 14 minutes, rotating the sheet half-way through to ensure even cooking. When done, they should be golden and slightly firm. Let the scones stay on the sheet for 15 minutes, then transfer to a wire rack to finish cooling.

Serve with raspberry preserves.

Savannah Peach

Savannah is my favorite city of the Deep South. I had the pleasure of spending much time with partner there. I would like to dedicate this scone to all the Georgian beaus —Kyle, Billy and Dean and the Georgian damsels —Betty, Liza and Carol. This lovely recipe will remind you of bygone days of elegant Southern mansions, manners, gentility as well as dashing blond suitors and delicate ladies. A scone that is…..Gone With the Wind. Try these with a little apricot or peach preserves. Also try a little peach Schnapps in a Ceylon tea. Peachy keen!

Ingredients:

1 cup of millet flour
1 cup of coconut flour
1/2 cup of sweet rice flour
1/2 cup of potato starch
1 tsp. of baking powder
1/2 tsp. of baking soda
1/2 tsp. of sea salt
1 tsp. of xanthan gum
2/3 cup of peach butter (apple butter could work too, but I was trying to stick with the peachy theme here (sugar-free is possible, sweetened only by fruit)
1/3 cup of agave nectar
4 Tbsp of organic palm oil shortening
1 cup of fresh or frozen diced peach pieces

Directions:

Mix all of the dry ingredients first in a large mixing bowl. Mix well and then fold in the peach butter and palm oil shortening with a spatula or fork. Make sure you do no over mix the batter. It should be a little sticky, but a firm biscuit like batter. Then add the frozen chunks of peaches. You could use fresh peaches as well if that is easier. But frozen works just fine...just make sure you do not let the peaches get defrosted while sitting out because it will add more water to the process before baking. Bake in a 375F oven for 20 minutes. Or until the bottoms are golden brown and crispy on the outside and moist in the middle. Serve hot with apricot or peach preserves and a cup of tea.

Savory Rosemary and Tomato

Sometimes one gets tired of serving sweet fruit scones. One day I attended a scone lecture at my local Whole Foods in Long Beach. The lecturer cooked this recipe. I thought this was a delicious and simple to make savory scone. I have always loved rosemary as a favorite savory spice. Just serve this scone with a cup of tea and a little melted vegan butter, or you may dip them foccacia style with some olive oil, balsamic vinegar and fresh herbs.

Ingredients:

- 3 cups of all purpose flour (or try Bob's Red Mill Gluten Free All Purpose Baking Flour plus 1 tsp of xantham gum)
- 2 Tbsp baking powder
- ¼ cup of coconut sugar
- ½ tsp salt
- ½ tsp ground black pepper
- 1/3 cup of extra virgin olive oil
- 1 .5 cups of tomato sauce
- 1 tsp Bragg's apple cider vinegar
- 2 Tbsp for fresh rosemary, chopped

Directions:

Preheat the oven to 400 degrees Fahrenheit. Lightly grease a large baking sheet.

In a large mixing bowl, combine flour, baking powder, sugar, salt, and pepper.

In another bowl, combine wet ingredients and rosemary.

Make a well in the center of the dry ingredients and pour in the liquid. Gently mix with a wooden spoon.

When the batter is loosely holding together, turn it onto a lightly floured work surface and gently knead until a soft dough forms. Do not over mix. Some patches of flour are good. Add a little extra flour if the dough seems sticky. Divide dough in two and form each section into a 6-inch disk. Slice each disk into six pieces (cut in half and then cut each half). Or if you are more relaxed and don't need your scones to be pretty, you can just scoop the dough into 8-12 mounds on the cookie sheet (like drop biscuits).

Place scones on the baking sheet and bake 14-16 minutes or until the tops are firm. Remove and let cool a bit on plate or cooling rack. Serve either warm or at room temperature.

Serve with some olive oil and balsamic vinegar mixed with herbs like rosemary, thyme, oregano and sage. Or serve with fresh vegan butter.

~Sir Andrew's Cranberry with Lemon Glaze~

A lemon-cranberry holiday scone. This scone has a jovial sunny disposition to brighten up any dreary foggy Fall day.

Ingredients:

For The Scones:

½ c plus 2 Tbsp unsweetened almond milk
½ tsp apple cider vinegar
¾ c coconut flour
1 Tbsp coconut sugar
2.5 tsp baking powder
¼ tsp salt
¼ c cold vegan butter
⅔ c dried orange cranberries

For The Glaze:

½ c plus 2 Tbsp powdered sugar
2.5 tsp freshly squeezed lemon juice
Zest from 1 lemon
Splash of vanilla extract

Directions:

Preheat oven to 450F.

Line a large cookie sheet with parchment paper.

In a small bowl, stir together almond milk and vinegar. Set aside to curdle.

In a large bowl, sift together flour, sugar, baking powder, and salt.

Using 2 knives or a pastry cutter, cut vegan butter into flour mixture.

Add milk mixture and cranberries to flour mixture and stir just until dough comes together. The dough should be relatively dry and not sticky, but if you can't get it to roughly form a ball, just stir in another tablespoon of milk.

Form dough into a sphere and flatten slightly.

Roll out dough to about 2" in thickness.

Using a sharp knife, slice dough (like a pizza) into 6 or 8 even triangles.

Arrange slices on cookie sheet and bake for 12-14 minutes, or until the tops are just beginning to turn golden. (be sure the slices do not touch)

Transfer scones to a cooling rack and let cool for a few minutes while you prepare the glaze.

In a small bowl, beat together powdered sugar, lemon juice and zest, and vanilla. Mixture should be easy to drizzle -- not so thick as to require spreading, and not so thin as to be watery. Add a little powdered sugar to thicken it up, or another squeeze of lemon juice to thin it out as needed.

Drizzle scones with glaze while still slightly warm and serve with Lemon or Orange curd.

Sir James Decadent Dark Chocolate-Pecan

I have to admit this is one of my favorite dessert scone recipes. It combines some of my favorite flavors together. Serve this scone with a dessert or flavored Ceylon. Black Currant, and berry teas are a nice compliment. Traditional Vintage Rose tea, chocolate dessert teas or rooibos red also work well. Enjoy this sinful but healthier scone.

Ingredients:

- 1 cup of chopped pecans
- 2 cups of spelt flour (or you may use whole wheat)
- 1 Tbsp of baking powder
- 1/3 cup of maple syrup (trust me, use Grade B dark amber)
- 2 tsp ground cinnamon
- 1 tsp of ginger
- Dash of nutmeg
- ½ tsp sea salt
- 1 cup of coconut milk (cold)
- 1 tsp vanilla extract
- 3 ozs of the darkest chocolate (at least 70% cacao). You may use a chocolate bar ground up into bits. (Just don't eat the bar before making your scones. I love dark chocolate so I'm always tempted)

Directions:

Preheat oven to 375° F and place the pecans in a single layer on a baking sheet. Toast the nuts in the oven until fragrant, (about 5 minutes). If you like drizzle a light coating of maple syrup to candy them.

In a medium mixing bowl, combine the flour, the toasted pecans, baking powder, ginger, cinnamon, nutmeg and salt in a bowl and whisk together.

Stir in coconut milk, maple syrup and vanilla extract. Keep mixing until wet and dry ingredients are fully incorporated.

Add chopped dark chocolate and stir until distributed.

Form dough into a circle that's about an inch deep all around. Cut the circle into 8 even slices.

Place on the baking sheet. Bake for 18-20 minutes or until lightly golden brown. OMG these are so yummy!

This is an excellent fall and winter chocolate scone. The flavors are like pecan pie mixed with dark chocolate. Totally rich and satisfying.

I often serve this scone for Harvest Teas, Halloween and Murder Parties and Christmas teas. It is my favorite dessert scone!

Sir Matthew's Blackberry

This scone has an eccentric pairing of juicy boysenberries and lavender. Delicious and totally unexpected. I usually serve this scone in the late winter season. I know you will enjoy this. Try it with a cup of Black Currant or Boysenberry Ceylon tea.

Ingredients:

3 cups spelt flour
1/3 cup coconut sugar
1 Tbsp dried lavender
2 1/2 tsp baking powder
1/2 tsp baking soda
3/4 tsp salt
3/4 cup cold unsalted vegan butter, cut into small cubes
3/4 cup cold coconut milk
1 cup fresh blackberries (you can used thawed and drained berries from the freezer although the scones will have a more purple color)

Directions:

Place a rack in the upper third of the oven and preheat oven to 400 degrees F. Line a baking sheet with parchment paper and set aside.

In a mixing bowl, sift together flour, sugar, lavender, baking powder, baking soda, and salt. Cut in butter (using your fingers or a pastry cutter) until mixture resembles a coarse meal. Work the butter into the dry ingredients until some of the butter flakes are the size of peas and some are the size of oat flakes. In another bowl, combine egg and buttermilk and beat lightly with a fork. Add to flour mixture all at once, stirring enough to make a soft dough. Fold in the blackberries.

Turn out onto a floured board and knead about 15 times. Roll or pat out into a 1-inch thickness. Cut into 2-inch rounds using a round cutter or cut into 2×2-inch squares. Reshape and roll dough to create more scones with excess scraps. Place on an ungreased baking sheet. Brush lightly with a little coconut oil sprinkle with coconut sugar. Bake for 15-18 minutes or until golden brown on top. Serve warm. Scones are best the day they're made, and though they can be frozen and lightly reheated in the oven if you need a future treat. Serve with blackberry preserves.

Sir Peter's Chocolate Grand Marnier

Rich and delicious, this satisfying chocolate scone is flavored with a little Grand Marnier.

Ingredients:

2 cups almond flour
⅓ cup coconut sugar, plus extra for sprinkling
1 Tbsp baking powder
½ tsp salt
½ tsp ground cinnamon
¼ cup refined* coconut oil
½ cup unsweetened vanilla almond milk, plus extra for brushing
2 Tbsp fresh orange juice
Zest of 1 orange
¼ tsp vanilla extract
1 Tbsp Grand Marnier
⅔ cup vegan chocolate chips (I prefer dark cacao)

Directions:

Preheat oven to 375 F. Line a large baking sheet with parchment paper.

In a medium bowl, whisk together 2 cups flour, ⅓ cup sugar, baking powder, salt, and cinnamon. Cut in margarine using a pastry cutter, until the texture is crumbly.

Add ½ cup almond milk, orange juice, Grand Marnier, zest, and chocolate chips, and mix with a wooden spoon. Do not over mix; the dough should be sticky and wet.

Transfer the dough to a lightly floured surface and liberally flour the top of the dough. Pat the dough into a circle (1" thick).

Cut the dough into 8 triangular slices. Transfer to the prepared baking sheet, leaving 2 inches between each slice. Brush the tops with almond dairy milk and sprinkle with sugar.

Bake for about 15 minutes, or until golden. Allow it to cool before serving. If you like you can drizzle some melted chocolate on top and garnish with orange slice.

Spencer Key Lime

This would be a perfect summer scone choice and pairs will with Southern Sweet Iced Tea, Old-Fashioned Lemonade or Pirate Iced tea. Inspired by my Grandma Sarah's Key West key-lime pie.

Ingredients:

- 3 cups of coconut flour
- 4 tsp baking powder
- ¾ tsp salt
- ¼ cup of coconut sugar
- 1 Tbsp key lime zest

80

- 8 Tbsp of vegan butter (Earth Balance works)
- ½ cup of toasted shredded coconut plus 2 Tbsp of toasted shredded coconut
- ¼ cup of chilled key lime juice
- 2 Tbsp vegan cream
- 1 tsp of coconut sugar (decorating)
- Thin Key lime slices (optional plate garnish)

Directions:

Heat the oven to 375F. In a large mixing bowl, whisk together the flour, baking powder, salt and sugar. Whisk in the lime zest. Then cut in the butter until the mixture is crumbly. Stir in the toasted shredded coconut, then stir in the coconut milk and limejuice just until incorporated; the dough will be crumbly and look dry. Knead in the bowl a few times to bring the dough together into a single mass.

Turn the dough out onto a lightly floured work surface and press into a circle roughly 7 inches in diameter and 1 inch thick. Cut the dough into 8 wedges, and place the triangles on a parchment-lined baking sheet.

 Brush the wedges with the cream and sprinkle over the coconut sugar. Bake on the center rack until golden, about 25 to 30 minutes. Remove the scones to a rack to cool slightly. Serve warm or at room temperature. Serve with Southern Iced Tea, Tropical Iced Tea, Pirate Iced tea, or white and green tea blends. Reminds me of lazy summers with my friends and family in Key West!

Soups

Autumn Butternut Squash

This delicious butternut squash soup combines other favorite fall flavors such as apples, cinnamon and nutmeg. It is a nice twist on the standard recipe.

Ingredients:

- 1 medium yellow onion (chopped finely) about 1 cup
- 1 celery (chopped finely) about ¾ cup
- 1 carrot (peeled and chopped finely) ¾ cup
- 2 Tbsp butter (try Earth Balance)
- 1 frozen bag of butternut squash cubed (thawed to room temperature)
- 1 tart Granny Green apple peeled, cored and chopped
- 3 cups of vegetable broth (no salt or at least low sodium)
- 1 cup of filtered water
- ½ tsp cinnamon
- ¼ tsp nutmeg
- Dash of cayenne pepper
- Garnishes (fresh parsley, chives and pepitas)

Directions:

Heat a large thick-bottomed pot on medium-high heat. Melt the butter in the pot and let it foam up and recede. Add the onion, carrot, and celery and sauté for 5 minutes. Lower the heat if the vegetables begin to brown.

Add the butternut squash, apple, broth and water. Bring to boil. Reduce to a simmer, cover, and simmer for 30 minutes or so, until the squash and carrots have softened.

Use an immersion blender to purée the soup, or work in batches and purée the soup in a standing blender.

Add pinches of nutmeg, cinnamon, and cayenne. Add salt and pepper to taste. Garnish with chopped fresh parsley or chives and pepitas.

Avgolemono

This is a vegan version of the delicious Greek lemon-chicken soup.

Ingredients:

- 1 quart low sodium vegetable broth
- ¼ cup long-grain organic Basmati white rice
- 3 Tbsp yellow pea protein powder (I use Naked Pea brand)

- 1 cup unsweetened almond milk
- 2 Tbsp cornstarch
- ¼ tsp turmeric
- 1/3 cup finely chopped chicken style seitan
- 2 Tbsp vegan margarine
- 1/3 cup fresh lemon juice
- Zest from 1 small lemon
- ¼ cup chopped fresh parsley
- Sea salt and black pepper to taste
- Fresh dill (garnish)

Directions:

Add vegetable broth, rice, and pea protein powder to medium stockpot. Bring to a boil, and then lower heat, cover, and simmer for 25 minutes, until rice is cooked.

Meanwhile, in a small bowl, mix the almond milk, cornstarch, and turmeric with a fork or whisk and set aside.

When 25 minutes is up, re-stir the almond milk mixture, and add to soup. Stir well, until thickened.

Add seitan, margarine, lemon juice, and lemon zest to soup. Mix well, and test for tartness. If more tart flavor is desired, add extra lemon juice.

Add parsley, salt, and pepper to taste. Stir well.

Serve with some freshly snipped dill, if desired. This recipe will double well.

Black Lentil Chili

For those that have sensitive stomachs I created this delicious lentil chili. I found the black (beluga) lentils cook the quickest and are easier to digest then kidney beans, or even red lentils. In addition I found the black lentils are actually more nutrient dense. Enjoy this delicious hearty chili. This would be a good choice for men's tea, or outdoor festivities.

Ingredients:

- 1 large brown onion (chopped) about 2 cups
- 1 large red bell pepper (chopped)
- 6 cloves of garlic minced
- 1 Tbsp chili powder
- 1 tsp ground cumin
- 1 tsp of oregano
- 1 tsp smoked paprika
- ½ tsp of chipotle chili powder
- 1 cup of baby black lentils (rinsed)
- ¼ cup yellow squash (cut into small cubes)

- 4 cups of no salt or low sodium vegetable broth
- 1 16 oz can of fired roasted tomatoes
- 1 tsp balsamic vinegar
- Dash of sea salt to taste

Directions:

Heat your pressure cooker. Add the onions and cook until they begin to brown, adding water by the tablespoon if they start to stick. Add the peppers, squash and garlic and cook for another couple of minutes, adding water as needed.

Add all the dry spices and the lentils and cook while stirring for another minute. Stir in the vegetable broth and tomatoes. Lock the lid in place, and bring to high pressure (switch to high pressure setting on electric PC and set timer for 10 minutes). After 10 minutes at high pressure, remove from heat or turn off and allow pressure to come down naturally for at least 10 minutes.

Use a quick release method to release the pressure and open the lid carefully. Stir and check that lentils are tender; if not, cover loosely with the lid and heat on low ("warm" setting) until they are soft. Add the vinegar, soy sauce, and salt to taste. If the chili seems too thick, add additional broth or water. Check seasonings and add extra to taste. Serve sprinkled with chopped fresh parsley or cilantro. Also you may use a scoop of vegan sour cream on top.

If you don't have a pressure cooker, follow the first steps to brown the vegetables in a large Dutch oven or pot. Then simply cook, covered, on low until the lentils are done, adding additional water or broth if it gets too thick. Allow at least 30 minutes.

If you can't find black beluga lentils, try using French green lentils, also known as puy lentils. (Note you may adapt this recipe to make in a large cauldron on the stove you will just have to watch that ingredients do not burn—stir regularly)

Casablanca Carrot Couscous

This is an exotic North African favorite and perfect for a more mysterious and unusual Autumn soup.

Ingredients:

1 large onion, grated
3 cloves garlic, minced
2 tsp grated ginger
1½ tsp paprika
1 tsp coriander
¾ tsp dried thyme or oregano
½ tsp ground fennel
½ tsp turmeric
¼ tsp ground black pepper
Pinch of cinnamon
4 cups shredded carrots (about 6-8 carrots)

8 cups vegetable broth (or 4 cups broth 4 water)

1 bay leaf

1 tsp lemon zest

¾ tsp sea salt

2 small tomatoes, peeled, seeded, and diced

½ of a jalapeño, other chili pepper, seeded and left whole

¼ cup whole-wheat couscous

2 tsp lemon juice

¼ cup chopped cilantro or parsley

Directions:

In a pot over medium-high heat, sauté the onion in 1 Tbsp olive oil for 5 minutes. Add another 1 Tbsp of olive oil to the pot and sauté the garlic and ginger for 30 seconds. Next, add the paprika, coriander, thyme/oregano, fennel, turmeric, black pepper, and cinnamon and sauté the spices for 10 seconds.

Finally, pour in the water, then add the carrots, bay leaf, vegetable broth powder, lemon zest, salt, chopped tomatoes, and jalapeño. Bring the soup to a boil, and then reduce heat to medium-low. Simmer the soup for 10-15 minutes.

After it has simmered, discard the bay leaf and put 4 cups (or about half) of the soup into a blender jar and carefully blend until smooth.

Return this smooth portion back to the pot.
Stir in the couscous and lemon juice and let the soup sit for five minutes off the heat. After 5 minutes, stir in the cilantro or parsley, taste for seasoning, and serve.

Cauliflower and Vegan Cheddar

This soup is my vegan twist on a New England specifically Connecticut favorite. This is a is also a favorite of children as it tastes super "cheesy" and creamy.

Ingredients:

2 Tbsp olive oil

1 large onion, finely chopped

2 medium celery stalks, diced

2 cloves garlic, minced

4 medium potatoes, peeled and cut into 1/2-inch dice

1 medium head cauliflower, finely chopped

2 tsp salt-free seasoning blend

1 tsp good-quality curry powder

1 tsp cumin

1 to 1 1/2 cups unsweetened rice milk

1 cup grated cheddar-style nondairy cheese, plus more for garnish

2 Tbsp nutritional yeast, or more, to taste, optional

1 1/2 cups thawed frozen green peas

2 to 3 Tbsp minced fresh dill, or 2 teaspoons dried

Salt and freshly ground pepper to taste

Directions:

Heat the oil in a large soup pot. Add the onion and celery and sauté over medium heat until the onion is translucent. Add the garlic and continue to sauté until the onion is golden.

Add the potatoes, cauliflower, and enough water to barely cover the vegetables. Stir in the seasoning blend, curry, and cumin. Bring to a gentle boil, then cover and simmer until all the vegetables are tender, about 20 to 25 minutes. Remove from the heat.

With a slotted spoon, transfer half of the solid ingredients to the container of a food processor. Process until smoothly pureed. Stir back into the soup pot with the remaining soup. Or, simply insert an immersion blender and process until half of the ingredients are pureed. Melt some vegan cheddar cheese on top.

Cherry and Dumplings

Loving the flavor of cherries especially when they are in season around my birthday in February, a friend told me about this vegan soup recipe that was in her family for 5 generations. This is a traditional Russian soup from St. Petersburg. A delicious and unusual soup to serve at your next tea party.

Soup:

- 4 cups of frozen dark cherries (defrosted)
- 1 cup of pomegranate juice (pure, no concentrated blend)
- 1 cup filtered water
- ¼ cup of coconut sugar
- ¼ tsp ground cinnamon (and 2 cinnamon sticks)

Dumplings

- 2 cups all purpose flour
- 2 tsp baking powder
- Dash of sea salt
- 1 cup unsweetened vanilla almond milk

Directions:

In large saucepan, place the cherries, water, sugar and cinnamon. Bring to a boil. Cook for 15 minutes or until cherries until tender. Adjust sugar, if necessary, depending on tartness of cherries.

For dumplings, combine the flour, baking powder and salt; stir in milk. Drop by teaspoonfuls into boiling soup. Cover and cook for 10-15 minutes or until dumplings are fluffy. Serve immediately. Yield: 8 servings. You may serve this chilled as well.

Chilled English Cucumber

Chilled English Cucumber is a British spring and summer tea favorite soup, and it pairs well with both hot and iced teas. I like to serve this soup for summer garden teas, or wedding showers.

Ingredients:

- 1 lb organic English cucumbers, roughly chopped
- 2 small avocados cut into small pieces
- ¼ cup fresh lime juice
- ¾ cup water
- 1 tsp sea salt
- ½ tsp sea black pepper
- Chopped tomato, cilantro (garnish)

Directions:

Place the cucumbers, avocados, limejuice, water, sea salt, and pepper into a blender.

Process ingredients until smooth.

Taste and add more salt/pepper if you like.

Transfer the soup to a large bowl or Tupperware and chill in the fridge for at least an hour before serving.

Garnish with fresh, chopped tomato and cilantro if you like.

Chilled Georgian Peach

Anyone who knows me, knows my love of Savannah, Georgia. One beautiful summer back in 1994, I had a Victorian Southern tea luncheon and made this soup, it was a big hit. This is a delicious and elegant soup for spring and summer brunches and Southern "Gone With the Wind" style tea ceremonies. "I do declare… I love this soup."

Ingredients:

- 4 cloves of garlic (minced)
- 1 Tbsp virgin olive oil
- 2 1/4 cups fresh peaches, peeled, pitted and chopped
- ½ cup diced sweet onion
- 1 tbsp curry powder
- 1/8 tsp of turmeric
- ¼ cup brown sugar
- ¼ cup of Moscato (not carbonated/fizzy)
- 1 cup vegetable broth
- ½ cup coconut milk
- Sea salt and black pepper to taste
- Garnish with peach slices, cilantro and a dash of vegan sour cream

Directions:

Preheat oven to 275 degrees F. Roast garlic cloves on a baking sheet for about 30 minutes, or until golden but not burnt.

Heat the oil in a medium saucepan over medium heat; sweat the onions and peaches until softened. Season with curry powder, turmeric, roasted garlic, and sugar. Cook over medium to low heat until caramelized, about 30 minutes. Deglaze the pan with Chardonnay wine, and then stir in the vegetable stock.

Remove from heat, and puree the soup in a blender or food processor, and strain through a fine sieve. Stir in the coconut milk, and season with salt and pepper. Reheat if desired, before serving and then re-chill.

Chilled Nectarine

An Italian friend was visiting her family in Tuscany, and told me about this unusual summer soup. I had to tweak the recipe a bit from it's no-vegan original recipe that calls for chicken broth but I think this recipe still works well, when one is going for a tea luncheon with a touch of the Italian.

Ingredients:

- 7 ripe nectarines (Skin removed)
- 2 cups of organic baby spinach (thoroughly washed)
- ½ cup of parsley
- 1/3 cup filtered water
- Dash of cinnamon and nutmeg

Directions:

Chop nectarines into small cubes and keep half a nectarine aside to slice into thin slices for garnish. Add the cubes of nectarine to your blender.

Add spinach and parsley and dash of spices to the blender. Blend till smooth.
Chill soup for 30 minutes. Serve chilled with slices of nectarine and parsley for garnish.

Chilled Raspberry Chambord

This romantic Parisien inspired chilled soup is perfect for weddings, anniversaries, and Valentine's Day. I have always been a huge fan of the tartness of fresh red raspberries and this soup pairs so well with salads, scones and teas. It is one of my chilled favorite and even once served it for my own romantic anniversary tea.

Ingredients:

1. 1/3 cup of organic cranberry juice
2. 1/3 cup of coconut sugar
3. 5 1/3 cups of fresh raspberries (12 raspberries saved)
4. 1 1/3 cups plus 2 tbsp of sour cream (or vegan equivalent)
5. 1 Tbsp of Chambord, Cilantro for garnish

Directions:

In blender blend cranberry juice, sugar, 5 1/3 cups of raspberries. Strain and discard seeds. Add Chambord (optional)

Stir in sour cream, and chill for 2 hours. Serve in small bowls or cordial glasses top with raspberries, ½ tsp of sour cream, and cilantro for garnish.

Creamy Tomato

This rather 1970s retro recipe reminds me of Campbell's tomato soup with a much healthier vegan twist. I used to enjoy this soup as a child watching my favorite cartoons on the tele.

Ingredients:

- 1 medium brown onion, chopped
- 2 tsp minced garlic
- 1 can diced tomatoes
- 1 tsp oregano
- 1 tsp dried basil
- 1 tsp apple cider vinegar
- 1 cup vegetable broth
- ½ cup unsweetened almond milk
- Salt and pepper to taste

Directions:

Heat a large greased or nonstick-sprayed pot over medium high heat. Add onion and cook, stirring occasionally, until golden, about 5 minutes. Stir in the minced garlic and cook for another minute. Add the tomatoes, oregano, basil, and apple cider vinegar, and bring to a boil. Once boiling, add the broth and almond milk and bring to a boil once again.

Using your blender, puree the soup until smooth (or feel free to leave it a bit chunky if you love texture). Salt and pepper to taste. Pour the soup into four bowls (or 1 really big one if you're super hungry), top with vegan cheese if desired, and serve!

Creamy Wild Rice

This hearty Mid West soup is great for cold Winter tea gatherings. It has a touch of the American Indian, and a earthy feel.

Ingredients:

3/4 cup raw cashews, soaked overnight and drained
Potato, cooked (skin intact)
1 can white beans, thoroughly rinsed
1 tsp oil of choice (I used olive oil)
1 yellow onion, diced

3 cloves garlic, minced
1 celery, diced
1/2 cup wild rice, un-cooked
1/2 cup black rice, par-cooked or soaked overnight and drained (I use forbidden black)
4 cup vegetable broth
1/2 Tbsp yellow or white miso
1 and 1/2 tsp. white balsamic vinegar
2 and 1/2 tsp. nutritional yeast
1/4 cup white wine
1/4 tsp. freshly ground black pepper
Salt, to taste
Herbs de Provence (to taste)
(Optional) fresh parsley & crackers, for serving

Directions:

In a blender or food processor, combine the cashews, cooked potato (feel free to leave the skin on), and white beans until completely smooth, stopping to scrape down the sides as needed. This may take a few minutes. Add some broth as needed to blend.

In a large saucepan, heat the oil over medium heat. Add the onion, garlic, and celery, along with a sprinkle of salt, and stir. Continue cooking until softened, about 3 minutes.

Add the wild rice and brown rice and stir. Cook for another 1-2 minutes.

Add the rest of the broth and bring the mixture to a boil. Reduce to a fast simmer and cook for about 15 minutes, or until wild rice is significantly softened.

Whisk the miso together with a bit of water to thin it out. Add it to the pot along with the vinegar, nutritional yeast, white wine if using, and black pepper.

Stir in the cashew, white bean and potato mixture. If you're not using a high-speed blender, you should pour the mixture into a mesh sieve first, using a spatula to push it through.

Continue to cook the soup at a steady simmer, stirring frequently to prevent the rice from sticking to the bottom of the pan. Add more water or broth if needed, or to thin. Take the soup off the heat when the wild rice is done, approximately 15-30 minutes. This will depend on your preference for chewier vs. softer wild rice.

Season the soup to taste. This soup needs to be salted pretty aggressively to cut through the richness, but some vegetable broths are saltier than others, so just play it by ear. I also Herbs to Provence to give it a slightly savory flavor.

⟶❧ Creamy Zucchini Dill ❧⟵

This creamy Southern Italian soup is perfect for spring and summer tea luncheons.

Ingredients:

¼ cup yellow onion, diced
1 small clove garlic, chopped

A few stems from the dill, left whole
½ cup vegetable broth
Salt & pepper
4 cups fresh zucchini cut in a small dice [about 20 ounces or 4 smallish squash]
2 Tbsp fresh dill fronds, snipped in small pieces with scissors
¼ cup canned coconut milk

Directions:

Place the onion, garlic, dill stems and vegetable broth in a 3 quart saucepan.

Add a pinch each of sea salt and freshly ground pepper.

Bring up to a simmer and cook over medium heat for 3 or 4 minutes.

Add the zucchini, a bit more salt & pepper, and return to a simmer.

Cook about 10 minutes, until the squash is very soft.

Remove the dill stems and discard.

Put the zucchini mixture in the blender, along with the fresh dill fronds.

Be careful blending hot ingredients - it is best to remove the center part from the blender lid, and hold a folded kitchen towel over the opening while blending.

Pulse the blender a few times to get things going, and then blend on high speed until the mixture is completely pureed.

Add the coconut milk [stirred so that it is well mixed and creamy], and pulse a few times to incorporate.

Taste and add additional salt if needed. You can thin it with a bit more vegetable broth if it is too thick for your taste.

Garnish with julienned zucchini skin, a few dill fronds.

Serve immediately, refrigerate leftovers. Serves two as a lunch or light dinner, 4 as an appetizer. Easily doubles or triple to serve more people, but do the blending in batches.

Ethiopian Peanut Soup

This exotic African soup is an autumn and winter favorite and also one that children tend to like because of it's creamy peanut butter consistency.

Ingredients:

- 3 cups vegetable stock
- 2 (15 oz) cans of coconut milk
- 1 cup diced yellow onion
- ½ cup diced celery

- 4 large cloves of garlic (minced)
- 4 cups of sweet potato (in ½ inch cube pieces0
- 1 ½ cups chopped tomatoes
- Sea salt to taste
- ¼ tsp ground black pepper
- Pinch of cayenne pepper
- Juice of one lime
- ¾ cup of creamy organic peanut butter
- 3 Tbsp of fresh finely chopped cilantro
- ½ cup roasted peanuts (garnish)

Directions:

Place the vegetable stock in a 3-quart pot over medium-high heat. Add all the remaining ingredients, except the peanut butter, cilantro, and peanuts, and cook for 15 minutes, stirring occasionally.

Remove about 1 cup of the liquid and place it into a small bowl. Add the peanut butter and stir until creamy. Return the mixture to the pot, stir well, and cook for 5 minutes, stirring occasionally.

Add the cilantro, stir well, and garnish with peanuts before serving.

I like to serve this delicious and exotic soup with a cup of rooibos (African red bush) tea.

French Onion Soup

This twist on the traditional French Onion soup has no beef stock. It is completely vegan. It is simple to make. I got a similar recipe from a seminar at Whole Foods Market. I just feel my seasoning and the wine add a bit more flavor.

Ingredients:

- 4 large sweet onions thinly sliced
- 2 Tbsp red wine vinegar
- ¼ cup of French red wine, Cabernet or Pinot Noir
- 6 cloves of garlic, thinly sliced
- 2 bay leaves
- 1 tsp fresh chopped thyme
- 1 tsp rosemary
- ½ tsp ground black pepper
- 1 baguette (slices are used for garnish)
- ½ cup of cashew nut cheese
- Fresh cut chives or scallions for garnish

Directions:

Heat a medium pot over high heat. Add onions and cook over high heat, stirring often until onions are dark brown and caramelized, about 15 minutes. Add vinegar and use a wooden spoon to scrape up any bits from the bottom of the pan. When vinegar has evaporated, add garlic, bay leaves, thyme, black pepper and 6 cups water and wine. Reduce heat to medium-low and simmer about 40 minutes and then remove bay leaves. Ladle onion soup into oven-safe bowls. Top with a slice of baguette and spread each slice with 1 tablespoon of cashew cheese. Place in a hot oven or under the broiler for 5 to 7 minutes, or until cheese is warmed and golden. Garnish with chives or green onions and serve.

Golden Cream of Mushroom

This delicious cream of mushroom is vegan and an excellent choice for traditional English tea luncheons. It is surprisingly rich with a beautiful golden color.

Ingredients:

- 16 oz of button mushrooms (cleaned thoroughly)
- 3 cloves of garlic minced
- 1 cup of sweet onions diced finely
- ½ cup of cashews soaked in water for four hours
- 4 cups of golden vegetable stock (plus 2 tbsp)
- ½ cup unsweetened almond milk
- ½ cup of sherry or dry white wine
- 1 tsp dried thyme
- 4 Tbsp of No Salt Seasoning
- 1 Tbsp of flour (almond works well)
- Ground pepper to taste
- Fresh parsley (garnish)
- Dash of paprika (garnish)

Directions:

Heat a medium soup pot over medium-high heat. Add the diced onions and two tablespoons of vegetable stock and stir. Water sauté the onions, adding small of amounts of veggie stock when needed to prevent sticking, for 5 minutes or until translucent. Add the garlic and cook for an additional 2 minutes. Add sliced mushrooms and cook for 5 minutes, stirring often. Add a little veggie stock if need, but the mushroom will add enough liquid you will probably not need to do this. Raise heat to high and add white wine, cook for five minutes stirring often.

Add 4 cups of vegetable stock, dried thyme and no-salt seasoning to pot and stir. Cover and simmer on low-heat for 15 minutes.

In a food processor or high-powered blender, puree soaked cashews (drained of water) and ½ cup unsweetened non-dairy milk of choice (I used almond milk). Add 1 cup of soup and puree until smooth and creamy. Slowly whisk in soup and cashew puree to the pot and stir.

In a small bowl, add one tablespoon of flour. Whisk in 1-2 tablespoons of vegetable stock until smooth. Slowly whisk into soup and simmer for an additional 5 minutes or until desired thickness.

Remove from heat and season with freshly ground pepper, to taste. Ladle soup into bowls and garnish with ground paprika and fresh chopped parsley.

Hawaiian Miso

This soup reminds me of the Japanese-Hawaiian miso soups I experienced while I was visiting Waikiki. A similar soup was served to be at a swanky Japanese restaurant and it paired well with a traditional sen cha.

Ingredients:

- 4 cups filtered water
- ½ cup green chard (slice into super thin strips)
- ½ cup chopped green onions
- ¼ cup of cubed extra firm sprouted tofu
- 4 Tbsp white miso paste
- ¼ cup of nori (seaweed) cut into strips
- A dash of sea salt
- Fresh parsley and dill (garnish)

Directions:

Place water in a medium saucepan and bring to a low simmer.

Add nori and simmer for 5-7 minutes.

In the meantime, place 3 Tbsp of miso into a small bowl, add a little hot water and whisk until smooth.

Then add to the soup and stir. This will ensure it doesn't clump.

Add remaining ingredients to the pot and cook for another 5 minutes or so. Taste and add more miso or a pinch of sea salt if desired. Serve warm.

Irish Potato-Leek

This is a delicious vegan version of traditional Irish potato soup. This is a great hearty choice for tea party soup. This soup has a traditional working man's high tea feel. For the average and less sophisticated palate.

Ingredients:

- 4 quarts of vegetable stock (divided)
- 1 Tbsp olive oil
- 2 large leeks trimmed and chopped
- 2 oz of dry white wine
- 8 large Yukon gold potatoes peeled and quartered
- 1 tsp sea salt, plus additional to taste
- Fresh dill and parsley (garnish)

Directions:

In a large pot, bring 2 qt stock to a simmer.

In a large saucepan, heat oil on low. Add leeks and sauté, stirring occasionally, until soft but not colored, about 7 minutes. Stir in wine and cook until liquid evaporates.

Add hot stock and potatoes to leeks. Simmer until potatoes are softened, about 15 minutes. Remove from heat.
With an immersion blender, purée soup until smooth. (Alternatively, purée soup in batches in a blender.) If necessary, bring remaining stock to a simmer and add to soup, as needed, to reach desired consistency. Season with salt and dill, to taste. If using, garnish with parsley or dill. Throw on some oyster crackers (salted).

Potage Saint-Germain (French Split Pea Soup)

This delicious split pea soup has a French country feel. It is hearty and satisfying. I created this soup after a soup that was served at my favorite Southern Californian French restaurant called The Magic Pan. It also reminds me of Quebecois split pea soup. So hearty and delicious.

Ingredients:

- 1 Tbsp of extra virgin olive oil
- 1 brown onion (chopped finely)
- 1 bay leaf
- 3 cloves of garlic (minced finely)
- 2 ½ cup of split green pea
- 1 ½ tsp sea salt
- 7 ½ cups of water
- 3 carrots peeled and finely chopped
- 3 stalks of celery finely chopped
- 3 potatoes diced
- ½ cup of chopped fresh parsley
- 1 generous tsp of Herbs de Provence (or more depending on taste)
- ½ tsp of ground black pepper
- ¼ cup of sherry or dry white wine

Directions:

In a large pot over medium high heat, sauté the oil, onion, bay leaf and garlic for 5 minutes, or until onions are translucent. Add the peas, salt and water. Bring to a boil and reduce heat to low. Simmer for 2 hours, stirring occasionally.

Add the carrots, celery, potatoes, parsley, Herbs de Provence and ground black pepper. Also add the wine. Simmer for another hour, or until the peas and vegetables are tender.

Garnish: Fresh parsley, saltine crackers, or pepitas.

Pumpkin Harvest Soup

This is a deliciously creamy and rich pumpkin soup. One of my favorites for the fall season.

Ingredients:

- 1 can of organic pumpkin puree
- 1 can of organic full fat coconut milk
- ½ cup filtered water
- 1.5 tsp nutmeg
- ½ tsp cinnamon
- ¼ tsp ground coriander
- 1 tsp Himalayan sea salt
- ¼ tsp ground black pepper
- 2 Tbsp plus 1 tsp pure maple syrup (B)
- 2 cinnamon sticks
- 2 bay leaves

Optional harvest croutons

- 2 slices of whole grain bread
- ¼ cup of coconut oil melted
- 1 tsp cinnamon
- 1 tsp ground nutmeg

Directions:

In a medium sized saucepan combine the pumpkin, and coconut milk over medium heat. Whisk until smooth.

Add in your water, and continue to stir.

Now mix in your spices, and maple syrup.

Toss in your cinnamon sticks, and bay leaves.

Bring to a low simmer, and heat for 15 minutes.

Remove the cinnamon sticks, and bay leaves before serving.

Croutons:

Pre-Heat your oven to 375 Degree F.
Slice your GF bread into small crouton sized squares.
Line a baking sheet with parchment paper.
In a mixing bowl combine your coconut oil, and ground cinnamon and nutmeg. Toss the bread pieces until coated.
Bake for 10 minutes, flipping half way through.

96

Russian Borscht

I have to admit I was not a fan of Russian cuisine until I dined at a Russian tea room when visiting San Francisco and had a delicious borscht similar to the recipe. I admit I don't like the vulgar smoky taste of Russian Caravan tea, but this paired well with hearty black tea English tea blend.

Ingredients:

3 small (or 2 big) beetroots, peeled and grated
2 carrots, peeled and grated
¼ cabbage, finely chopped
2 onions, finely chopped
1 small package of tomato paste
4 garlic cloves minced
Half a cauliflower, florets separated
A few rosemary leafs and/or sage leafs
1 tsp turmeric
1 tsp paprika
1 Tbsp coconut sugar
2 bay leafs
Juice from half a lemon
5 Tbsp olive oil
Salt and pepper, to taste
Water

Directions:

Warm the olive oil (5 tbsp) in a big pot and add the onions and garlic and fry for a couple of minutes, add the rosemary leafs and/or bay leafs, turmeric (1 tsp), and paprika (1 tsp) and keep frying for a few minutes until translucent.

Add the beetroot, carrots, tomato paste (small package), sugar (Tbsp) lemon juice (1/2 a lemon), 1 Tbsp of salt, and ½ a cup of water and stir

Bring to a simmer and cook on low heat for 15 minutes, while paying attention, if the water has completely evaporated add a bit of water

Add 14 cups of water, bring to a boil, and keep cooking on medium heat for 15 more minutes

Add the cauliflower (1/2) and cabbage (1/4) and keep cooking for 10 more minutes

Turn off the heat, taste and add salt/pepper as needed

Optional: spread some parsley or coriander on top of the soup. You may also add some vegan sour cream.

Spencer Cream of Asparagus

My favorite soup is cream of asparagus. This is a staple soup and also a lovely rich creamy soup for a traditional English tea luncheon.

Ingredients:

- 2 pounds of organic green asparagus
- 1 large brown onion (chopped finely)
- 1 Tbsp of vegan margarine (Earth Balance)
- 5 cups of vegetable broth
- ½ cup of cashew butter
- 1 Tbsp yellow pea protein (this makes the soup creamier)
- ¼ tsp of fresh organic lemon juice
- 2 garlic cloves minced
- A dash of Herbs de Provence

Directions:

Cut asparagus into ½ inch pieces

In a large pot, heat margarine over medium low until softened.

Add asparagus pieces, a dash of herbs de Provence (also sea salt and pepper to taste). Stir 5 minutes. Add onions, garlic, pea protein and broth. Simmer covered for 20 minutes until asparagus is very tender.

Add ½ cup of cashew butter to a blender and your soup mixture. Puree in a blender till smooth

Season with some lemon juice. Serve hot. Throw on some oyster crackers (salted)

Spencer Sweet Pea with Mint

Sweet pea is grown at the Spencer estate (Althrop) in Northamptonshire. I created a vegan English sweet pea soup that is perfect for spring or summer season. Enjoy!

Ingredients:

- 5 cups of sweet peas (or a bag of frozen peas (thawed)
- 2 cups of vegetable stock (please use organic with no salt added)
- 2 cups of filtered water
- 1 cup of finely chopped sweet onion
- ½ cup fresh mint (finely chopped)
- 1/3 cup of fresh parsley (finely chopped)
- ¼ cup of fresh finely chopped chives (for garnish)
- 2 Tbsp of coconut oil
- 2 tsp sea salt
- ½ tsp ground black pepper

Directions:

In a large saucepan add the coconut oil and onion, cook over medium-low heat for 5 to 10 minutes, until softened.

Add the vegetable stock and water and increase the heat to allow the mixture to come to a boil.

Add the peas and cook for 3 to 5 minutes (very quick cooking), until the peas are tender. If you're using frozen peas it will only take 2-3 minutes.

Taking the pot off of the heat, add in fresh herbs, salt, pepper, and adjust for seasonings.

Next, pour half of the mixture into the blender (or divide the mixture in thirds) and puree/blend a little at a time until the entire mixture is creamy.

Garnish with fresh cut chives, raw pumpkin seeds or sprinkle with vegan parmesan cheese. Also garnish with a little parsley or mint leaves.

Sweet Potato Curry

This exotic and traditional English Empire Victorian soup has a rich Indian flavor, and is perfect with a hot cup of spicy chai tea. This is an autumn and winter flavor with a more exotic twist.

Ingredients:

- 1 medium white onion, diced
- 4 cloves of garlic minced
- 1 large sweet potato, cubed
- 2 Tbsp yellow curry powder
- ¼ tsp chipotle or cayenne powder
- ¾ tsp seas salt and ½ tsp black pepper
- 3 cups of coconut milk
- 2 cups of chickpeas
- 3 Tbsp coconut oil
- ½ tsp yellow curry powder
- ¼ tsp sea salt
- ½ tsp garlic powder
- ½ tsp ginger powder
- Pinch of cayenne

Directions:

Preheat oven to 400 (for chickpeas).

Then start the soup by sweating the onions in a large pot over medium heat in 1/2 Tbsp coconut oil

Cook for a few minutes and then add garlic and stir.

Season with 1/4 tsp each salt and pepper and stir.

Add sweet potatoes, curry powder, chipotle (or cayenne) and stir.

Cook for 5 minutes, stirring frequently.
Add 1/4 tsp more salt and pepper, coconut milk and cover.

Bring to a simmer and then reduce heat to low. Simmer for 25 minutes more.

In the meantime, prep your chickpeas by tossing them in coconut and spices and spreading evenly on a baking sheet. Bake for 25-30 minutes or until crispy on the outside and slightly soft on the inside. Remove and set aside for serving.

At the end of 25 minutes, taste and adjust seasonings as needed. I added about 1/4 tsp more salt and a pinch more chipotle. Then puree using an immersion blender, food processor or blender.

Transfer back to the pot if needed and keep heat on low until ready to serve.

Tomato Basil Bisque

This savory and delicious Italian favorite is great for any tea luncheon and I love the pairing of tomato and basil. I sometimes will serve this with a savory rosemary-tomato scone over traditional sweeter fair. This also pairs well with summer iced tea.

Ingredients:

3 Tbsp extra-virgin olive oil, plus more for garnishing
4 cloves garlic, minced
1 medium yellow onion, diced
1 red bell pepper, roughly chopped
2 28-ounce cans whole peeled tomatoes in juice
1 small head cauliflower, roughly chopped
1 tsp dried oregano
1 tsp dried basil
Dash of red pepper flakes (optional)
½ tsp sea salt, more or less to taste
3 Tbsp nutritional yeast flakes
½ to 1cup water (if needed to thin soup)
Fresh basil, chopped (optional)

Directions:

Add olive oil to a large stockpot and heat over medium heat.

Add in garlic and onion. Cook for 3-5 minutes until tender.

Add in the red bell pepper and cook for another 2 minutes.

Add in the tomatoes, cauliflower, oregano, basil, and red pepper flakes (be sure to submerge the cauliflower chunks in the tomato liquid as much as possible -- it will seem like there is too much cauliflower, but there is just enough)

Bring the mixture to a boil. Reduce heat, cover, and allow the mixture to simmer vigorously for 25 minutes.

Turn off heat and purée mixture with an immersion blender for 5-10 minutes or until the mixture is very smooth. If you don't have an immersion blender, you can add the mixture to a blender in batches or a large food processor (return soup to pan once done blending).

Add in salt (to taste) and nutritional yeast. Simmer on low for an additional 10-15 minutes, stirring occasionally. If soup is thicker than desired, add in ½ to 1 cup water and whisk into soup.

Ladle soup into bowls. Drizzle with olive oil and top with chopped fresh basil, if desired. Also sprinkle with vegan parmesan.

Tom Kha Gai (Thai Coconut Soup)

This traditional vegan Thai soup is perfect nourishment all year round. I find the medicinal herbs also help when one is sick with a cold. I prefer it to traditional chicken noodle soup. It pairs well with green, white and other Asian teas.

Ingredients:

- 1 Tbsp extra virgin olive oil
- 3 cloves garlic, minced
- ½ red onion sliced
- 1 carrot, sliced thin
- 1 cup shitake mushrooms, sliced
- 2 small red chili peppers
- 1 ½ cups vegetable broth
- 1 12 oz can coconut milk
- 6 thin slices of raw organic ginger
- 6 1 inch slices lemongrass
- 1 lime (juice from)
- 1 16 oz package of extra firm sprouted tofu
- 2 Tbsp chopped fresh cilantro

Directions:

In a large soup or stockpot, sauté the onion, garlic, carrots and mushrooms in oil for just a few minutes until lightly cooked.

Reduce heat to low and add the vegetable broth, coconut and remaining ingredients, except for cilantro.

Allow to simmer over low heat for at least 15 minutes. Stir in fresh cilantro just before serving.

Enjoy your vegan Thai coconut soup!

Vegetable Quinoa

This delicious hearty Tex Mex soup adds some regional flavor to your next tea luncheon.

Ingredients:

- 2 Tbsp extra virgin olive oil
- 1 yellow onion diced
- 1 carrot, chopped
- 2 celery stalks, thinly sliced
- 3 cloves garlic minced
- 1 large sweet potato peeled and chopped
- 2 cups chopped butternut squash
- 1 cup yellow squash
- 3 bay leaves
- 4 cans vegetable broth (14.5 oz each)
- 2 cans (15 0z) diced tomatoes
- 1 cup of red quinoa
- 1 Tbsp rosemary
- 2 tsp thyme
- 2 cups chopped Italian Tuscan kale
- Sea salt and black pepper to taste

Directions:

Heat olive oil in a large stockpot over medium heat. Add onion, carrot, and celery and cook until onions are translucent, about 5 minutes. Add the garlic, sweet potato, butternut squash, and bay leaves. Cook until vegetables are tender, about 10 minutes. Stir occasionally so they don't stick to the bottom of the pan.

Add the vegetable broth, tomatoes, and yellow squash. Stir in the quinoa and season with fresh rosemary and thyme. Cook for 15 minutes or until quinoa is soft. Stir in the kale and cook for an additional 5 minutes. Season with salt and black pepper, to taste. Serve warm.

Willie Wonka Chocolate

This crazy wacky unusual soup is perfect for the chocoholic and the kid within us all. As a child, I loved the story of Willy Wonka and the Chocolate Factory and I often serve this tea for kids' tea parties or a zany twist on a traditional tea party. People are always blown away by chocolate soup.

Ingredients:

1 cup unsweetened vanilla almond milk
1/4 cup coconut milk
1 /3 cup soaked and drained apricots (the dark ones, soaked about 10 minutes in hot water)
1/4 cup crushed pecans
2 tsp cornstarch
1/4 cup cacao nibs

1/2 cup cocoa powder
1/4 tsp vanilla extract
Cinnamon and sea salt for serving

Directions:

Heat coconut milk and almond milk in a double-boiler over medium heat.

While milks heat, whisk together cornstarch, cacao nibs, and cacao in a bowl.

Process pecans and apricots in blender until they form a paste (should be a little bit chunky).

Add pecans/ apricots and chocolate mixture to double-boiler and whisk until evenly combined.

Add vanilla and continue to whisk for 3-4 minutes more, until the soup thickens and cacao nibs melt.

Top with a little cinnamon and a tiny pinch of Celtic sea salt.

Yankee Chowder

This is a delicious and creamy vegan version of Boston clam chowder. It is much healthier. Enjoy!

Ingredients for "clams":

- ½ cup of roughly chopped shitake and maitake mushrooms
- ¼ cup of dry white wine
- ½ tsp celery seed
- 1 tsp vegan butter of choice

Soup Base:

- ½ medium yellow onion (chopped finely)
- 2 celery stalks (rinsed and finely chopped)
- 3 medium carrots (rinsed, peeled and finely chopped)
- 1/3 cup of frozen corn
- 1 tsp dried thyme
- 3 tbsp gluten-free flour
- 1 medium potato cut into 1 inch cubes
- 3 cups vegetable broth (no salt or low sodium)
- ½ cup unsweetened almond milk
- ¼ cup fresh parsley (finely chopped)

Cream base

- 1 cup cauliflower lightly steamed
- ¾ cup unsweetened almond milk
- 1 Tbsp vegan butter
- ¼ tsp sea salt

- ¼ tsp of cracked pepper

Directions:

For the clams:

In a large saucepan (this is what you are using to make the soup so make sure it is big enough) sauté the mushrooms with the vegan butter over medium high heat.

Add the white wine and stir until it is completely absorbed.

Stir in the celery seed. Remove from heat and place the mushrooms on a separate plate.

Cream Sauce:

Blend everything together in a high-speed blender. If it is too thick to blend add a tablespoon of almond milk at a time until desired consistency. Adjust seasonings according to preference.

Soup Base:

Over medium-high heat, sauté the onions, celery, carrots, corn, and thyme together until the onions are translucent.

Throw in the gluten-free flour and mix until well-combined.

Add the broth and almond milk. Bring to a boil, stirring often.

Add the potatoes and cream base. Allow to fully heat through (approx. 10-15 minutes).

Add the mushrooms and chopped parsley last and heat another 2-3 minutes.

Season according to taste. Garnish with fresh parsley. Add oyster shaped saltine crackers.

Salads

Ambrosia Tropicana

This delicious fruit salad is inspired by my time I spent in my youth performing on Cruise Ships in the Caribbean. This delicious recipe is reminiscent of salads I had in the French Antilles, especially around the time I was performing at Buccaneer's Creek, for Club Med in Martinique. This lovely fruit salad pairs well with pirate rum iced tea, red tea and tropical flavored black ice teas like mango, papaya or passionfruit.

Ingredients:

¼ cup of coconut sugar
¼ cup of water
2 Tbsp. of white rum
4 Tbsp. limejuice
2 cups of mango (ripe, cubed)
1 cup of green grapes
2 cups of kiwi fruit (cubed)
4 tbsp. of coconut flakes

Directions:

Combine sugar and water in small saucepan. Bring to boil and cook about 1 minute until sugar dissolves. Remove from heat stirring in rum and limejuice. Cool completely.

Combine fruit and rum syrup in a bowl and toss gently. Sprinkle with coconut. Chill for 30 minutes. Serve in parfait glasses. Garnish with lime wedge.

Aztec Quinoa with Citrus Dressing

This Aztec inspired salad brings the exotic and tangy citrus flavors of Mexico. The salad is a nice regional twist to traditional English tea salads. This salad is for the world traveler, and more adventurous, and therefore I sometimes serve this salad for Cinco de Mayo tea parties or for my Victorian steampunk adventurers.

Ingredients:

6 cups of mixed greens of choice (consider herb greens, arugula, baby spinach and Tuscan kale)
1 cup of cooked red quinoa
½ cup canned corn (drained)
1 cup of black beans (cooked and seasoned with equal pinches of sea salt, cumin, garlic powder and cayenne pepper)
¼ cup diced purple onions
1 blood orange in segments (no seeds and peeled)
½ avocado (ripe, chopped)
¼ cup cilantro (shredded or chopped)
½ ripe avocado (sliced)
4 Tbsp. limejuice

3 Tbsp. orange juice
2 tsp. raw honey (or may sub. Xylitol or agave)
2 tsp. hot sauce
¼ tsp. cumin
1/8 tsp. chili powder
Pinch of sea salt and black pepper
1 Tbsp. cilantro (fresh, minced)
4 tbsp. avocado or coconut oil
Garnish: (pepitas, black olives, shredded carrots)

Directions:

Begin if you haven't by preparing quinoa by thoroughly rinsing ½ cup of red quinoa in a fine mesh strainer, then bringing to boil with 1 cup of water in a small saucepan. Once boiling reduce heat to simmer and cook on low for 15-wo minutes. The kernels should open up to a lovely curly consistency. This will yield 1 cup of cooked quinoa to set aside.

Meanwhile: Prepare salad ingredients by chopping all vegetables, segmenting orange and warming black beans (seasoning with salt, cumin, chili powder and garlic powder. In a large bowl toss veggies and beans with greens and cooked quinoa.

Prepare dressing by adding all remaining ingredients into a blender until creamy. Taste and adjust as needed. I often add a bit more hot sauce. If you prefer a vinaigrette leave out the avocado and simply whisk together salad dressing ingredients. You may put the salad dressing in a decanter to be added on later or toss dressing with the salads. After placing servings on to plate feel free to garnish with black olives, pepitas, shredded carrots, or tortilla strips.

Blood Orange and Almond

This vibrant orange salad, adds vibrant color to your tea table and perfect for Autumn and Winter holiday teas. This pairs so well with a traditional black English winter solstice spice tea or chai.

Ingredients:

1 small bunch (about 8 leaves, stems removed) curly kale, washed, dried, and chopped
4 blood oranges
1 cup chopped red bell pepper
3/4 cup sliced or slivered almonds
4 Tbsp hemp oil
2 tsp lemon juice
2 tsp maple syrup B
Sea salt and black pepper to taste

Directions:

Remove the skins and pith from the oranges. Cut three of them into segments and set the fourth aside for dressing.

Combine the non-segmented orange, the olive oil, the lemon, the maple syrup, and the salt and pepper in a blender and blend to combine. If your blender isn't very strong, you can use 3 tbsp blood orange juice in place of the whole orange. Set dressing aside.

Place the kale in a large mixing bowl. Massage the vinaigrette into the kale with your hands. You can use as much as you like; I like a very well-dressed kale salad!

Add the sectioned oranges and almonds and pepper to the salad. Re-mix, and serve.

Caesar

This vegan Caesar has a retro 1960s Ceasar's Palace Vegas feel. I love to serve this salad for retro lounge 1950s-1960s tea parties.

Caesar Dressing Ingredients:

1/2 c cashews (soak overnight)
1/4 c hemp
1/4 c nutritional yeast
1/4 tsp salt
2 lemons juice
Black pepper
3 pitted dates
1 tsp kelp granules
 3/4 c water
2 large stalks celery

Blend all ingredients together in a high-speed blender, or, if you haven't got one, soak the nuts first and put it all in a regular blender. Serve over romaine lettuce and any other veggies you like. I, for one, kicked up traditional Caesar (which is basically romaine, and nothing more) with some cherry tomatoes, fennel, avocado, and celery and black olives.)

Chinese Cole Slaw

This Chinese style cole slaw reminds me of slaw I had as a side dish while I was visiting China Town in San Francisco. This salad pairs well with traditional Chinese style teas. My favorite is oolang.

Dressing

> 2 Tbsp Rice Wine Vinegar
> 1 Tbsp Lemon Juice
> 1 Tbsp Agave or Raw Honey
> 2 Tbsp Soy Sauce
> 3 Tbsp Grapeseed Oil or Sesame Seed Oil
> Sea Salt & freshly ground Pepper
> 2 Large Garlic Clove – smashed minced to a paste with the salt
> 1 Tbsp Fresh Ginger - finely minced or grated

Coleslaw

> 2 Tbsp Sesame Seeds - toasted
> 6 cups Cabbage Red and Green - thinly sliced or shredded
> 1 red Bell Pepper - thinly sliced

3 Green Onions - finely sliced on the bias
¼ cup Fresh Cilantro - torn into larger pieces
1 Tbsp Lemon Zest

Instructions

Prepare the dressing first by combining all of the ingredients in a medium glass bowl. Stir until all is well combined, and set aside.

In a sauté pan over medium high heat, gently toast the sesame seeds until golden brown. Let it cool

In a large bowl combine all of the fresh slaw ingredients except the sesame seeds and lemon zest.

Pour over the dressing and toss well. Let it rest for at least 20 minutes so that the salad has a chance to absorb the dressing.

Just before serving sprinkle with the toasted sesame seeds and lemon zest. Enjoy!

——❦Galician Gypsy Rice ❦——

This traditional Galician Northern Spanish rice salad recipe has been in my family for generations on my mother's side. This Berea recipe is reminiscent of the flavors one would find in A Caruña. The dried fruit mixes nicely with the chewy black rice for a hearty fall or winter salad. I like to serve this with my favorite apricot Ceylon tea.

Ingredients:

2 cup of black rice
4 Tbsp apple cider vinegar
6 Tbsp raw honey
Dash of ground cinnamon
½ cup of rose water
¼ cup of black currants
¼ cup of dried cranberries
¼ cup of dried apricots (cut into bite sizes)
¼ cup of finely chopped scallions
¼ cup of finely chopped carrots
¼ cup of finely chopped celery
½ cup of red seedless grapes (cut into small bites)
½ cups of chopped toasted walnuts

Directions

Cook the black rice as instructions say on the package. Drain and rinse in cold water and set aside.

In a small bowl mix together apple cider vinegar, raw honey and rose water and a dash of cinnamon. If the glaze dressing is too thick at a little more rose water and/or vinegar. If it is too water add a bit more honey.

In a large salad bowl toss all ingredients with the rose/honey dressing. The salad should have a sticky shiny glazed consistency. Not too water. Chill for an hour then serve.

Hemp Seed Tabouli

This quirky twist on the traditional Lebanese style tabouli is perfect for your hippie, yogi friends. I made this once for a simple yoga tea kirtan and everyone ate it up quickly.

Ingredients:

1 cup fresh parsley (minced)
1/2 cup fresh mint leaves (minced)
1/4 tsp sea salt (I used 1/4 + 1/8 teaspoon)
2-3 large red tomatoes diced
1 cup shelled hemp seeds
2 Tbsp hemp oil (I used olive oil)
2 Tbsp freshly squeezed lemon juice

Directions:

Mix all ingredients and toss gently. Chill in airtight container for at least 1 hour before serving.

Japanese Cucumber

I once had a boyfriend named Chris who passionate about Japanese culture. This simple cool as a cucumber salad is a great choice for very hottest summer tea fares. It will actually help your body cool down and cucumber cleans the palate so you can really absorb the natural flavors of your tea pairing. Go for a light green, white or floral tea. I especially like jasmine pearl.

Ingredients:

2 medium organic cucumber peeled and thinly sliced
¼ cup of rice vinegar
1 tsp of sesame oil
1 tsp of coconut sugar
¼ tsp sea salt
2 tbsp of toasted sesame seeds

Simply add all ingredients together and chill (letting marinate) for 2
2 hours. Serve cold with a cup of sen cha.

Jicama and Melon Summer

This Tex Mex cool summer melon salad is a nice unexpected change from more English traditional salads. I like to serve this with a soft white or green tea.

Ingredients:

1 large jicama (peeled and cut into ¼ inch strips)
3 navel oranges (peeled and sectioned)
1 honeydew melon (scooped into small balls or cut into cubes)
½ cup pomegranate seeds
1 cup of fresh limejuice

2 sprigs of cilantro
1 tsp. sea salt
½ tsp. chili powder (optional)

Instructions:

Simply toss all the ingredients together in a bowl and chill. Other ideas: toss in some shredded coconut, or fresh berries (I prefer blueberries, red raspberries, or black berries), fresh pineapple cubed, passion fruit (cubed), or cantaloupe (cubed). Another way I make this is with rose water and ½ Tbsp. of raw honey. The rose water makes the fruit taste esp. fresh and is perfect for a spring affair. Watermelon is always another good choice. Remember part of being a talented vegan cook is allowing yourself to experiment and tweak recipes to your liking!

——❧Lebanese Falafel❧——

When I lived briefly in Laguna Beach with my partner at the time, we both loved to eat regularly at the local Lebanese restaurant. Falafels became an instant favorite. This salad pairs well with exotic African and Middle Eastern style teas.

Ingredients:

1 (6 oz) package falafel mix, prepared (Near East brand)
1 lb mixed herb greens
3 cups baby spinach
2 cups cherry tomatoes (halved)
¼ cup of black olives (no pitts)

Tahini Dressings:

2 tsp extra virgin olive oil
½ cup Tahini
3 Tbsp lemon juice
2 tsp balsamic vinegar
3 garlic cloves (minced0
¼ tsp paprika
2 tsp dried dill

Directions:

For the dressing, heat the 2 tsp of oil in a small saucepan over medium heat and add the garlic. Lightly cook until fragrant, and then remove from heat.

Put all dressing ingredients into a blender and blend until smooth.

Slowly add a little water until you reach your desired thickness/thinness. Scrape into an airtight container and let it sit in the fridge for at least 30 minutes before serving.

Prepare the falafel mix and roll into balls or little patties. Cook in a light olive oil until browned all over. Remove from the pan and drain on a thick paper towel to get rid of excess oil.

Arrange the greens on a plate and top with falafel patties, tomatoes, and black olives and drizzle on the tahini dressing.

Niçoise

My vegan take on this traditional French salad favorite. I use a generous amount of capers and use Grey Poupon for a tangy mustard dressing.

Ingredients:

1 to 1.3 lbs of organic French green beans
2 large Russet potatoes
6 large tomatoes
2 Tbsp Bragg's Apple Cider Vinegar
¼ cup of *Grey Poupon*
Sea salt
Ground lemon black pepper
1 generous tbsp of capers
¼ cup of small green Sevilla olives

Directions:

Cook the beans and potatoes separately in boiling water. Leave to cool and slice the potatoes into small bite size squares and cut the green beans into bite sizes.

Quarter the tomatoes and arrange them with the beans and potatoes on individual salad plates.

Combine the oil, vinegar, mustard and seasoning then pour over the salad.

Slice the olives finely, combine them with the capers and sprinkle this over the salad.

Quebeçois Pear and Arugula

One of my favorite cities I have visited is Quebec. I fell in love with the old world feel of the city and the national delicious Canadian flavors. I also experienced a high tea at the Chateau Frontenac. My partner Billy and I spent a romantic weekend there where we both enjoyed the regional flavors of pears, maple syrup and pecan. I love to serve this salad especially in the Autumn months. It pairs well with holiday and flavored teas.

Ingredients:

3 ripe Anjou pears
Juice of two organic lemons
1/3 cup of dried cranberries
1/3 cup chopped pecans (toasted)
½ cup of spiced apple cider
1 tbsp Bragg's apple cider vinegar
½ tsp ground cinnamon
1/3 cup of maple syrup (B)
¼ cup extra virgin olive oil

1 bag 6 oz arugula
Black pepper and sea salt to taste

Directions:

Preheat the oven to 375°F. Cut the pears into slices, about 6 slices per pear, removing the cores and seeds.

Whisk the apple cider, apple cider vinegar, lemon juice, maple syrup and 1 tablespoon of the olive oil in a bowl. Gently toss the pear slices with the mixture.

Arrange the coated pear slices, core side up, in a baking dish. Bake the pears, basting every 8-10 minutes with the basting mixture, until tender, about 40-50 minutes. Remove and let cool to warm or room temp. Whisk together the remaining olive oil and ½ cup of the basting mixture. Toss the arugula with the dressing, pecans and cranberries and divide among six salad plates. Top each salad with 3 pear slices, season with salt and pepper. (Alternatively, if you prefer equal distribution, toss only the arugula with the dressing, and then sprinkle the pecans and cranberries on top before adding the pear slices.

——✹Salade Tangiers✹——

This exotic salad is perfect for the adventurer explorer. I serve it regularly for steampunk teas or teas with an exotic atmosphere. I picture this as perfect for a sensual Victorian British empire parlor.

Salad Ingredients:

1/2 bag of herb greens
1 avocado cut into small cubes
1 jar of pickled red beets (cut into cubes)
1 cup of cooked sweet potatoes (cut into small cubes)
1/2 cup of pomegranate seeds
Small can of tangerines
1/4 cup of dried black currants

Dressing

Pomegranate Vinegar

Toss ingredients with pomegranate vinegar.

Shogun Sea Slaw

This unique twist on slaw is perfect for Asian themed tea gatherings. I have served this for Chinese New Year, or as a Bhuddhist yoga tea luncheon.

Ingredients:

For the dressing:

1/2 cup orange juice (fresh or bottled)
1/2 cup carrot juice (fresh or bottled)
2 Tbsp mellow white miso
1 Tbsp tamari
1 tbsp sesame oil
1/4 cup olive oil
2 pitted dates

For the salad:

8 oz (1/2 package) kelp noodles, rinsed and snipped with a scissor into small pieces
2 cups tightly packed, shredded red
2 cups tightly packed, grated carrot
1 cup tightly packed, curly kale, finely chopped
1/2 cup chopped cilantro
1/4 cup chopped basil
1 green onion, chopped
2 Tbsp black sesame seeds

For the tempeh:

8 oz. tempeh
1 Tbsp coconut oil
Tamari as needed

Directions:

To prepare the dressing, blend all ingredients together in a blender till smooth. Dressing will make about 1 1/4 cups.

Mix all salad ingredients together in a large mixing bowl.

Slice the tempeh into thin strips (about 1/2 inch thick). Heat a Tbsp of coconut oil in a medium pan till hot, then add as many pieces of tempeh as you can. As soon as it starts sizzling, add a nice dash of tamari. Allow it to brown on one side (shouldn't take long--2 minutes or so), flip, and brown on the other side. Add more oil and tamari as needed.

Toss the salad with as much dressing as you like. I like this salad to be generously dressed, so I'd suggest 1/2-2/3 cups. To serve, top the salad with the seared tempeh strips and a sprinkle of seeds.

This is a twist on a traditional Spencer family recipe dating back as far as the late 1700s. It has a regal traditional English feel with a touch of French court. Go heavy or light on the vegan mayo depending on your tastes. I tend to go light on the mayo and a little heavier on the Dijon. I adjust the recipes to my guests.

Ingredients:

1.5 lb bag of small potatoes (red, blue if possible) quartered
1 tsp sea salt
5 Tbsp vegan mayo
1 Tbsp Grey Poupon
3 Tbsp pickle juice
¼ tsp sea salt
¼ tsp paprika
Lemon black pepper to taste
¼ cup grated carrots
¼ cup thinly sliced celery
3 Tbsp dill finely chopped
2 Tbsp garlic dill pickles finely chopped
1 Tbsp red onion chopped and soaked in ice water for 10 minutes
2 Tbsp green onions finely chopped
2 Tbsp capers
2 Tbsp green bell pepper finely chopped
¼ cup red bell pepper finely chopped
Garnish paprika and dill

Instructions:

In a large pot, cover the quartered Creamer potatoes with cold water, add 1 tsp of salt and bring to a boil over high heat. Turn down to a simmer and cook until tender, about 10 minutes. Do not overcook.

In a small bowl, combine the vegan mayo, Grey Poupon, pickle juice, paprika, ¼ tsp salt, and black pepper. Add the dressing to the potatoes while they're still warm. Mix with a fork, mashing slightly to thicken the dressing.

Cool the potatoes and dressing in your fridge or freezer until they are room temperature or cooler.

Gently mix in all the remaining ingredients: carrot, celery, dill, pickles, red onion, green onion, red and green bell pepper and capers. Taste and adjust the seasoning.

Refrigerate for at least 1 hour before serving. The flavors will merge and intensify if you refrigerate overnight before serving. Garnish with paprika and dill.

Tahitian Tropical with Spicy Mango Dressing

Bring a touch of the British-French explorer to the South Pacific with this exotic tropical spring and summer salad. I love the exotic blending of flavors and the macadamia nut feels extremely unusual and interesting in your salad. This pairs so deliciously well with tropical mango or passionfruit iced tea, or flavored iced red teas.

Salad Ingredients:

Package of extra-firm tofu, pressed to remove extra liquid
Lemon pepper seasoning
1 Tbsp macadamia nut oil
1 bag of herb greens (rinsed
1 red bell pepper, stemmed, seeded and thinly sliced
1 small jicama, peeled and cut into matchsticks
1 avocado
½ cup of cubed strawberry papaya
¼ cup toasted macadamia nuts
Fresh cilantro, for garnish (optional)
Garnish fruit (thin slices of mango)

Spicy Mango Dressing

Mango, peeled and cubed
2 Tbsp macadamia nut oil
Juice of 1 lime
¼ tsp crushed red chili flakes (or more for spicier dressing)

Directions:

Heat macadamia nut oil in a medium skillet on medium-high heat. Cut the tofu into 1-inch cubes and season with lemon pepper seasoning. Add to skillet and fry, tossing every so often, until golden on all sides. Remove from skillet and set aside to cool.

While tofu is cooking, make the dressing. Add all the dressing ingredients to a blender or food processor and season with salt. Blend until pureed.

In a large salad bowl toss herb greens with red pepper slivers, jicama matchsticks, cubed papaya, macadamia nuts. Garnish with fresh cilantro, thin slices of mango. Drizzle dressing over and serve.

Tempeh Garden

This is one of my favorite entrée salads. It is hearty and great for a spring or summer tea. I like the slightly nutty consistency of the tempeh and I go for generous mayo.

Ingredients:

16 oz of tempeh (get the sprouted nut if you can find)
¼ cup of sweet pickle relish
¼ cup of finely chopped celery
¼ cup of finely chopped red onion

¼ cup of finely chopped red bell pepper
¼ cup of finely chopped green bell pepper
¼ cup of raw sunflower seeds (unroasted unsalted)
¼ cup of scallions (use the white onion, cut very thin)
2 Tbsp of Tamari
2 Tbsp of Italian curly parsley (chopped very fine)
2 Tbsp lemon juice
½ tsp finely minced garlic
1 tsp of ground cumin
1 tsp dry dill weed
1 cup of vegan mayonnaise

Directions:

Prepare the tempeh first breaking it into chunks and steaming it over boiling water for about 15 minutes.

Set aside and allow to cool.

Assemble the rest of the ingredients in a large bowl adjusting the amounts according to your preference.

Finely crumble the cooled tempeh into the bowl and combine with the chopped vegetables.

Add the mayonnaise last.

Chill before serving.

Serve with blue corn tortilla chips

Tex Mex BBQ Tofu

Though I'm disgusted by red meat, I won over a few of my die-hard carnivorous Texan friends with this tofu alternative. A much healthier salad for those who love barbecue. This s a hearty masculine Tex Mex salad and I especially serve it for men only tea gathering. I sometimes serve this with iced tea when I'm having few of the guys over to play board games.

Ingredients

8 cups chopped romaine lettuce
4 medium tomatoes, chopped finely
2 avocados, chopped
1 can black beans, drained and rinsed
1 cup corn
2 cups shredded carrots
1 16 oz. package extra firm sprouted tofu, drained and pressed as described above
1 cup BBQ sauce, DIVIDED
½ cup vegan mayo

¼ cup unsweetened almond milk
⅛ cup chopped parsley
1 tsp cayenne pepper
1 tsp. garlic powder
Salt/pepper

Directions:

Chop the pressed tofu into cubes. Place in a bowl and cover with ½ cup BBQ sauce. Toss to evenly coat. Marinade for at least 20 minutes.

Make the dressing: whisk together the mayo, almond milk, chopped parsley, cayenne pepper, garlic powder, 3 tbsp. BBQ sauce and pinch salt/pepper

Preheat the oven to 400 degrees F. Remove the tofu cubes and place on a lightly greased baking sheet. Bake for 15 minutes. Remove, flip cubs and lightly brush with remaining BBQ sauce- you might not use it all. Place back in oven and cook for another 10-15 minutes.

Assemble the salads: Place all ingredients in a large bowl and toss together.

Garnish with blue corn tortilla chips

Tofu Tostada Tropicana

This colorful vegan fiesta tostada has the nice hint of sweetness from the fruit. It is a surprising twist and perfect for al fresco summer teas pool side.

Ingredients:

6 organic corn tortillas (I prefer red or blue corn for a more festive look)
Vegan cooking spray
Pinch of sea salt
2 tbsp. extra virgin olive oil or avocado oil
½ yellow onion (diced)
2 garlic cloves (minced)
1 red bell pepper (medium, diced)
12 oz. firm sprouted tofu (drained, pat dry and cut into small cubes)
1 tsp. chili powder
½ tsp. cumin
Limejuice
¼ cup of chopped cilantro
Small cherry tomatoes (cut in quarters) about a cup
¼ cup of pepitas
1 avocado (chopped)
½ cup mango (chopped)
½ cup Mexican papaya (chopped)
½ cup of fresh pineapple (chopped)

Instructions:

To make the baked tortilla shells, preheat the oven to 400 F. Spray each side of the corn tortilla with cooking spray. Season with a pinch of sea salt. Place tortillas on a large cookie sheet and bake until crispy and lightly browned. Approx. 3-5 minutes. Remove from the oven and flip the tortillas. Place back in the oven for an additional 3-5 mins. Set aside to cool.

Pour oil in a large bottom skillet over medium heat. Add onion and cook until tender and golden: about 5 minutes. Stir in minced garlic and cook 2 more minutes. Stir in red peppers and pepitas and cook for an additional 3-4 minutes. Toss in all fruit and remaining ingredients.

Add tofu cubes and season with the chili powder, cumin, sea salt and pepper to taste. Squeeze fresh limejuice over the tofu and cook until brown on each side. About 5 minutes. Stir in fresh cilantro.

Place tropical tofu mixture onto tostada shell. Garnish with diced tomatoes, diced or sliced avocado, cilantro, and lime wedges.

Note: Feel free to add other favorite toppings: vegan cheese, black beans, salsa, vegan sour cream, black olives, and hot sauce are all great ideas!

Watermelon

This Charleston, South Carolina Southern chilled fruit salad favorite is perfect of spring and summer outdoor teas especially if you are lucky enough to be able to serve this on the veranda of some Queen Anne Victorian mansion. Well one can dream…..

Ingredients:

3 cups of seedless watermelon (cubed)
1 cup of star fruit (cubed) if you can't find this delicacy try 1 cup of cubed kiwi fruit
2 cups of cucumber (thinly sliced)
A spritz of rose water (if you can't find it leave it out of this recipe)
½ cup of freshly chopped mint leaves
¼ cup of limejuice
1 Tbsp. of orange juice
1 Tbsp. of white rum
1 Tbsp. of raw honey
Garnish (dash of coconut flakes)
Pinch each cinnamon and nutmeg and a sprinkle of fennel seeds.

Instructions:

This is so simple, combine all ingredients and toss. Chill for a couple of hours. Then garnish with coconut flakes, and sprinkle with cinnamon, nutmeg and a couple of fennel seeds.

Desserts

Apple Strudel

This is my vegan alternative for traditional German apple strudel. This is a perfect dessert choice for Oktoberfest and fall and winter festivities. Anyone who knows me knows that I'm most attracted to Germanic blonde types so this is best served by either a buxom blonde biergarten hostess named Heidi or Ute, or a strapping muscular blonde boy in lederhosen named Dieter and Hans. Add a little German or Viennese twist to your next tea luncheon with this dessert favorite.

Ingredients:

1 Pepperidge Farm Puff Pastry Sheet, defrosted
3 Tbsp sugar
1 1/2 Tbsp all-purpose flour
1/2 tsp cinnamon
1 pinch nutmeg
1 pinch allspice 1 pinch salt
2 to 3 apples, peeled and thinly sliced
1 Tbsp lemon juice
2 Tbsp Earth Balance margarine,
Melted Sugar, for topping

Directions:

Defrost the puff pastry according to package directions (it takes approximately 30 to 40 minutes to defrost one sheet). Preheat the oven to 375 degrees F. Combine the sugar, flour, cinnamon, nutmeg, allspice, and salt. Toss the sliced apples with the lemon juice and then coat with the dry spice mixture. Place the apples in a line down the middle. Fold the dough over and tuck in the ends. Brush the strudel with the melted margarine and sand generously with sugar. Using a serrated knife, make several diagonal slashes in the strudel. Bake for 35 minutes until golden and puffy. Let it cool for an additional 20 to 30 minutes before slicing, and then serve.

Blueberry Cobbler

I am wild about blueberries any time of year, and this is one of my favorite cobbler recipes. This is a perfect dessert for late night mystery and Gothic Victorian theme teas. This dark delicious dessert reminds me of late foggy nights in New Orleans or Savannah, perfect to share with your favorite ghoulish companion whether it be a furry werewolf or hypnotically erotic vampyr.

For the cobbler biscuit dough:

1 1/3 cups almond flour
3 Tbsp. coconut sugar, divided
1 1/2 tsp. baking powder
1/2 tsp. salt
5 Tbsp. melted nonhydrogenated, nondairy butter

1/2 cup vanilla almond milk 1-2 Tbsp. vanilla almond milk or melted nondairy butter (for brushing on top of dough)
1 tbsp. coconut sugar (for brushing on top of dough)
1 tsp vanilla extract

For the filling:

4-5 cups blueberries
1/2 cup coconut sugar
2 Tbsp. almond flour
1 tsp. grated lemon or lime zest (optional)
1 tbsp maple syrup B

Directions:

Preheat the oven to 375°F. Have ready an ungreased 8- or 9-inch square baking pan or 8-inch-by-10-inch rectangular baking pan at least 2 inches deep.

To make the biscuit dough, combine the flour, 2 tablespoons of the coconut sugar, baking powder, and salt. When completely combined, add the nondairy butter and the 1/2 cup of milk. Stir just until you form sticky dough. Set aside.

To make the filling, wash and pat dry the blueberries. In a large bowl, combine them with the sugar, maple syrup, flour, and lemon zest, if you're using them. Spread evenly in the baking dish.

Using a tablespoon, scoop the dough over the fruit. There will be just enough to cover the fruit. Either leave the dough in shapeless blobs on the fruit or spread it out. Brush the top of the dough with the remaining 1 to 2 tablespoons of milk or butter and the 1 tablespoon of sugar. Bake until the top is golden brown and the juices have thickened slightly (about 45 to 50 minutes). Let cool for 15 minutes before serving.

Makes 6 to 8 servings.

Blueberry Pie

Do you see a pattern? Yes I love blueberries and blueberry pie is a delicious favorite all year round. I prefer blueberries to other pie fillings as it is not to sweet and pairs well with nearly all tea choices. This is also an American favorite, perfect for the 4th of July, or summer picnic teas.

Filling

6 cups of fresh blueberries
½ cup sugar
3 Tbsp flour or tapioca starch
1/4 tsp cinnamon
1 Tbsp lemon juice
Pinch salt

Crust

1 1/3 cups all purpose flour

1 1/3 cups whole-wheat pastry flour
1 tsp salt
2/3 cup high-oleic safflower oil
6 Tbsp almond
½ to 1 tsp sugar

Prep:

Heat the oven to 400 degrees.
In a large bowl, combine the sugar, starch/flour, cinnamon and salt. Add the lemon juice and blueberries, stirring gently to combine.
Meanwhile, whisk the flour and salt in a medium mixing bowl. Pour the oil in a glass measuring cup and add the milk, without stirring. Pour this mixture into the flour and stir briefly, just until combined. Divide the dough in half and form two balls. Roll the piecrust out immediately; do not refrigerate.

Place a piece of wax paper on your work surface, putting a few drops of water under the paper to keep it from sliding around. Put one ball on the paper and use your hands to press it into a 6-inch circle. Top with another piece of wax paper and roll it out with a rolling pin to a 12-inch circle (the edges may extend beyond the top and bottom of the wax paper slightly, but you can loosen it with a knife when you lift the dough.) If your circle is uneven, simply tear off a piece from one part and add it to another – it's easy to make repairs, before or after the dough is in the pan.

Remove the top sheet and turn the dough over into a 9-inch pie pan, pressing to remove any air pockets. Pour in the filling. Roll out the second disc between fresh wax paper and place it on top of the pie. Fold the top crust under the bottom all the way around, and crimp the edges. Cut some slits in the top and sprinkle with the sugar.

Bake at 400 degrees for 10 minutes, then reduce the heat to 350 and bake about 40 to 50 minutes, until the crust is lightly golden and the filling is bubbling. Cool four hours before serving

⇒❧ Castagnaccio (Vegan Chestnut Cake) ❧⇐

I was first introduced to this delicious traditional vegan recipe while visiting an old friend, Antonio who was born in Rome. He is also vegan and mentioned that his family has made this vegan cake for almost 100 years. What is amazing is the original recipe is vegan! Leave it to the Romans to be progressive! Antonio and I shared this cake on my terrace listening to Vivaldi while we shared a dark roast coffee laced with Amaretto. A romantic dessert to serve your sweetheart! Though this is a traditional Roman coffee cake it pairs well with hearty teas. You can find barley and other teas with a more coffee consistency.

Ingredients:

- 9 oz of chestnut flour (sifted). Note: Chestnut flour might be difficult to find. Antonio had it imported from Rome. However I bought a bag on Amazon.com
- 1.5 cups of water
- 1 1/3 oz. crushed chestnuts
- 2/3 oz. pine nuts
- 1 cup black juicy raisins
- 1 sprig of rosemary
- Olive oil (extra virgin)

Instructions:

Preheat oven to 350F. In a large mixing bowl combine chestnut flour and water; stir until you have a smooth mixture (neither too watery or too thick). To be sure not make the batter too liquid, add the water a little at a time. You may need more or less than 1.5 cup. Stir in 2/3 cups of raisins.

Spray a baking loaf pan with non-stick spray or you may grease the pan with olive oil. Sprinkle the rosemary, pine nuts, chestnuts and remaining raisins. Drizzle a little extra olive oil on top and back for 30 minutes. It is ready when the surface begins to crack. Slice and serve with your favorite tea pairing.

Cherry Cobbler

One of my favorite desserts is cobbler. Cherry is also a favorite especially around my birthday in February. I add a few things like dates to this recipe to give it a distinctive flavor. This is also a completely raw recipe! This dessert can be served all year round. I serve it in February or as a patriotic dessert choice around the 4th of July.

Ingredients:

For the Cherry Filling:

3 cups dark cherries, pitted
1 tsp maple syrup B
1/2 teaspoon lemon juice

For the Crumble Topping:

1 cup crushed pecans
1 1/3 cups pitted medjool dates, tightly packed
2 tbsp hemp seeds
1 tbsp chia seeds
1/4 teaspoon sea salt

Optional:

Raw whipped cream, for topping

Toss the cherries with the maple syrup and lemon juice. Divide them into four ramekins or other small serving bowls.

In a food processor, pulse together the walnuts, medjool dates, hemp seeds, chia seeds, and salt. Continue pulsing until the mixture is crumbly and broken down, but not quite sticky the way you'd want a snack bar base to be.

Divide the topping over the four bowls and serve with whipped cream, if desired. If you have extra topping left over, it will work nicely over oats, as a smoothie garnish, or served with fresh berries!

Chocolate Berry Parfait

Chocolate and berries is always a good pairing and this dessert is great not only for romantic teas but for the kiddies. This recipe is easy to adapt in presentation. I sometimes add little animal cookies for kid, or rose petals on the dish for romantic teas.

Ingredients:

1 cup semisweet chocolate pieces
1 12oz package of silk style soft tofu
1/3 cup of maple syrup B
2 Tbsp of Frangelico
1 1/2 cups fresh blueberries, blackberries and raspberries
3 Tbsp cranberry juice
2 Tbsp maple syrup B
1 Tbsp of blackberry brandy
Fresh blueberries, blackberries/boysenberries, raspberries

Directions:

For mousse: In a double boiler or a small heavy saucepan, cook and stir chocolate over low heat until melted. Set aside.

In a food processor, combine tofu, 1/3 cup maple syrup and hazelnut liqueur. Cover and process until mixture is smooth. Add melted chocolate. Cover and process until well-combined and creamy, scraping down the sides as needed. Cover and chill for 2 to 4 hours.

For berry puree: In a food processor, combine 1 1/2 cups blueberries, cranberry juice, the 2 tablespoons maple syrup and raspberry liqueur. Cover and process until mixture is smooth.

Spoon half of the berry puree into the bottom of eight chilled 8- to 10-ounce glasses, such as margarita, martini, parfait or dessert glasses. Top with half of the chilled mousse. Top with the remaining mousse and berry puree. Garnish with additional fresh blueberries. Cover and chill any leftovers up to 24 hours.

Chocolate Hazelnut Fudge (No Bake)

I'm a huge fan of hazelnut and this decadent delicious no bake dessert is a great all year round. The additional of a little Frangelico makes it just the more sinful.

Ingredients:

1/2 cup virgin coconut oil
1/4 cup raw hazelnut butter
1/2 cup cocoa powder (or raw cacao powder)
1/2 cup pure maple syrup B
1 Tbsp pure vanilla extract
1 Tbsp of Frangelico (optional)
Pinch fine grain sea salt, to taste
3/4 cup raw hazelnuts, roughly chopped

Directions:

With electric beaters, beat together the coconut oil and almond butter.
Sift in the cocoa powder and beat again until combined.
Pour in the maple syrup, vanilla, and salt and beat until smooth.
Stir in the hazelnuts.
Line a loaf pan with a piece of parchment paper. Scoop the chocolate mixture into the pan and spread out until even. I took another handful of hazelnuts, broke them up, and sprinkled over the top of the fudge for extra crunch and good looks.
Freeze uncovered for about 1 hour, or until solid. Slice into small squares and prepare to be seduced.

Coconut-Pineapple Cake

This Key West tropical favorite is similar to my grandmother's recipe. A perfect tropical dessert which pairs well with f ruity ice teas, or lighter white and green tea blends.

Ingredients For Cake

1 cup plus 4 tablespoons coconut milk, divided
1 cup shredded coconut
1 20 oz can crushed pineapple
¾ cup earth balance vegan buttery sticks
1¼ cup sugar
1 tsp vanilla
3 cups sifted whole-wheat pastry flour
4 tsp baking powder
¾ teaspoon salt
2½ Tbsp egg replacer
4 Tbsp coconut milk
2 Tbsp water

Frosting

1 package vegan/dairy free frosting mix
2 Tbsp plus 1 tsp coconut milk
8 ounces softened vegan cream cheese
2 cup flaked coconut

Directions:

Preheat oven to 350 degrees, Grease 2, 9 inch round cake pans.
Place shredded coconut in a mesh sieve over a bowl. Bring 1cup coconut milk just to a boil in a small saucepan. Pour warm milk over shredded coconut to reconstitute, reserving the liquid. Pour pineapple and liquid into sieve with coconut also reserving pineapple juices.
In a medium bowl sift flour, baking powder and salt together.
Whisk until frothy, egg replacer, remaining 4 tablespoons of coconut milk and water in a small bowl.
In the bowl of a stand mixer, cream butter, sugar, vanilla and egg replacer mixture.
While slowly mixing, alternate adding reserved coconut milk and pineapple juice mixture with dry ingredient flour mixture. Scrap down the sides.
Add shredded coconut and pineapple and mix until just incorporated.
Pour evenly into cake pan. Bake for 25-30 minutes until a tester is removed clean.

Allow cakes to cool in the pan completely. After cake is cooled refrigerate for at least 2 hours or overnight before frosting.

Mix all frosting ingredients together with an electric mixer. Frost cake. Sprinkle flaked coconut on top of frosting and press coconut into the sides of the cake with your hand. Refrigerate again to allow frosting to set.

Enjoy!

Diá de Muertos Pumpkin Harvest Flan

This dessert is perfect for Mexican Day of the Dead or Halloween fall style teas. The dessert ads some ethnic flavor to a more traditional English tea service.

Ingredients:

6 Tbsp. brown sugar
1 cup water
12 ozs.soft tofu (drained) or silken tofu (drained)
¾ cup of pumpkin puree (approx. ½ of 13 oz. can)
1 cup of unsweetened vanilla almond milk (or soy milk)
2.5 Tbsp. of tapioca starch (or cornstarch)
½ cup brown sugar (3/4 a cup for sweeter flan)
1.5 tsp of vanilla extract
Dash of sea salt
1 Tbsp. of pumpkin spice (or ½ Tbsp of cinnamon/1/2 Tbsp of nutmeg)

Directions:

To make Caramel: - boil sugar and water in a small saucepan until it is thick. You will know it's ready when the caramel does not drip from a spoon. - pour caramel into a pan/mold (I use flan mold) and manipulate the dish to spread the caramel on sides of pan and then make sure caramel is evenly covered on the bottom of pan - Set aside to let caramel cool and harden in pan at room temperature

To make Flan: - Preheat oven to 350 F Place all filling Ingredients in a food processor fitted with a metal blade and process until smooth and completely combined. - Scrape into the caramel lined pan. Gently smooth top - Place the pan/mold in a larger roasting pan and fill the surrounding area with hot water until it reaches up to the same height as the flan mixture. - Bake for 45 minutes - Allow flan to cool in pan completely before refrigerating it for at least 4 hours (ideally overnight) covered with foil or saran wrap. - To unmold the flan, simply run a knife around the sides, place an upside down serving platter over the flan then invert really quickly. For traditional Spanish flavor serve with pirouette cookies.

Additional notes:

Can substitute pumpkin puree for butternut squash puree. For a Cuban flair sprinkle shredded coconut on the top.

Empanadas (Fruit Turnovers)

These traditional Spanish/Mexican turnovers are a nice regional dessert change to serve at your next tea.

Ingredients:

2 cups of unbleached flour (may substitute any gluten free flour-I prefer rice flour)
2 Tbsp. of evaporated cane sweetener or liquid xylitol
2 tsp of sea salt
2 tsp of baking powder
1/3 cup of vegetable shortening
½ cup of water
1 jar of pineapple preserves or 1 can of guava paste (check in the Cuban section of gourmet store) or 1 jar of *Knott's* boysenberry preserves—a California favorite! Or any favorite preserve works.
Agave nectar

Instructions:

In a large bowl mix flour, cane or xylitol sweetener, salt and baking powder.

Add shortening and use fingers to mix thoroughly.

Add water and kneed together.

Cover dough and place in the refrigerator for about 10 minutes.

Pre-heat oven to 350F

Roll out dough on a large floured surface and cut circles about 3.5 inches in diameter (your mix should make 12 circles)

Place your favorite filling in the center of each circle and lightly dab the edges with agave nectar. Note: You may use any preserves you like! Pineapple is the most traditional Mexican. But I have tried this recipe with Guava (for a Cuban twist), and my favorite is Boysenberry preserves. I even tried this recipe once with Indian mango chutney that worked well for a spicy exotic flavor.

Seal edges together with a fork

Line a baking sheet with parchment or wax paper and bake for 15 minutes.

Remove sheet from the oven and glaze empanadas with agave nectar.

Set sheet back in oven and broil empanadas until golden brown.

Serve hot or cool with your favorite cup of tea.

Georgian Peach Cobbler

This traditional Georgian dessert is a favorite all year round. It brings back great days I spent with my partner Billy in Savannah, or with friends and family in the state. A perfect compliment to Southern Plantation themed tea parties.

Ingredients:

1/2 cup of coconut sugar
2 Tbsp cornstarch
4 cups of freshly sliced peaches
1 cup water
Ground cinnamon and nutmeg for sprinkling
1 cup almond flour
1 tbsp coconut sugar
1.5 tsp baking powder
1/4 tsp sea salt
3 Tbsp of Earth Balance
1/2 cup of vanilla almond milk

Directions:

Preheat oven to 400 degrees F.

Combine sugar and cornstarch in a saucepan.

Add in water and peaches.

Bring to a boil.

Stir constantly for 1 minute.

Pour into a baking dish and sprinkle with cinnamon.

Combine flour, sugar, baking powder, and salt.
Cut in margarine until mixture has a cookie dough like consistency.

Stir in almond milk until mixed.

Drop by spoonfuls on the fruit (It won't cover it completely, but will when it bakes).

Bake for about 25-30 minutes.

Granita Caffè Cioccalata

Anyone that knows me knows I'm a huge fan of dark chocolate. Granita is a traditional low calorie shaved ice dessert. When looking at recipes, I noticed traditional granita is often light fruit flavors and I have rarely seen rich chocolate variety, usually reserved for gelato. This recipe is perfect for chocolate lovers and does not have all the heavy cream and egg of gelato. This is also a great dessert to serve for those who prefer coffee to tea (God forbid).

Ingredients:

- 2 cups of chilled brewed coffee (do use a dark roast)
- 2/3 cups of xylitol or granulated sugar
- 2/3 cup cocoa powder
- 1 tsp pure vanilla extract
- 3 oz of dark chocolate (finely chopped: Try to find at least a 75% dark bar)
- Garnish with bits of chocolate bar, fresh mint or a dash of shredded coconut, and a cherry.

Directions:

In a medium saucepan over medium heat, whisk coffee, sugar and cocoa powder till melted and smooth. Whisk in vanilla and chocolate bar bits until smooth. Transfer to a bowl and chill until cold. Usually 2 hours at least.

Transfer mixture to plastic container (like an ice cream carton) and freeze. Briefly stirring with fork once every hour, for about 5 hours. Continue to freeze until completely frozen solid. Approx.3 more hours.

Break up with a fork before serving. Place in ice cream dishes and garnish as recommended. You can freeze individually before serving to prevent premature melting.

Granita Muscato

Granita is a simple to make flavored ice with less calories than gelato, spumoni or tortoni. It is flavorful and easy to make. After searching through over 100 Granita recipes, I decided to explore the flavors of an Italian fruity wine with peaches. This turned out absolutely delicious. It is a light flavorful and colorful granita! Enjoy.

Ingredients:

- 4 cups of peeled slice juicy peaches
- 1 bottle of Italian Muscato (be sure not to buy the fizzy cheap carbonated Muscato. I prefer a medium sweet Muscato with a light vanilla peach or pear overtone.
- 3 cups of water
- ¾ cup of xylitol, or sugar
- Garnish: Fresh Mint leaves

Instructions:

Combine peaches and wine in a food processor or blender blending until super smooth. Strain the mixture through a sieve or mesh strainer into a large bowl. Discard any solids.

Combine 1 cup of water and sugar or xylitol in small saucepan; bring to a bowl, stirring until all the sugar dissolves. Remove from the heat; stir in gently 2 cups of water.

Combine peach and sugar mixture in a 13 X 9 Pyrex baking dish, stirring and whisking. Freeze 6 hours until firm stirring at least twice in the first 2 hours.

To serve: Either let thaw to where it is soft enough to scoop out. Or better yet, using a grater shave off ice into ice cream dishes or martini glasses. It should look a bit like a snow cone. Garnish the granita-shaved ice with fresh mint leaf and serve.

———❧Holiday Date Squares❧———

One of my families' holiday favorite dates squares are a perfect choice for Xmas themed holiday teas and pairs well with spicy Winter solstice tea, chai or ciders.

Crust

1.5 cups of whole raw almonds
1.5 cups of gluten free oats
1/2 tsp of sea salt
10 Medjool dates (pitted and roughly chopped
1/4 cup of coconut oil
1/2 tsp cinnamon
1/2 tsp nutmeg

Filling

25 Medjool dates (pitted and roughly chopped)
1/2 cup of filtered water
1/2 tsp cinnamon
1/2 tsp nutmeg

Directions:

Line a square pan (I used 8in x 8 in) with two pieces of parchment paper going opposite ways. In a food processor, process the almond, salt, and oats until a fine crumble forms. Now add in the dates and process until crumbly again. Melt the coconut oil and add to the mixture with spices and process until sticky. You can add a tiny bit more oil if the dough is too dry. I didn't need to though! Remove from processor, set aside 3/4 cup of the mixture for later, and press the rest of the mixture very firmly and evenly into the pan.

Grab your pitted and roughly chopped dates and water and process in the food processor until a paste forms. You will have to stop and scrape down the sides of the bowl often. You can add a tiny bit more water if needed, but you want the paste quite thick. Scoop out the date mixture onto the crust and gently spread with the back of a wet spatula until even.

Sprinkle on the 3/4 cup of mixture you set aside and gently press down with fingers. Refrigerate in the fridge until firm for at least 1 hour, preferably overnight. Cut into squares and serve. Store in the fridge or freezer.

Jungle Jimmy Frozen Chocolate Bananas (With Adult Variation)

Children and adults alike love chocolate frozen bananas, they can be playful, or phallic depending on how you choose to look at them. They are a great choice for hot summer days and pair well with iced tea.

Ingredients:

4 large bananas (unpeeled and not overly ripe)
16 oz of semisweet chocolate chips or 16 oz of dark carob or dark chocolate chips (My fav!)
2 Tbsp of vegan margarine
Garnishes of choice (chopped walnuts, pecans, hazelnuts or peanuts, coconut flakes)
Adult variations: 2 tbsp of either *Kahlua* or *Frangelico*

Instructions:

Carefully thread each banana through with a small chopstick or skewer about halfway, and then remove the peels. Peeling after inserting the skewer will help it stay together and not poke through the other side. Or you cannot use a stick for adult variation.

I prefer sticks for children and do not use sticks for adult variation.

Melt chocolate and margarine in a double boiler over medium low heat. Be sure to stir and watch that chocolate doesn't burn! Add your Kahlua or Frangelico for adult variation (also rum works nicely as well).

Dip each banana in chocolate, coating thoroughly.

Roll the dipped bananas in the nuts or coconut and place on wax paper lined baking sheet. Transfer to the freezer for at least 1 hour. For adult variety I cut them into bite size shapes and display them in a kaleidoscopic arrangement on a platter with fresh strawberries, blueberries, blackberries, pineapple spears and mango cubes. The colors create quite a beautiful presentation. I then sprinkle all the fruit with coconut flakes. So easy, elegant and yummy.

Key Lime Tarts

A simple family twist on key lime pie, this dessert pairs well with lighter white/green tea blends or Southern style iced teas.

Ingredients:

Crust:

1 1/4 cups graham cracker crumbs (about 1 sleeve graham crackers)
1/4 cup (4Tbsp) vegan butter, melted (such as Earth Balance)

Filling:

1 cup raw cashews, soaked for 4-6 hours (or overnight), then drained
3/4 cup light or full fat coconut milk, well shaken
1/4 cup coconut oil, melted
3-4 large limes or 6-7 key limes (1 Tbsp zest, 1/2 cup juice)
1/3 - 1/2 cup agave nectar (depending on preferred sweetness)

Instructions:

Preheat oven to 375 degrees F and line a standard muffin tin with 12 paper liners.
Add graham crackers to a food processor and process until you achieve a fine meal. Then add melted butter and pulse to combine.
Distribute evenly among muffin tins and press down with a glass or spoon to flatten. Bake for 10 minutes or until golden brown. Remove and set aside to cool.
Add all filling ingredients to a blender and blend on high (or liquefy) until creamy and smooth. Taste and adjust flavor as needed, adding more lime zest/juice for more tart, or more agave for added sweetness.
Pour filling into muffin tins and tap on counter to release air bubbles. Top with a bit more lime zest and loosely cover.
Freeze for 2-4 hours or until firm. Remove from the freezer for 10-15 minutes to thaw before serving. Will keep covered in the freezer for up to 2 weeks, though best when fresh.

Lavender-Lemon Cheesecake

Crust

1/2 cup dates
1 1/2 cup nuts (I used almonds and cashews)
3 Tbsp melted coconut oil

Cheesecake

3 cups cashews
3/4 cup lemon juice
2/3 cup agave nectar
3/4 cup melted coconut oil 1 tsp salt
3 tsp dried lavender
1 tsp vanilla extract

Coconut Whipped Cream

1 can full fat coconut milk
3 Tbsp powdered sugar
1-2 tsp vanilla

Crust

Blend all ingredients together in a food processor.

Line a cake pan or pie tin with non-stick or waxed paper. Press mixture into the sides and bottom of pan.

Refrigerate to set, about one hour.

Cheesecake

Blend all ingredients together in food processor until smooth and creamy, about 2-3 minutes.

Then taste test…

Pour batter into set crust and refrigerate for several hours or overnight before removing from wax paper and serving!

Lemon Bars

Lemon bars are a simple colorful dessert that pairs well with hot and iced teas. This is a perfect simple summer dessert and my dad's favorite.

For the crust:

1 cup flour
⅓ cup coconut oil, melted
½ cup powdered sugar

For the lemon filling:

1 ripe banana
Zest and juice of 3 lemons
¾ cup granulated sugar or coconut sugar
1 tsp vanilla extract
2 Tbsp cornstarch
2 Tbsp all-purpose flour or almond flour
Powdered sugar, for dusting

Directions:

Preheat oven to 350 degrees F. Grease an 8x8 pan and set aside.

In a small bowl, stir together the flour, coconut oil, and powdered sugar until the dough comes together. Press into the bottom of the greased pan and bake for 7-9 minutes, until the edges are golden brown. You don't want to over bake the crust, or it will become too hard after you add the filling. Set aside.

In a medium bowl with a handheld mixer, beat together the banana, lemon juice and zest, sugar, vanilla extract, cornstarch and flour until fairly smooth and combined.

Bake for 30 minutes, until filling it set. Allow to cool and refrigerate for at least 1 hour, until cool.

Dust with powdered sugar before serving garnish with lemon slices

Mango Madness Cheesecake

This twist on an English Empire dessert brings a touch of the exotic to your tea ceremony. This is perfectly paired with tropical ice teas or a spicy hot chai, rooibos or Darjeeling Indian blend.

Base

1 1/2 cups almonds
1 cup medjool dates (no pitts)
1/2 cup dried coconut
1/4 tsp vanilla extract
Tiny pinch of sea salt

Filling

2 1/2 cups cashew (soak overnight)
3/4 cup coconut oil
1/4 cup lucuma powder
1/2 cup coconut cream
1 1/2 ripe mangos chopped + 1 mango sliced for decoration
3/4 cup agave
1 tsp vanilla extract

Directions:

In a food processor, mix all the ingredients for the base until it form a nice dough and is broken down to the texture you prefer.
Press the dough evenly into the base of a spring form pan, I used a 10 inch. Set aside.

In a high powered blender, process the cashews, coconut oil and cream, agave, vanilla and chopped mango until it is creamy.

Pour the filling into the base and place it in the fridge to set, best over night.

For decoration I used sized mango and passion fruit plus a coconut cream.

You can test the mixture at this point by spooning a Tbsp into a container and setting it in the fridge for 15 minutes. If you can cut the filling cleanly then it's perfect. if not then add an extra couple of Tbsp of coconut oil. I always add extra in my recipes to avoid that problem.

Peanut Butter Balls

Children especially love this simple dessert or this is great to serve for those who love peanut butter. I personally find peanut butter a little too ordinary for my sophisticated palate but these seem to go fast when I serve them.

1 cup 100% natural peanut butter (crunchy)
3.5-4 Tbsp pure maple syrup B
2-3 Tbsp coconut flour (I used 2)
Fine grain sea salt, to taste (I used 1/4 teaspoon)
 6 Tbsp gluten-free rice crisp cereal
3/4-cup dark chocolate chips
1/2 Tbsp coconut oil

Directions:

Stir the jar of peanut butter well before using. In a large bowl, mix together the peanut butter and maple syrup vigorously, for 30-60 seconds, until it thickens up. It will go from runny to thick during this time.

Stir in the coconut flour until combined (if your PB is dry, you might be able to skip this step or only use half). We're looking for a texture that isn't too sticky, but not too dry either. Let it sit for a couple minutes to firm up as the coconut flour will continue to absorb moisture with time. Add a touch more coconut flour if necessary. Or if it's too dry, add a touch more syrup.

Add salt to taste and stir in the cereal.
Shape into small balls (I made about 15).

In a small pot, add the chocolate chips and coconut oil and heat over low heat, stirring frequently. Once half the chips have melted, remove from heat and stir until completely smooth.

With a fork, dip the balls into the melted chocolate. Tap off excess chocolate on the side of the pot and place the ball on a plate or cutting board lined with parchment. Repeat for the rest. Save any leftover melted chocolate for later.

Place balls in the freezer for around 6-8 minutes until mostly firm.

Dip a fork into the leftover melted chocolate and drizzle it on top of the balls to create a "sophisticated" design like the baking diva you are.

Freeze the balls for another 10-15 minutes, until the chocolate is completely set. If you can wait that long, you win life.

Note: 1) I'm not sure if other liquid sweeteners will work in this recipe (and firm up the peanut butter the same way as maple syrup does), therefore I can't recommend any. A friend did tell me that agave nectar worked for her though! 2) I recommend only using 100% natural peanut butter for this recipe. You just want to see roasted peanuts on the label (and maybe salt, if it's salted). The *no-stir* kinds made with oil and sugar might not work the same way. The PB I used was very drippy. If your PB seems dry, you probably won't need to use all of the coconut flour. Experiment.

 Pecan Bars

A staple dessert in the South, pecan bars are a nice dessert to serve all year around but especially in the Fall for your special tea gathering. I especially like to serve them for Halloween or Thanksgiving tea luncheons.

Ingredients:

For the crust

1 cup Medjool dates, pitted
1 cup raw pecans
1 cup unsweetened shredded coconut
1 Tbsp coconut oil
1/2 tsp fine sea salt

For the filling

1 cup Medjool dates, pitted
2 Tbsp pure maple syrup B
2 Tbsp coconut oil
1 cup raw pecans
1/4 cup water, or more as needed for blending
1/4 tsp fine sea salt
1 cup of additional pecans, for topping
Optional: 1 1/2 cups dark chocolate chips, divided for filling/topping

Directions:

Line an 8″ x 8″ baking dish with plastic wrap, for easy removal of the bars.

In a large food processor, combine the crust ingredients and blend until a sticky dough is formed. Press the crust into the lined baking sheet, using your hands or a spatula to smooth it out.

For dark chocolate pecan pie bars, melt 1 cup of dark chocolate chips and pour the melted chocolate over the crust, using a spatula to spread evenly.

Place the crust in the freezer to set, while you prepare the filling.

For the filling, combine all of the ingredients in a high-speed blender, or food processor, and blend until thoroughly combined. You may need to stop and scrape down the sides, or use a tamper, to keep everything blending smoothly. Adjust sweetness to taste, if necessary.

Remove the crust from the freezer, and pour in the filling, using a spatula to smooth the top. Sprinkle the additional cup of raw pecans over the top, and gently press them into the filling for easy serving. Drizzle an additional 1/2 cup of melted dark chocolate chips over the top, if desired.

Pistachio Matcha Torte (Raw)

This is one of my first recipes I created using matcha green tea powder. I feel it came out great, as I really like the nutty taste of pistachios. This dessert pairs best with the nuttier green and white tea blends.

Makes a 7" French torte

Crust

2/3 cup raw almonds
1/3 cup raw pistachios
2 Tbsp shredded coconut
1/3 cup black juicy raisins
1 tsp water

Grind the almonds to flour in a food processor. Add the pistachios, coconut, and raisins. Process until the raisins are completely broken down. Add the water and pulse to combine. Press into the bottom of a 7" spring form pan.

Filling

1/2 cup water
1 cup cashews
1/2 cup raw pistachios
1/3 cup maple syrup B
2 1/2 - 3 tsp matcha powder
1 tsp pure vanilla extract
1/2 cup melted coconut oil
Few drops stevia, if desired

Blend the water, cashews, pistachios, maple syrup, matcha powder, and vanilla in a high-speed blender until smooth. Add the coconut oil and blend to incorporate. Taste and add a few drops of stevia if desired. Pour over the crust and chill in the freezer for 5-6 hours. Transfer to the fridge and chill for 12 hours.

Chocolate Drizzle

2 Tbsp maple syrup B
1 Tbsp raw cashew butter
1 Tbsp cacao powder, sifted
1 Tbsp melted coconut oil

Whisk all ingredients together in a bowl or jar. Drizzle over the cake. If the mixture starts to thicken too quickly, set it over a bowl of hot water to make it more fluid again. Drizzle over the chilled cheesecake and garnish with chopped pistachios.

Pfeffernüsse (Spiced Nut Cookies)

These spicy gingerbread style German cookies are a perfect choice at Christmas time. I love these cookies and they always make me feel warm and cozy (especially when shared with my sexy blonde German friends). I love to serve this with a sugar plum flavored black tea, a masala chai, or traditional English winter tea blend or Earl Grey.

Ingredients:

2 1/4 cups flour (gluten free spelt flour may be used)
1/4 teaspoon baking soda
/2 tsp ground cinnamon
1/2 tsp ground cloves
1/2 tsp ground nutmeg
1/2 tsp ground allspice
1/4 tsp freshly ground black pepper
1/2 cup vegan margarine at room temperature (I usually prefer Earth Balance brand)
3/4 cup brown sugar, gently packed
1/4 cup molasses
Egg replacer for 1 egg (I like Ener-g or Bob's Red Mill brand)
1/2 tsp vanilla
1 cup powdered (confectioner's) sugar

Instructions:

Pre-heat oven to 350 F and lightly grease two baking sheets. First, prepare your dry ingredients. Combine the flour with the baking soda, cinnamon, cloves, nutmeg, allspice and pepper. Set aside. Using an electric mixer, beat together the vegan margarine, brown sugar and molasses until well combined and as light and fluffy as you can get it. Then add in the prepared egg replacer and vanilla, again beating until well combined and as fluffy as possible.

Gradually beat in the dry ingredients, mixing until well combined. *Pfeffernusse* cookie dough isn't as moist as other cookie doughs, and it may seem a bit crumbly. That's ok. Roll the cookie dough into 1-inch balls, and place them on prepared cookie sheets. Do not flatten. If the dough is too crumbly, you can moisten your hands a bit when rolling the dough. Bake the cookies for 13-15 minutes, until just starting to crack; do not over bake. Allow the cookies to cool, then gently roll in powdered sugar until completely coated - no skimping. These are pfeffernusse cookies, not crinkles! They must be completely coated in sugar to get the right effect. You can place the sugar in a bag or a bowl and gently roll the cookies around. I prefer the bowl method. Enjoy your egg-free vegan *pfeffernusse* cookies.

Pumpkin Pecan Pie

Anyone who knows me knows my favorite flavors are of Fall, my favorite time of year. Pumpkin and pecan blend so perfectly with a touch of Maple for this traditional Autumn dessert.

Crust

2 1/2 cups all-purpose flour

1/2 cup pecan pieces

1 tsp fine sea salt

1 Tbsp sugar

1 cup non-hydrogenated vegetable shortening

Filling

1 (16-ounce) package extra-firm lite silken tofu, drained

1 (15-ounce) can pumpkin purée

1/2 cup sugar

1/4 cup plus 2 tablespoons maple syrup, divided

1 tsp pure vanilla extract

1/2 tsp fine sea salt

1 tsp ground cinnamon

1/2 tsp ground ginger

1/4 tsp ground cloves

1 cup pecan halves, divided

Non-dairy topping (optional)

Directions:

For the crust, pulse flour, pecans, salt and sugar in a food processor until pecans are finely ground. Add shortening and pulse until almost combined, then add 3 Tbsp ice water and pulse until just blended. Gather dough into two balls then press each into a disc. Wrap each in plastic wrap and chill for several hours until firm. When ready to make the pie, set one disc out at room temperature for 15 minutes to soften slightly. On a floured surface, roll out dough into a (10- to 11-inch) circle and carefully transfer to a (9-inch) pie plate. Press crust back together where needed and crimp edges as desired; chill until ready to use. (Reserve remaining pie dough for another use.) Preheat the oven to 400°F. For the filling, blend tofu in a food processor until creamy and smooth. Add pumpkin, sugar, 1/4 cup of the syrup, vanilla, salt, cinnamon, ginger and cloves and purée until smooth; set aside.

  Reserve 8 pecan halves as a garnish then toss remaining pecans with remaining 2 Tbsp syrup and arrange evenly on the bottom of the pie shell. Pour pumpkin filling into pie shell and bake until just set and a toothpick inserted in the center comes out clean, about 1 hour. Set pie aside to let cool then top with non-dairy topping, if you like, and decorate with reserved pecans.

Raspberry Chocolate Cheesecake

This awesome recipe comes from a friend in England. I especially love making this for Valentine's Day. This is a romantic aphrodisiac dessert perfect for any romantic tea luncheon or ceremony such as weddings, anniversaries or romantic first date teas.

Ingredients:

Base

1 cup almonds
1 cup desiccated coconut
12 dried dates
A little coconut oil for greasing the tin

Filling
1 cup cashews
1/2 cup coconut oil
2 cups raspberries
1/3 cup coconut nectar (you can use agave or rice malt syrup if you prefer)

Top

7/8 cup cacao butter
1 1/2 Tbsp coconut nectar
2 heaped Tbsp cacao powder
1 tsp vanilla extract

Pop your almonds, desiccated coconut and dates into a high-speed blender and blend on a low speed until the mixture becomes slightly sticky. You want it to hold together when you press a small amount between your thumb and forefinger.

Press into the base of an 8-inch springform tin which has been lightly greased with coconut oil.

Next, put the cashews into your blender and blend on a low to medium speed until they have become a nut butter consistency.

Add the rest of the filling ingredients and mix on a medium speed until smooth and silky.

Pour cheesecake mix into the spring form tin and refrigerate either overnight or until set. Or if you're in a hurry, you can just freeze it for a couple of hours.

For the top, grate your cacao butter into a small bowl and then melt gently over a small saucepan of simmering water (this is called a double boiler). For your dessert to still be considered 100% raw, do not heat above 115 degrees F (keep checking with a food thermometer). It takes a little longer this way, but the cacao butter will still melt.

Once your cacao butter is melted, whisk in the coconut nectar, cacao powder and vanilla extract.

Decorate the top of your cheesecake with the chocolate, then pop it back in the fridge to set. I also top this cheesecake with raspberry in little heart motives.

Hint: If you have any chocolate topping mix leftover, pour onto a tray that has been lined with baking paper and refrigerate. Once hardened, it can be broken into shards to use when decorating another dessert. Or just eat it on its own. Yum!

Tiramisú (Raw Vegan)

This traditional Italian dessert is in my top 5 desserts. I adore it but wanted to find a healthier version. This recipe is raw and vegan! Truly amazing. I think it is my best original dessert recipe! Try it.

Ingredients:

Crust

- 1 cup of almonds (soaked overnight)
- 1 cup pitted dates (soaked overnight)
- 1 Tbsp of ground coffee (use a dark French Roast)

Vanilla Crème

- 2 cups of creamy cashew butter (try to get one with no salt)
- ¼ cup coconut oil (liquid)
- ¼ cup dates (soaked over night)
- 1.5 Tbsp of pure vanilla extract
- Pinch of salt

Chocolate Crème

- 1/3 cup of coconut oil
- 4 Tbsp of cacao powder
- 3 Tbsp of maple syrup (Grade B Dark Amber)
- ½ tsp of vanilla extract

Instructions:

1. **For the crust:** Process ingredients in a food processor until combined. Press into a loaf pan or mold.

2. **For the vanilla crème**: Blend all ingredients until creamy, pour on top of crust and place in the freezer for 10 minutes.

3. Melt coconut oil in a pot over the stove. Turn off heat and add the rest of the ingredients. Pour chocolate sauce on top of hardened vanilla cream, place in the freezer for 10 minutes, or until chocolate layer hardens. Dust before serving with more cacao powder to your liking. Cut and serve.

Tortoni Venezia

Tortoni is a frozen almond gelato or sorbet (depending on the region of Italy it is from) mixed with bits of cherries and sometimes biscotti almond cookie. I have always loved the taste of almonds and thus this was a real treat for me as a child. I searched all over the internet for a vegan Tortoni recipe but couldn't find anything that satisfied until I concocted this simple substitute version.

Ingredients:

- 1 quart of vanilla soy or coconut ice cream. Some soy ice creams lack the creaminess of gelato, thus I prefer coconut ice cream.
- 1.5 cups of crushed almond biscotti or almond cookies. Think cookie crumb size. Macaroon cookies also work. I prefer almond biscotti .
- 1 cup of finely chopped almonds
- red and green maraschino cherries rinsed and cut in halfs. (about ½ a cup)

Directions:

Thaw ice cream till it is soft. Put ice cream in a large mixing bowl. Mix in cookie crumbs. Put portions into small ice cream dishes. Sprinkle with more chopped cookie crumbs, chopped almonds and top with red/green cherries (This will also be the colors of the Italian flag (white, red and green). Very patriotic!

Put bowls of ice cream in the freezer to firm up and frost the ice cream glasses for an old fashioned parlor feel.

Winter Peppermint Patties

A typical Winter favorite chocolate and min pair well for a cool breezy holiday dessert. I like to pair this with herbal mint mélanges, chocolate teas, or white holiday tea blends

Ingredients:

1/2 cup raw cashews, soaked over night
1/2 cup coconut oil
4 Tbsp agave nectar
2 Tbsp unsweetened vanilla-almond milk
1 tsp peppermint oil extract
3/4 cup dark chocolate chips
1/2 Tbsp coconut oil

Directions:

Place cashews in a bowl and cover with water. Let soak overnight.
Drain and rinse the cashews after soaking.
Add cashews, liquid coconut oil, agave, almond milk, and peppermint extract into a blender.
Blend on the highest speed until completely smooth. This should take about 3 minutes.
Line a cookie sheet with parchment paper and grab mini cupcake/candy liners. Add a half
Tbsp of filling into each liner. Place on the cookie sheet. Repeat until you don't have any

filling left (you should get about 24). Freeze, uncovered, for 30-35 minutes, or until firm to the touch.

After freezing, quickly pop the patties out of the cupcake liners and set each on top of their respective liner. Return to the freezer for 15 minutes to firm up even more.

Meanwhile, melt the chocolate and coconut oil in a saucepan over low heat. When half of the chips have melted, remove it from the heat and stir until all the chips are melted. Allow the chocolate to cool slightly for a few minutes before dipping the patties.

Remove the patties from the freezer and dunk them into the melted chocolate with a fork. Tap the side to shake off excess chocolate and place on parchment paper. Do this step as fast as possible so the patties don't melt. Note: Some of you are having trouble with the chocolate thickening up as you do this step. If this happens, I suggest heating the chocolate again over low heat to thin it back out. The cold peppermint patties are probably causing it to thicken with time. Another option is to just drizzle the chocolate on top of the patties.

Return the patties to the freezer until set, for about 10 minutes, until the chocolate coating is firm. Store leftover patties in the freezer/fridge until ready to enjoy!

1) you can sub in your favorite liquid sweetener for agave, if desired. Just know that the flavor will change depending on the sweetener you use. 2) See the bottom of this post for a nut-free version and more tips on making this recipe. 3) If you have melted chocolate leftover, spread it into a parchment paper lined plate and freeze it.

Beverages

California Cadillac Margaritas

Though I rarely drink, this California cocktail is my absolute favorite. If you are serving alcohol at your tea gathering, this sexy delicious cocktail will add a California coastal twist to your next gathering.

- 1.5 oz 100% blue agava tequila
- 1 oz Gran Marnier
- 3/4 oz fresh lime juice
- Margarita sea salts

Shake 100% blue agava tequila with grand marnier and limejuice and strain into a chilled salt-rimmed cocktail glass. Garnish with lime slice. Or serve on the rocks.

Champagne Mimosas

This champagne cocktail is perfect for any special holiday occasion, wedding, or anniversary tea dinner. I often serve this for New Year's Eve for friends' wedding receptions.

For 8 Mimosa Cocktails

1 750 ml bottle chilled dry sparkling wine

3 cups (750 ml) chilled orange juice (freshly squeezed is best)

1/2 cup (118 ml) Grand Marnier or triple sec

Fill 8 champagne flutes 1/2 full with chilled sparkling wine. Top with orange juice. If you are using, top mimosa with 1 Tbsp of Grand Marnier or triple sec. Garnish with a strawberry, mint leaf or orange slice.

French Lavender Lemonade

This delicious Old-Fashioned lavender lemonade is perfect for spring and summer al fresco tea luncheons, picnic style tea luncheons. Lavender is also a color associated with gay, lesbian and transgendered people, so this is perfect for Pride tea events. The Victorians were also especially fond of lavender and I often serve this lemonade regularly

1 cup raw honey
12 cups of clean water
1 drop of essential oil of lavender (or more depending on how much you like)
6 lemon, peeled and squeezing
Lavender sprigs for ornamental with lemon slices

Mix all ingredients and chill in the fridge for 1 hour
Serve in tall ice tea classes with ice, lavender sprigs and lemon slices

Iced Southern Sweet Tea

A staple of the South, Southern Sweet tea is perfect for hot balmy spring or summer day tea gatherings or for just enjoying by yourself or with a friend. I like to have this tea on my balcony in the Summer months with a simple scone while I read a good novel.

3 family-sized tea bags (I used Luzianne)
10 cups water, divided (can add more to adjust sweetness)
Pinch of baking soda
1/2 cup of coconut sugar
Lemon slices and fresh mint leaves for garnish

Instructions

In a large bowl, heat 2 cups of water in the microwave until boiling (about 10-12 minutes)

Add a pinch of baking soda.

Drop in the tea bags.

Let tea steep for 5-7 minutes.

Carefully remove tea bags and discard. Do not press on tea bags.

Add sugar and stir until sugar completely dissolved.
Pour into a serving pitcher (preferably glass not plastic)

Add in 8 cups of cold water.

Refrigerate until ice cold.

 Fill a glass with ice and fill with tea. (Tip make ice tea ice cubes as ice can water down the flavor of your tea.

Garnish with fresh lemon slices and mint leaves.

Long Island Ice Tea

I rarely drink but when you are in the mood to get a little tipsy with "the girls" or "the guys" this cocktail usually does the trick. This cocktail is also perfect for New York or Great Gatsby roarin' 20s themed tea parties.

1 part vodka
1 part tequila
1 part rum
1 part gin
1 part triple sec
1 1/2 parts sweet and sour mix
1 splash Coca-Cola®

Mix ingredients together over ice in a glass. Pour into a shaker and give one brisk shake. Pour back into the glass and make sure there is a touch of fizz at the top. Garnish with lemon.

Old English Apple Cider

This traditional apple cider is perfect for cold afternoon and evening tea gatherings. I love to serve these with cinnamon sticks in copper Colonial style mugs. One of my favorite things to do is sip this by the fire on a foggy evening while I watch an atmospheric classic film noir or maybe watch The Tudors, Downton Abbey or Penny Dreadful on the tele.

6 cups apple cider

1/4 cup real maple syrup B
2 cinnamon sticks
6 whole cloves
6 whole allspice berries
1 orange peel, cut into strips
1 lemon peel, cut into strips

Pour the apple cider and maple syrup B into a large stainless steel saucepan.

Place the cinnamon sticks, cloves, allspice berries, orange peel and lemon peel in the center of a washed square of cheesecloth; fold up the sides of the cheesecloth to enclose the bundle, then tie it up with a length of kitchen string. Drop the spice bundle into the cider.

Place the saucepan over medium heat for 5 to 10 minutes, or until the cider is very hot but not boiling.

Remove the cider from the heat. Discard the spice bundle. Ladle the cider into big cups or mugs, adding a cinnamon stick to each cup if desired.

Old-Fashioned Lemonade

An Old-Fashioned American favorite, this is a perfect addition to any spring or summer tea brunch. I love to make this in a decorative decanter and display with slices of lemons. Simple and refreshing on a hot day.

- 6 large organic lemons
- 1 cup of coconut sugar, xylitol or stevia
- 6 cups of cold filtered water

Juice the lemons to make 1 cup of juice. To make your labor easier, FIRMLY roll the lemons between your hand and counter top before cutting in half and juicing.

In a gallon pitcher combine 1 cup lemon juice, 1 cup sugar, and 6 cups cold water. Stir. Adjust water to taste. Chill and serve over ice in zombie glasses garnished with fresh mint and lemon slice.

Old-Fashioned Strawberry Lemonade

This is a delicious Southern California twist on old-fashioned lemonade. When I first moved to Southern California from Florida as a child I was excited to see all the fresh strawberry groves. I love this refreshing and healthy lemonade choice and it pairs well with summer scones, light soups and salads, and summer desserts.

- 8 large organic strawberries cut in half
- 2 Tbsp coconut sugar
- 7 cups of filtered water
- 1 cup of coconut sugar
- 2 cup of freshly squeezed organic lemon juice

Place strawberries in a blender; top with 2 tablespoons sugar. Pour 1 cup water over sugared strawberries. Blend until strawberry chunks transform into juice.

Combine strawberry juice, 6 cups water, 1 cup sugar, and lemon juice in a large pitcher; stir until blended. Chill before serving. Serve in tall zombie glasses with ice, garnished with lemon slice and mint leaf.

Pear Cider

A festive twist on traditional apple cider, pear cider is perfect to serve around Thanksgiving or Christmas…a hot coazy partridge in a pear tree feel. This is a hot and spicy warming drink for tea dinners by the fireplace.

16 whole allspice
8 whole cloves
4 (3-inch) cinnamon sticks
6 cups unsweetened pear juice
2 cups pear nectar

Place allspice, cloves, and cinnamon in the center of a coffee filter or an 8' square of cheesecloth. Gather edges into a sack, and tie sack with a small piece of kitchen string. Combine spice sack, pear juice, and pear nectar in a 3-quart saucepan. Cover with lid, and cook on low for approximately 3 hours.

Throw away the spice bag. Serve hot

Pirate Rum Iced Tea

Anyone who knows me, knows I was obsessed with pirates as a young boy. Growing up with a dad and relativels from Key West, Florida, this sexy Caribbean ice tea became a staple. I often host Goth themed or pirate theme teas and this is a favorite. I also see this served often at Renaissance and Medieval May faires.

12 black Ceylon, or English Breakfast tea bags
2 Tbsp of Spiced Rum
2 Tbsp of Coconut Sugar

Brew tea as indicated. Take tea bags out, and dissolve sugar and rum. Store in the fridge for at least 4 hours. Serve in tall zombie glasses (use tea ice cubes so you do not water down the tea. Garnish with fresh mint leaves or a parasol with pineapple slice and red cherry. Or a slice of lime, lemon or orange.

Raspberry Lemonade

This tart blending of fresh raspberry with lemonade is a nice change from the more traditional lemonade recipe.

- 1 cup fresh rinsed raspberries
- 2/3 cups of coconut sugar or stevia
- 1 cup lemon juice
- 2 cups of filtered water

In a small bowl, with a potato masher or spoon, mash 1 cup rinsed fresh raspberries (6 oz.) with 2/3 cup sugar. Let stand 10 minutes. Press through a fine strainer into a pitcher (at least 1 1/2 qt.); discard seeds. Stir in 1 cup lemon juice and 2 cups water. Taste and add more sugar if desired. Pour into tall, ice-filled glass and garnish with lemon slice and raspberry.

On the following pages I have included several themed tea party ideas including sample menus, tea pairings and suggested decorations. Feel free to add your personal touches, and mix and match recipes from this book. The tea party section is here to give you some creative ideas as to what is possible. Enjoy your healthy *Vegan Tea Time*.

Baby Shower Tea Luncheon

Objective: *Celebrate the upcoming birth of a new baby with a festive tea luncheon. This can been an all woman baby shower ladies' luncheon or for family and friends of both genders. If you know the sex of the baby you can adapt decorations and menu to more girly pink or blue boy. I often like to start a baby shower tea around 10:30 am or 11:00 as a more formal brunch, but light fare afternoon teas or elegant evening baby showers work just as well.*

MENU

Tea Sandwiches

Artichoke
Lady Anne's Lemon-Dill
Lady Caroline's Strawberry Patch
Tofu "Eggless"

Canapé

Pesto Baguette Bites

Scones

Apricot
Lemon Poppyseed

Soups

Chilled Raspberry
Creamy Wild Rice

Salads

Caesar
Blood Orange and Almond

Desserts

Chocolate Berry Parfait
Lavender-Lemon Cheesecake

Tea Recommendations:

Royal English Breakfast (selected)
Vintage Rose (floral-scented)
Berry Ceylon (decaffeinated)
Spearmint (herbal)

Note: I usually serve an herbal tisane tea which is appropriate for an expecting mother and I usually avoid excess caffeine. Sometimes making up a lemonade in the spring and summer months is adviced

Decorations:

Blue for Boys: For baby boys consider having blue flowers, and boy motifs such as choo-choo trains, teddy bears, fire engines, and other ideas that suggest the male sex. I have seen some pretty creative floral displays and decorations for baby showers. My favorite was a Steampunk Baby shower with a train theme. There were copper metal trains with floral settings, as well as hot air balloon lanterns. It was pretty magical.

Pink for Girls: For baby girls choose pink flowers, and girl motives such as ballerinas, Barbie dolls, porcelain Victorian dolls and perfume bottles. One of the most outrageous baby shower teas I went to had a French Shabby Chic theme. The woman who hosted dyed her poodle pink. The whole house looked like Coco Channel's fashion boutique in shades of white black and pink. There were Eiffel Towers on the tables, with little Barbie dolls in pink berets and Channel outfits hanging off of theme. All the food was pink. Pink lemonade, pink scones, and even pink watermelon soup (my recipe!). What a lovely and crazy way to celebrate the birth of a baby girl. Get creative!

Have a table for gifts: Be sure to create a beautiful display table to show off baby shower gifts. A guest book/gift book is often a good touch. Acknowledge presents with thank you letters.

Music: Keep it ultra elegant and soothing such as:

Classical piano music
Harp Music: French Impressionist Composers (Debussy, Ravel, Satie, and Fauré)
 Soft Light Baroque: Vivaldi, J. S. Bach
Soft cocktail piano selections

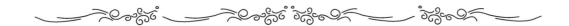

Bridal Shower Tea Luncheon

Objectives: *A bridal shower is one of the most important occasions in a woman's life. A bridal shower luncheon can be just for the bride, her mother and sisters and girl friends or more and more the groom and his family attends. You can adapt a bridal shower to a more intimate informal luncheon or a swanky elegant champagne black tie and gown tea dinner.*

MENU

Tea Sandwiches

Cucumber
Lady Emily's Raspberry-Rose
Matcha-Mango
Tahini Goddess

Canapé

Mushroom and Caramelized Onion Polenta Bites

Scones

Fraises Lavande
Sir James Decadent Chocolate-Pecan

Soups

Chilled Nectarine
Golden Cream of Mushroom

Salads

Niçoise
Quebecois Pear and Arugula

Desserts

Granita Muscato
Key Lime Pie

Tea Recommendations:

Champagne Breakfast (selected)
Black Currant (fruit):
White Diamond (white):
Tropical (herbal):

Champagne Mimosa (for toast) or your favorite red and white wines

Wedding or bridal shower tea luncheons or more formal tea dinners are a great way to celebrate this joyous time in someone's life. When I host a bridal shower or wedding tea party I like to first meet with the "couple" to discuss their themes, there wedding colors, music choices, and menu. Wedding showers can be ultra elegant for 100 people in Victorian or Edwardian splendor or simple more modern affairs. Also with advancements finally in human rights for all, gay and lesbian weddings are more common. I know several gay and lesbian couples that have hosted wedding shower tea luncheons. Here a few important suggestions:

Meet with the couple! This is so important! You want to discuss the date and place of their wedding, where they are registered, and their wedding colors. You can then plan out floral arrangements, menus and music choices for the bridal shower/wedding shower.

Tie themes together: Everyone has different tastes. It is important that the wedding or bridal tea reflect the personality of the honored couple! A friend had a gorgeous English Baroque style wedding ceremony around the winter solstice in a Gothic style cathedral. Her color scheme was rich burgundy and crème tones mixed with Christmas poinsettias, and pine. There coordinating wedding shower tea pulled all these ideas together perfectly. We served spiced tea, cider and festive holiday favorites that mixed well with the wedding color. I also enjoy having electric candles (as they don't smoke and don't cause fire hazards) I place them in decorative lanterns among the flower displays.

Music Programming: The music should reflect the taste of the honored couple. Music can range from traditional classical music, jazz and pop standards to the latest music trends. Feel it out and make sure the music does not under mind the ability to have intimate conversations. I do not recommend loud rock music hip-hop and rap. If these genres happen to be the tastes of the wedding couple, you might decide to have a dance floor, or play more contemporary quieter music like smooth jazz or easy listening adult contemporary while dining.

- Soft classical music
- Soft cool jazz vocals
- Harp music
- Easy-listening adult contemporary
-

Create a beautiful display table: Have photos of the couples, scrapbooks of photos, a guest book, and a table for guests to leave wedding presents.

Consider having guests get instant cameras at their place settings so they can take photos to be included in a final wedding album.

Busy Bee Summer Tea Festival

Objective: *A spring or summer tea luncheon that can be held indoors or outdoors with a bee theme. The colors are black, white and yellow. This can also be done as a business style tea or brainstorming tea. Busy Bee can also be just an outdoor garden, backyard, poolside, beach party or countryside tea.*

MENU

Tea Sandwiches

Lady Anne's Lemon-Dill
Galician Apricot
Monsieur Poire-Bleu
Tarragon-Herb

Canapé

Beet- Nectarine

Scones

Mary-Anne Blueberry Lemon
Spencer Key Lime

Soups

Avgolemono
Chilled Georgian Peach

Salads

Tempeh Garden
Watermelon

Desserts

Georgian Peach Cobbler
Lemon Bars

Tea Recommendations:

English Breakfast with Honey (selected)
Luscious Lemon (flavored)
Tropical Sencha (green)
Apricot Brandy tea (flavored)
Old-Fashioned Lemonade

Spring and summer are the perfect time for a sunshine picnic style down home American tea party. Consider serving this tea al fresco in the backyard, poolside, or out at the park on the greens. You might also go for Country Fair calico feel. Maybe even decorate the backyard like a farm with haystacks, country music, square dancing, and outdoor games. Here are a few suggestions to make your busy bee festival fun and memorable for the whole family.

Flowers and Decorations: Think bee and honey. Have a beautiful bee hive glass ice tea dispenser with fresh Old Fashioned Lemonade. Yellow and Black checkered linens, picnic baskets, tables with yellow roses, daisies or other yellow flowers, hay stacks, Old Fashioned Mason jars for ice tea or lemonade. Yellow and Black dishware, Old Fashioned place settings or even silver tin plates that suggest the Old West.

Music: Bluegrass Country, Fiddlers, Banjos, Country Music, Ragtime Parlor Piano, and Dixieland.

Dancing: Square dancing, Country Line Dancing

Country Western Theme: Dress in your best Cowboy/cowgirl clothes. Or come calico old West.

Live Music: Consider hiring a bluegrass band, Cajun band, Country Western performers, Dixieland band, or a ragtime parlor pianist.

Out Door Games: Pin the tale on the donkey, 3 legged races, and bingo with prizes.

Pool Parties: Have your tea and food poolside in colorful tropical plastic dishware. Maybe tea in loungers floating on the water.

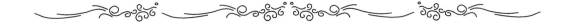

Candlelit Classical Music Dinner Tea

Objective: An elegant candlelit dinner tea with either live classical music such as chamber music, singer-pianist or piano recital.

MENU

Tea Sandwiches

Basil-Tomato Grilled Cheese Panini
Lady Dolores' Ginger-Carrot
Figgy Cheese
Lady Anne's Lemon-Dill

Canapé

Dijon Potatoes

Scones

Autumn Carrot
Cherry Almond

Soups

Black Lentil Chili
Cauliflower and Vegan Cheddar

Salads

Caesar
Salade Tangiers

Desserts

Cherry Cobbler
Pistachio Matcha Torte

Tea Recommendations:

Ceylon or Darjeerling (selected
Jasmine Pearl (scented):
Earl Grey (decaffeinated):
White Pomegranate (white)

An elegant tradition in European homes of the 17 and 1800s were late night dinner parties, tea and salon gatherings for in house chamber music, solo piano and vocal ensemble recitals. Famous composers such as Franz Schubert, Franz Liszt, Frederic Chopin and Edvard Grieg often visited wealthy homes of patrons to partake in dinner, desserts, tea and scones, and a light concert. My favorite painting of Gustav Klimt entitled "Schubert at the Piano" shows the composer at the piano and elegant woman in art nouveau regalia illuminated by candlelight. Candlelight and classical music do indeed create the magical background for a tea dinner.

You can keep this tradition alive by hosting a chamber concert, piano recital or vocal recital in your home with a dinner or evening tea and dessert. As a concert pianist I have enjoyed performing for such gatherings in elegant homes around the US. If you are unable to host a full recital or concert, you can still have some elegant classical music on the stereo and create a lovely atmosphere.

You could make your dinner a black tie swanky affair or opt for a more casual dinner. You may even decide to host an outdoor al fresco dinner on the veranda, patio, poolside, or in a gazebo. Here are a few simple suggestions:

Candles: Candles, candles and more candles! Light your home up with beautifully lit candelabras, lanterns, tea lights or dimmer switch on chandeliers. Lighting is key to create a romantic and intimate gathering. Also you might like to create floating candle table arrangements or hanging lanterns. Digital electric candles are also safe way to go if you are concerned about fire hazards or do no like smoke. I always use electric candles when children are present. Electric candles are less expensive then you might think and many have timers or you can adjust the brightness.

Table Settings and Floral Arrangements: Consider romantic table settings with Victorian China, silver and crystal and flower arrangements featuring elegant tea roses in various shades. I often like to use Depression era glass tea cups and saucers that look like jewels against the candle light.

Music:

Classical Piano: your favorites

Chamber Music: Works by Mozart, Haydn, Vivaldi, and Beethoven are good choices.

Opera: Operas by Mozart, Rossini, Donizetti, Verdi, Offenbach, and Puccini are good choices.

Chinese New Year
Tea Luncheon

Objective: Host a Chinese New Year's tea luncheon. You might choose to serve more traditional Chinese teas such as oolong or assam, and combine Chinese flavors with traditional English. It is your choice "how Chinese" you decide to go. Fortune cookies, and psychics who read tea leaves can be a fun added touch.

MENU

Tea Sandwiches

Basil-Tomato Grilled Cheese Panini
Matcha Mango
Tahini Goddess
Watercress

Canapé

Beet-Nectarine
Black Lentil

Scones

Dried Berry
Asian Pear

Salads

Shogun Sea Slaw
Watermelon

Desserts

Jungle Jimmy Frozen Chocolate Bananas (With Adult Variation)
Mango Madness Cheesecake (Raw, No Bake)

Tea Recommendations:

Oolong (selected)
Monkey King Jasmine (scented)
Orchard Oolong (fruit
China White (white)

The Chinese are famous for their exotic teas like Assams, oolongs and white needle. A great way to start of the New Year is with a Chinese themed tea. Bring the mystic Orient into your home with an exotic Chinese New Year celebration. A few suggestions:

Read up on the animal theme for the year and its element. For example I was born the year of the Monkey and my element for the year of my birth is Earth. You could create simple little cards with fortune "outlook" for the year. You my like to put fortunes into cookies or desserts for your guest, or hide a secret gold ticket where someone wins a prize.

Here are some other suggestions:

Flowers, Table Settings and Decorations: Traditional Chinese colors include rich reds, golds, black and jade green. Consider having little table touches of the animal for the year. Little figurines of monkeys, dragons, or horses might be a nice touch. Have dramatic Chinese red lanterns, tea lights and exotic floral arrangements. Incense holders smelling of opium is another exotic touch. Consider serving tea in traditional Chinese iron teapots, and having Chinese teacups. Of course you should consider serving Chinese teas such as oolong, jasmine scented, Assam or Chinese white needle tea blends. Hanging doorway beads is also an exotic touch, as well as large silk pillows and comfortable plush sitting areas. The Victorians in England were fond of sensual Chinese opium dens. You have guest wear silk pajamas and serve tea on the floor.

Hire a tea reader: Nothing is more fun then having a professional tea reader read your tea leaves, it also ads an air of mystery to your gathering.

Wear kimonos or silk pajamas. Make your tea into a pajama party. Wearing silk and satin pjs is a sensual and relaxing experience while indulging in tea.

Music selection: Exotica jazz with a Chinese orient feel such as the music of Martin Denny or Les Baxter. Classical exotic oriental selections like Puccini's *Turandot*. Traditional Chinese music.

Classic Hollywood Cinema Luncheon

Objective: Host a classic cinema inspired tea luncheon or dinner. This could be combined with awards ceremonies on television such as the Academy Awards, or for a more intimate movie night with friends. Or you can go all out with a costume dress up party where guests come dressed as their favorite actors/actresses or characters from famous movies.

MENU

Tea Sandwiches

King Charles (Black Bean, Guacamole and Mango Wrap)
Peruvian Sandwiches (Chocolate and Avocado)
Matcha Mango
Waldorf Astoria

Canapé

Stuffed Fiesta Mushroom Canapés

Scones

Krazy Boysenberry
Irish Soda Bread

Soups

Casablanca Carrot Couscous
Willie Wonka Chocolate

Salads

Ambrosia Tropicale
Tofu Tostada Tropicana

Desserts

Chocolate Hazelnut Fudge
Empanadas (Fruit Turnovers)

Tea Recommendations:

English Breakfast (selected)
Boysenberry (fruited)
Tropical iced Tea (fruit)

California Cadillac Margaritas

I am a movie historian that specializes in a few specific genres such as film noir, Pre-Code 1930s, MGM musicals, Alfred Hitchcock and Universal Horror movies. I throw a weekly tea dinner and a movie for a few close friends. I love this ritual of lighting candles, sharing dinner, tea and desserts and watching classic movies. The channel TCM (Turner Classic Movies) have excellent programming to choose from and even free online classes. I'm currently enrolled in their "Into The Darkness" film noir series.

Guests love the cozy home feel of lounging around in recliners and over stuffed couches and watching old movies on the big screen. I have also thrown Hollywood themed costume parties where guest come as their favorite movie stars. I once threw a 1950s style movie party and dressed up like fellow Aquarius James Dean. We watched *Rebel Without A Cause* and a few Marilyn Monroe flicks.

TCM makes an amazing parlor game called *Scene It*. Look for it at Barnes and Noble or online. It is a trivia pursuit type parlor game where guests have to guess movie clips, unscramble the names of famous actors, or answer trivia. I put together little gifts sets of dvds and tea for winners. So fun and everyone talks about my movie nights for months after.

Flowers and Decorations: Go for art deco style china, teapots and silverware. Deco vases full of gorgeous flower arrangement will work well. Consider postcards of your favorite movie actors/actresses for place settings. You might go for black and white flowers tied with silver ribbons to suggest the movies. Old Movie posters are also a great idea.

Music: Jazz Piano, movie and Broadway musical scores, or your favorite old Hollywood singers like Marilyn Monroe, Frank Sinatra, Marlene Dietrich.

Movie Suggestions:

Silent Movies: Those featuring Charlie Chaplin, Laurel and Hardy, Theda Bara, Ramon Navarro, Valentino.

Pre Code: *Baby Face, Red-Headed Woman, Three On A Match, Night Nurse, Sense of Beauty, The Cheat, 42nd Street, The Divorcee, Satan's Daughter.*

Film Noir: *Rebecca, Laura, Sunset Blvd, Maltese Falcon, Mildred Pierce, Citizen Kane, D.O.A., Night of the Hunter, Scarlet Street, Panic in The Streets, Criss Cross.*

Alfred Hitchcock: *Psycho, Vertigo, The Birds, North by Northwest, The Man That Knew Too Much, Rebecca, Saboteur, Stranger on A Train.*

MGM Musicals: *Singing In the Rain, The Wizard of Oz, An American in Paris, Show Boat, Gigi, Easter Parade, Brigadoon, Kismet, Meet Me In St. Louis, Harvey Girls.*

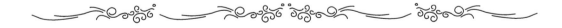

Edwardian Easter Tea Brunch

Objective: *Host a Turn of the Century, elegant Easter tea brunch. Think elegant Downton Abbey. Men and Women can wear there holiday bests and elaborate and styling hats and vintage styles is recommended. You can host your brunch inside or al fresco, especially if you a large garden, or backyard space for decorating. If children or present you can host an Easter Egg hunt or have someone dress up as the Easter bunny. Or you can keep this elegant adult. It is up to you.*

MENU

Tea Sandwiches

Lady Emily's Raspberry-Rose
Martinique Banana s
Monsieur Poire Bleu
Tofu Eggless

Canapé

Edwardian English Cucumber Canapés

Scones

Razzle Dazzle Raspberry
Sir James Decadent Dark Chocolate-Pecan

Soups

Chilled English Cucumber
Spencer Cream of Asparagus

Salads

Spencer Potato
Tempeh Garden

Desserts

Lavender-Lemon Cheesecake
Tortoni Venezia

Tea Recommendations:

Earl Grey (selected):
Vintage Rose (floral):
Pearl Peach (white):
Chocolate Mint (decaffeinated):

Raspberry-Lemonade

Easter Tea Brunch is a big deal in England and especially at Easter. After church services aristocrats in Edwardian society wearing their finest Sunday best and hats and bonnets would retire for tea brunches that were elaborately decorated.

Children would pick up their Easter baskets for Easter egg hunts, friendly games of crochet or cricket, card games, and sharing.

Flowers and Decorations: Decorate with pastel colored tea roses, colored Easter eggs, and baskets, floral pattern Victorian china and linens, birdcages, and anything that suggests springtime and nature.

Music: *Edwardian period classical music.* Debussy, Cyril Scott, English Parlor Music, harp and flute, classical chamber music, opera selections.

Easter baskets for guests: You can put simple Easter baskets together for your guests with some chocolate, tea assortment, scones to take home or other gifts.

Hats and Bonnets: Encourage your guests to wear fancy hats. You might have your guest vote on the most beautiful bonnet, the most outrageous hat etc and gift out parlor gifts.

Take Photos! Since everyone is dressed up take photos of all your guests and send them copies!

The EASTER BUNNY! Kids and adults alike can love meeting the Easter Bunny.

I have actually dressed up as the White Rabbit from *Alice in Wonderland* wearing a huge pocket watch. It was such a weird idea my guests were talking about it for weeks.

Fourth of July Tea Brunch

Objective: *Throw a patriotic red, white and blue, themed 4ᵗʰ of July tea brunch. You can go for an indoor or out door spread depending upon your mood and the weather. Backyard gardens, pool side, out in the Country or near the ocean are all good ideas. Or you can do a picnic tea brunch or dinner before firework displays.*

MENU

Tea Sandwiches

Artichoke
Lady Anne's Lemon-Dill
Lady Caroline's Strawberry Patch
Lady Mary's Blueberry Patch Tea
Waldorf Astoria

Canapé

Beat and Nectarine Raw

Scones

Aloha
Mary-Anne Blueberry Lemon Scones

Soups

Chilled Georgian Peach
Yankee Chowder

Salads

Ambrosia Tropicale
Spencer Potato

Desserts

Cherry Cobbler
Coconut-Pineapple Cake

Tea Recommendations:

Ceylon (selected):
Blueberry Ceylon (fruit)
Cherry flavored (decaffeinated)
White Island (white):

Old Fashioned Lemonade
Strawberries and Cream Ice Tea

162

Fourth of the July is a ritual for almost all Americans. We indeed enjoy our summer picnics, pool and beach parties, barbeques and fireworks. Here are a few ideas to make your Fourth of July tea magical! I have also included in the menu some recipes inspired by flavors from New England, The South, Hawaii and California.

Flowers and Decorations: I would consider red and white roses with blue flowers. Throw in some American Flags and other patriotic stars and ribbons. You might have a picnic style Old Fashioned style party. Maybe pick up red and white checkered picnic linens, some gas lanterns, and tea lights.

Or actually just pack a picnic basket and thermos of iced tea. Stores like Macy's or Bloomingdales sell gourmet picnic baskets with beautiful leather straps to hold china and silverware, a place for linen and compartments for food.

Another idea is to host a party poolside with lounge chairs, tables with umbrellas or in an old fashioned gazebo decorated with tea lights or hanging lanterns.

In the evening you could take your picnic tea basket to outdoor concert venues. I have often held picnic tea parties on the 4th while attending orchestral pops concerts with fireworks.

If you do not want to prepare a tea for the 4th, many local tearooms allow you to get a take out box of scones and pastries and large plastic cups of iced tea or lemonade. In California beachside, I can easily run to *Peet's* or other tearooms to pick up some tea and scones for the beach.

Music suggestions:

Ragtime Piano, New Orlean's Dixieland, Swing, Jazz, bluegrass country, Americana.

Gentlemen's Tea Luncheon

Objective: *An all men's gathering tea luncheon or dinner. This can be combined with playing board games, poker, or with watching sporting events. The feel should be masculine. Environments with comfortable leather couches and chairs, and dark woods work best. Think: Private men's clubs.*

MENU

Tea Sandwiches

Curried Tofu Salad
Reuben Club
Sir James (Nutella, Cream Cheese and Preserves)
Watercress

Canapé

Black Lentil Canapé

Scones

Irish Soda Bread
Sir James Decadent Dark Chocolate-Pecan

Soups

Autumn Butternut Squash
Golden Cream of Mushroom

Salads

Aztec Quinoa with Citrus Dressing
Caesar

Desserts

Blueberry Cobbler
Peanut Butter Balls

Tea Recommendations:

Russian Caravan (selected)
Vintage Rose (scented)
Black Current (decaffeinated
Gunpowder Green (green):

French Lavender Lemonade

Contrary to popular belief, many men enjoy sharing tea. It is still very popular in the U. K. but areas such as New York City, San Francisco and the South offer all male tea gatherings.

During the Victorian and Edwardian era the aristocratic sets would often pair off by gender. Women would retire to living room, a tea green house or veranda while Men would retire to a smoking room, game room or the library for intellectual conversation. Men often met for afternoon tea around 4 or 5 pm after a hard day at the office. Many men would discuss the politics and philosophies of the day; share in a competitive game of chess, checkers or card games, gamble, or share cigarettes and cigars.

Tragically homosexuality was illegal in the U. K. during the Victorian and Edwardian era and so gay man often held secret tea gatherings in student dorms on college campuses such as Oxford or Cambridge or private late night parties. Interesting traditions developed. Gay men often wore purple or lavender to distinguish themselves and prevent being arrested by undercover police. Gay men also wore gardenias in their lapels to distinguish themselves. In revolt to Victorian strict morality, heterosexuals as well as homosexuals often had private tea gatherings to unwind from the demands if protocol. Secret tea meetings were also created so men could discuss "banned" literature and music.

There is a huge renaissance gentlemen's tea movement starting. Visit the page on facebook: https://www.facebook.com/pages/The-Gentlemens-Tea-Room/1652043998347704

Flowers and Decorating: Men's gatherings prefer leather chairs, dark woods, and British Empire touches such as coat of arms, swords, and exotic world artifacts from Egypt, India, and The Orient. Think Indian Jones!

Music: classical, soft jazz or exotic music.

Parlor Games: Men enjoy playing games like Chess, Chinese Checkers, Checkers, Poker, Stratego, Monopoly etc. Have attractive board games available. Barnes and Noble is a great place to pick some up. I like to splurge and use elegant games instead of the cheap Target store variety.

Sports Tea: Your buddies will love watching "the game" with some finger sandwiches, hearty soups, scones, desserts and cup of tea.

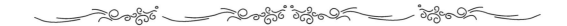

Great Gatsby's New Yorker
Tea Luncheon

Objective: *Host a lavish New York roarin' 20s style Great Gatsby estate in Long Island tea luncheon. You could host a costume party with 20s flapper/gangster attire. Create at the 20s with period music, costumes, and deco décor.*

MENU

Tea Sandwiches

Cucumber
Monte Cristo
Reuben Club
Waldorf Astoria

Canapé

Beet -Tangerine

Scones

Apple Harvest
Lemon-Ginger

Soups

Chilled Raspberry
Yankee Chowder

Salads

Blood Orange and Almond
Jicama and Melon Summer

Desserts

Apple Strudel
Raspberry Chocolate Cheesecake

Tea Recommendations:

English Breakfast (selected):
Earl Grey (scented black):
Strawberries and Cream (decaffeinated):
Spiced Green Apple (green)

Long Island Ice Tea

One of my favorite periods in history in the roaring 1920s. My mother's parents enjoyed this wild period in New York City. I can't even imagine how exciting it would have been to see the *Ziegfeld Follies,* attend Manhattan Supper Clubs, or attend the premiere of Gershwin's *Rhapsody in Blue* or better yet hanging out with Cole Porter at the Carlyle.

One of my favorite novels is *The Great Gatsby* by F. Scott Fitzgerald. The imagery of wild jazzy dinner parties at mansions on Long Island, dancing the Charleston amongst the lavish finery and art deco splendor is indeed an exciting prospect.

This is one of my favorite theme parties to show. This is due to Long Beach, California is known for having some amazing art deco attractions including the White Star line's *Queen Mary* cruise ship and hotel. Each September I attend the ship's Art Deco Festival, attending high tea on the Promenade Deck, and ballroom dancing in my 1920s finery. Here are some simple ideas to make your Gatsby party exciting with a great deal of razzle-dazzle.

Flowers and Decorating: If you happen to own art deco china or silver tea settings by all means use them! If not go for beautiful pastel roses such as those in lavender, pink, baby blue, peach, or canary yellow. Consider art deco vases. Another great touch is postcards of 1920s silent film stars, and an old 1920s style radio.

Dancing: If you have the space, like a ballroom consider playing 1920s big band music with Charleston, or some sexy tangos.

Costumes: Encourage your guest to come in 1920s period costumes. I love got get out my black and lavender pin striped double breasted and show off some of my favorite best silk art deco ties and slicking my blue black hair back like Valentino or Clark Gable.

Silent Movies: Consider showing some silent movies during your tea party. Charlie Chaplin or Laurel and Hardy for comedy. For something sexy and slightly naughty try some Valentino, Theda Bara or Louise Brooks in *Pandora's Box.* For a little darker atmosphere try some German Expressionist silent movies like: *Metropolis, Nosferatu,* and *The Cabinet of Dr. Caligari.*

Or show *The Great Gatsby* movie from the 1970s starring sexy Robert Redford, Mia Farrow and Linda Black.

Music: 1920s parlor piano music (Gershwin, Cole Porter and Irving Berlin), Paul Whiteman Orchestra, Bix Beiderbecke, Ray Noble, Louis Armstrong, or Josephine Baker are all great choices.

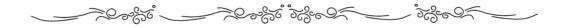

HALLOWEEN HAUNT TEA DINNER

Objective: *Serve a late night Halloween tea party. You can go all out and make it as outrageous as you like or keep it simple.*

MENU

Tea Sandwiches

Apple-Cashew
Donna Dolores Ginger-Carrot
Georgian Harvest
Pumpkin Harvest

Canapé

Fall Fig Canapé

Scones

Carnival Apple
Pumpkin Harvest

Soups

Casablanca Carrot Couscous
Sweet Potato Curry

Salads

Blood Orange and Almond
Salade Tangiers

Desserts

Castagnaccio
Diá de Muertos Pumpkin Harvest Flan

Tea Recommendations:

Earl Grey (selected)
Rooibos Pumpkin Spice (seasonal)
Masala Chai

Olde English Apple Cider

Anyone who knows me knows Halloween is my favorite holiday. I love to dress up in costumes, decorate wildy, and host haunt teas or costume parties. Halloween is a perfect time to get dramatic in your tea hosting. There are so many ideas that I will only include a few that should turn your Halloween party into a huge success.

Halloween Costume Party: Consider a costume party. You can reward the best costumes with tea gift sets. Or go for a specific theme such as *Vampire Tea Ball, 1920s Speakeasy, Victorian English Manor Tea,* or any idea that strikes your fancy.

Murder Parties: Murder parties are wickedly delicious. I host at least 2 a year. Halloween is the perfect time to host one.

Decorations: Obviously have dramatic evening lighting with jack-o-lanterns and eerie candles. Maybe even consider having guests arrive early to have some carving pumpkin time over with hot chai tea or cider with lots of cinnamon. YUM! Traditional games like bobbing for apples is fun. With the new digital media, you can create eerie paintings that move and change. Dry ice for fog our outdoor graveyard teas are also weird and wacky.

In addition consider decorating tables with fall flowers. I love the beautiful look of large blood red, orange and yellow sunflowers. Tres Vincent Van Gogh! Also throw a few maple leafs onto your dining table or coffee table.

Hire a psychic: One of my favorite jobs in my youth was working as a psychic, palm, tarot and tea leaves reader at two local Orange County New Age book Stores. My favorite was called: *Visions and Dreams.* There, I sat in this mystical Egyptian inspired tearoom. As a Goth boy of the 1980s, I used to wear a little Egyptian eyeliner and wear Gothic Victorian clothes. I actually got paid for sipping tea and reading people's fortunes. Another idea is to rent out an old mansion or if you are so fortunate to own one host a séance or maybe a little Ouija board if you dare.

Horror TV: One of my close friends is Louise Robey from the 1980s television show *Friday the 13th.* I loved this show and actually appeared as an extra in two episodes. The show centered on Mickey (played by Louise), and her cousin Ryan who inherits a creepy old antique shop with cursed objects they have to get back. Since I was a Friday the 13th baby, I especially love throwing Friday the 13th tea nights. We watch the series by the fire over tea. I'm yet to visit Louise in her beautiful home in France. Other great shows to watch are *Night Gallery, Twilight Zone, Tales From The Crypt* or *Elvira Mistress of the Dark.*

Horror Movie Night: Some of my favorites: *Burnt Offerings, The Shining, Carrie, The Omen, The Exorcist, Nightmare On Elm Street II, Frankenstein, Dracula, Phantom of the Opera (with Claude Raines), The Wolfman and Dunwich Horror.*

Music: Creepy pipe organ, harpsichord music. Horror movie soundtracks.

Goth bands: *Xymox, The Cure, Dead Can Dance, Siouxsie*

Harvest Tea Luncheon

Objective: *Host an elegant cozy Autumn tea luncheon with all the beautiful colors and flavors of the season.*

MENU

Tea Sandwiches

Apple-Cashew
Figgy Cheese
Georgian Harvest
Monsieur Poire Bleu

Canapé

Sweet Potato and Avocado

Scones

Chunky Monkey
Pumpkin Harvest

Soups

Pumpkin Harvest

Salads

Galician Gypsy Rice
Lebanese Falafel

Desserts

Apple Strudel
Pumpkin-Pecan Pie

Tea Recommendations:

Canadian Breakfast (selected)
Cinnamon Apple (fruited):
Masala Chai

Pear Cider

Anyone that knows me knows my favorite season if autumn. I love the fall colors and flavors of pumpkin spice, chestnuts, gingerbread and maple. A great way to show gratitude for all the wonderful things life has to offer is by throwing a harvest tea around Thanksgiving for your friends and loved ones. I often include a time of prayer and sharing of what we are all thankful for. Another great idea is to gift each tea guest with a small journal so they can begin the lovely habit of keeping a gratitude journal. I pick up beautiful but inexpensive journals at Big Lot's for only a few dollars. Barnes and Noble also have gorgeous journals to choose from. Another idea is having a tea where guest do a "visioning"; that is spending time to write down goals and desires for the upcoming year. I find it amazing what one can accomplish by creating a goal journal and writing thoughts down.

In the last year I have recorded 5 albums and released 3 books. I am amazed at how my creativity is flowing. I owe this burst of creativity to my spiritual support from my church and the act of visioning.

Here are a few simple Harvest Tea suggestions:

Flowers and Table Settings: Obviously decorate with rich fall colors of golds, crimson red, burnt orange, and chocolate browns. I love large table settings of sunflowers and wild flowers. Cornucopias of fresh fruit and vegetables can remind your guests of the benefits of a vegan plant-based diet and healthy organic eating. I love the look of maple leafs. I often just walk around the Bluff in my area collecting maple leafs that have fallen in all colors. I set them on my table spread.

Flavors: Obviously pick the recipes in this book that tie all the flavors of fall together brilliantly. The Menu guide will give you some of the best choices: cinnamon apple, pecans, pumpkin, gingered pear, maple syrup, cider, sweet potato, butternut squash, and figs. Oh my! Now I'm craving some maple oat scones with pecans and a cup of chai.

Candles and lighting: If you have access to a cozy fireplace, that is always a nice touch. Floating candles and candelabras are always a great idea. Also some pinecones, cinnamon scented brooms (I pick these up inexpensively at Trader Joe's) are also great ideas.

Music: Cozy fall themed cocktail piano and easy-listening orchestral albums, classical music, your favorite big band, singers and standards.

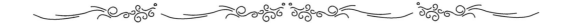

Indian Yogi Tea and Kirtan

Objective: *Host an English Empire Indian style tea for your yoga friends. You can transform your home into a yoga studio or decadent Indian opium den. Or make a sensual harem feel.*

MENU

Tea Sandwiches

Curried Tofu Salad
Figgy Cheese
Lebanese Cucumber
Matcha Mango

Canapé

Black Lentil

Scones

Apple Harvest
Cranberry Orange

Soups

Black Lentil Chili
Sweet Potato Curry

Salads

Blood Orange and Almond
Hemp Seed Tabouli

Desserts

Mango Madness Cheesecake
Pecan Bars

Tea Recommendations:

Masala Chai (selected):
5 Star Darjeeling
Tulsi Cinnamon Rose
Mango Iced Tea

Yogis often enjoy tea and sharing especially after a yoga workout or meditation. I myself enjoy sipping a spicy cup of Masala chai after a yoga workout with friends. I have often met new friends and healthy like-minded people at yoga studios and over tea.

A kirtan is a traditional gathering of Indian musicians with chanting and sung prayer called "mantra". Check your local area for yoga studios that offer tea gatherings and kirtans.

When I first moved from Newport-Mesa to Long Beach, I attended a yoga studio and Ayurveda Spa called *Omadawn*. There I met life time friends that include my dear friends Heidi, Jack, Issa, Dharma, Lonne and her radiant mother Laura who became my Reiki Mother and Master. Some of my fondest memories were kirtan gatherings at Laura's mystical home in Seal Beach. Since those days Laura and her daughter Lonne have moved to Austin, Texas. I still get together regularly with Heidi for tea in her home.

When I lived in Costa Mesa, California and was just beginning to learn about veganism, acupuncture, qi gong, yoga, and tai chi, I became close friends with my acupuncturist doctor Jeanne. Jeanne and I often attended hatha, kundalini and bikram yoga classes together as well as we took excursions down to the Deepak Chopra center or *Temple of Self Realization* in Encinitas, California. There we would meditate, attend yoga gatherings and kirtans and of course indulge in Masala chai tea.

The best chai tea I had was out of an Indian restaurant in Costa Mesa called *Mother India*. For local Southern Californians, you may make a short excursion trip to Little India in Artesia. There are several restaurants and Indian style tearooms.

It should be also noted that India was originally part of the British Empire and many Indian teas such as chai, and darjeerlings made there way into English high tea settings. English are often fond of their curries. (Try the delicious curry tofu sandwich recipe in this book).

Flowers and Table Settings: Any Hindu statues, incense burners, candles and exotic floral arrangements can give the feel of an Indian Tea. Another idea are colorful silk pillows and fabrics. I often serve Indian style tea on the floor in the evening surrounded by candles after a meditation.

Music: Try some traditional kirtan music, sitar or esraj music. Also there are many yoga inspired New Age cds with an Indian flavor or opt for some mid 60s Exotica jazz. For example: Martin Denny's *Taste of India*. Or maybe some Tantra Lounge Indian electronica? Get creative.

Incense: Incense is an important element of India. Try nag or golden champa.

Attire: Wear comfortable yoga attire or maybe silk harem pants. I love to throw yoga pillows around the floor and just lounge with friends with a cup of chai.

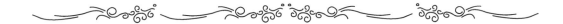

Japanese Tea Garden Luncheon

Objective: *Serve a traditional Japanese tea with the flavors of Japan. Obviously you will want to serve a traditional green or white tea, or matcha. If you are lucky enough to won a Japanese garden with a pond of coi fish, that would make a brilliant impression.*

MENU

Tea Sandwiches

Donna Dolores Ginger-Carrot
Matcha Mango
Sir James (Nutella, Cream Cheese and Preserves)
Watercress

Canapé

Bavarian Apricot Flower

Scones

Aloha
Asian Pear

Soups

Chilled Nectarine
Hawaiian Miso

Salads

Japanese Cucumber
Watermelon

Desserts

Lemon Bars
Mango Madness Cheesecake

Tea Recommendations:

Origami Sencha (selected):
Sweet Cherry Green (fruit):
Jasmine Green

Plum Wine

One of the most relaxing tea luncheons I ever had was when I was visiting a few friends in Hawaii near Honolulu. I attended a picnic style Japanese tea at a Buddhist Temple. It was one of the most beautiful scenes I have ever experienced. I sipped a lovely rare Japanese silver needle white tea which went perfect with a fruit bowl of pineapple and coconut ambrosia, miso soup and a vegan spring roll. The gardens had trees with cherry blossoms, bridges, lotus ponds and coi fish that I'm especially fond of.

When I moved to Long Beach I taught a local Doctor and his partner piano. His mid century modern home had a lovely backyard with a Japanese garden and coi fish. We often shared a cup of sencha out on his terrace.

Even if you do not have access to a Japanese Garden setting you can easily create the mood of Japan with some simple decorations and music. Here are some thoughts:

Flowers: Exotic Orchids, Lilies, Birds of Paradise and other tropical floral settings are good ideas. Also consider the simple touch of bamboo. Bamboo is inexpensive but can be a dramatic table setting.

Tea Settings: Serve tea in traditional iron teapots, or Japanese teacups and teapots.

Decorations: Japanese lanterns, screen lamps, fans, and other Japanese touches can make a huge difference.

Kimonos: Do not rule out wearing kimonos or making your party a casual pajama feel.

Spa Tea: Another idea would be to have your special loved one, spouse or significant other over and serve tea and then hire a massage therapist. Another idea is "girls" beauty day of massage, facials, painting nails and tea or a guy's day of massage and relaxation. This is a great idea for much needed R and R. One thing I have always loved about Japanese culture is the simplistic beauty, cleanly efficiency and the Japanese ability to stay in the now moment.

If you are not as familiar with Japanese teas, here is an opportunity to try out several unique teas mentioned in this book such as sencha, white tea, and matcha.

Music: Traditional Japanese Shakuhachi flute, creates a mystical tea feel. Or opt for some New Age Music with Japanese touches here are a few favorites:

Deuter's: *Buddha Nature, Bosho's Pond, Gardens of the Gods or Wind and Mountain*

London Afternoon Tea

Objective: *Create a traditional elegant London afternoon tea. You can specialize by adding additional themes of Victorian, Gothic Victorian, Edwardian, Elizabethan, Georgian.*

MENU

Tea Sandwiches

Artichoke
Basil-Tomato Grilled Cheese Panini
Cucumber
Lady Mary's Blueberry Patch

Canapé

Beet- Nectarine

Scones

Apricot
Razzle Dazzle Raspberry

Soups

Sweet Potato Curry
Tomato Basil Bisque

Salads

Jicama and Melon Summer
Tahitian Tropical with Spicy Mango Dressing

Desserts

Key Lime Tarts
Raspberry Chocolate Cheesecake

Tea Recommendations:

Earl Grey Lavender
Vintage Rose
Apricot Brandy
Gunpowder Green

Theme: *London Afternoon Tea*

London is my favorite city in Europe full of great sites to see like: The Tower of London, Buckingham Palace, Covent Gardens, The British Museum and much more. Londoners still stop in the afternoon to enjoy tea and scones with friends. Use this simple London theme to create a quiet, intimate and relaxing tea experience for you and a few friends.

Please don't feel that if you do not have a large home that you can not entertain and throw a successful tea gathering. The majority of my favorite teas are just getting together with one or two friends in my living room for afternoon tea and scones. I don't over decorate, just a few floral arrangements on coffee tables, and some candles for mood lighting. I also of course have something quiet and dreamy on the stereo like my classical or jazz albums, some soft harp music, or just the local classical station.

You might also like to use this opportunity with a few friends to watch some excellent documentaries on the estates of England. PBS put out an amazing series which are also now up on Netflix. Look for: *The Spencers of Althrop, Chatworth, Hyclere, and Windsor Castle.* Or you might decide to throw a *Downton Abbey* party.

I often get together with friends to watch a little BBC America or PBS shows over a cup of tea. (Actually any excuse to sit down and enjoy a hot scone is fine with me. LOL)

You might also use the opportunity to watch some videos with friends about tea prep, or get together to bake and create some of the recipes in this book.

If you are the type of person that feels overwhelmed by creating a full high tea, then have each guest make a dish. I do this often. In fact my friend Arlene is coming over for tea tomorrow and is baking a simple black currant scone. I'm making the soup and salad. Voila.

For decorating ideas look at English Tea rooms online. The most simple floral arrangement is just some tea roses in a vase. Keep it sweet and elegant. Also you can decide to have guest come in casual or more formal attire depending on the occasion.

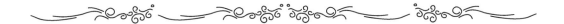

Mad Hatter Tea Party

Objective: *Host a fantastic whimsical and magical Alice in Wonderland Mad Hatter tea party.*

MENU

Tea Sandwiches

Cucumber
Lad Emily's Raspberry-Rose
Martinique Banana
Tofu "Eggless"

Canapé

Bavarian Apricot Flower

Scones

Fraises Lavande
Sir James Decadent Dark Chocolate-Pecan

Soups

Cauliflower and Vegan Cheddar
Willie Wonka Chocolate

Salads

Quebecois Pear and Arugula
Spencer Potato

Desserts

Blueberry Cobbler
Chocolate Raspberry Cheesecake

Tea Recommendations:

Earl Grey (selected)
Blackberry
Apricot Vanilla Crème
Chocolate Raspberry
Strawberry Lemonade

My favorite childhood story was *Alice in Wonderland*. Since childhood I have been fascinating by the outrageous characters and their unique personalities in this story. I am also amazed at the commentary Alice makes on Victorian values and morality. Since I was a child I have collected all things Alice! Working at Disneyland in Anaheim California in my youth as a ragtime pianist and keyboardist for their in house top 40 band, I began collecting *Alice* memorabilia. I have Alice in Wonderland tea sets, and a great deal of outrageous Cheshire Cat trinkets including: A Cheshire Cat sugar bowl, door mat, stuffed animals, blankets and even a glow in the dark Cheshire Cat watch.

Adults and children alike love Alice. Sometimes when I throw an *Alice in Wonderland* party I show either the 1950s Disney cartoon classic or the gruesome Tim Burton version.

Flowers: Obviously choose red and white roses. I often dye a few white rose petals red to give the illusion of "painting the roses red" from the story. Also I use floral arrangements in large teacups, and usually have my leather bound edition of Alice sitting on a display table. Also little trinkets such as porcelain white rabbits and Cheshire cats are nice touches. You may also have decks of cards or hearts put into the flower arrangements to create the court of the Queen of Hearts.

Table Settings: Go for red, black, pink or white settings, use fancy 3 story tiered high tea servers to display your outrageous array of diamond, heart, club and spade tea sandwiches, and fancy Alice inspired desserts. I love to add whimsical touches from the Disney movie. Children love little simple keepsakes. I have little gifts like Disney key rings, etc.

Costume Party: You could decide to make your Alice party a costume party. Boys can wear outrageous Mad Hatter hats. Girls could dress like Alice or the Queen of Hearts. Or have a crazy hat contest. Who every wears the most outrageous hat wins a prize such as a teacup and tea blend to take home.

Music: classical, soft jazz, or maybe Disney's *Alice in Wonderland* soundtrack

Marie Antoinette's Tea at Versailles

Objective: *Throw an elegant French Baroque Marie Antoinette tea. You can wear powdered wigs and go all out or just create a Baroque atmosphere.*

Menu

Tea Sandwiches

Cucumber
Lady Caroline's Strawberry Patch
Monte Carlo
Monsieur Poire Bleu

Canapés

Black Lentil Canapé
Dijon Potatoes

Scones

Fraises Scones Lavandes
French Vanilla

Soups

French Onion Soup
Potage Saint-Germain (French Split Pea Soup)

Salads

Niçoise Salade
Quebecois Pear and Arugula

Desserts

Chocolate Berry Parfait
Lavender Lemon Cheesecake

Tea Recommendations

Darjeerling
French Vanilla (flavored)
Gingered Pear White (white)
Strawberries and Cream Iced Tea

Champagne

180

A perfect opportunity to throw an outrageous and extravagant tea would be to host a "Marie Antoinette" tea party. You could have guests come in powdered wigs and finery. You can turn your home, tearoom into a Versailles salon, or opt for an elegant garden party. Here are a few simple ideas that can make this party fun, quirky, or elaborate and elegant.

Table Settings: Opt for gorgeous china, silver, crystal and little touches of the French court such as fleur de lys, and the French regal colors of blue and silver. You could go for a French Revolution theme a la *Les Miserables* with French flags and if you really want to get crazy at a few Guignol-esque touches with a working guillotine and decapitated heads. Just teasing, but then again I wouldn't be surprised if someone hasn't already thrown a gruesome French Revolution party. This party theme is great for those who celebrates Le 14 juillet (French Independence Day). The French even in the time of Marie Antoinette loved to gamble. A roulette table or card games would be appropriate. I once did a French themed Antoinette party and if a guest betted correctly on the roulette table, they won a small tea gift package. This went over well! Great fun. Champagne cocktails are appropriate.

As a professional harpsichordist, I love the opportunity to dress up like Mozart and perform. I once performed for Anne Rice's Vampire Ball in New Orleans and I played some Couperin and Scarlatti on a French 2 manual harpsichord. Harpsichord music, Mozart or Beethoven are great ideas for background music. In fact, historically Mozart was employed in Vienna by Emperor Joseph who was the brother of Marie Antoinette. A story goes that Mozart met Marie at age 6 and after playing at the French court, jumped into her arms as said "Will you marry me? Yes or no." Mozart was such the cheeky Aquarius.

An 18th century vampire tea might be just the thing too for those Goth boys and girls out there. A perfect ambiance for a little flirting and seduction.

I once attended a rather erotic Marie Antoinette Salon Tea Party where strip poker was actually played. A bit outrageous, but with all the layers of 18thc clothing the anticipation was intense. Note: no one actually got butt naked. But again for those adult swinger types this might be a perfect theme. Oh and of course "let them eat cake."

Chandeliers, candles and crystal is appropriate.

Music: French Baroque, Mozart, Haydn, Baroque opera especially those by Lully or Rameau.

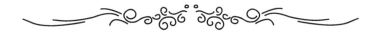

Mother's Day Tea Brunch

Objective: *Host a Mother's Day spring high tea brunch.*

MENU

Tea Sandwiches

Cucumber Tea
Lady Emily's Raspberry-Rose
Tahini Goddess
Waldorf Astoria

Canapé

Bavarian Apricot Flower

Scones

Lemon Poppyseed
Savannah Peach

Soups

Avgolemono
Chilled English Cucumber

Salads

Melon and Jicama
Tempeh Garden

Desserts

Granita Muscato
Lavender Lemon Cheesecake

Tea Recommendations:

Champagne Breakfast (selected0:
Vintage Rose (floral)
Peaches and Cream (fruit)
Springtime Plum and Pear (green):

Mimosa

Nothing says Mother's Day like a beautiful tea brunch honoring your mom. Ladies after church often like to wear fancy hats and finery. This is a tradition not only in England but throughout the United States as well.

It is traditional that if your mother is still alive to give her red roses, or you may decorate for your tea with red roses. If your mother has passed on then white roses is appropriate.

Actually a beautiful colored pastel tea rose may be used in decorating for a Mother's Day Tea Brunch. Pick your mother's favorite tones. I prefers lavender tea roses mixed with ivory. When I was in Savannah I attended a Mother's Day tea luncheon decorated with beautiful peach colored roses. The effect was dazzling.

Of course you will want get out the best china, silver, and crystal, and play with ideas. Be sure to set aside a table for Mother's Day gifts.

Music is essential for creating the perfect elegant ambiance. Here are a few suggestions:

Classical Piano:
Jazz Piano
Classical Harp Music
Baroque Masters: Vivaldi's *Four Seasons,* J. S. Bach *Brandenburg Concerti*
Soft Jazz Vocals: Julie London, June Christy, Johnny Hartman,
Frank Sinatra
Soft Pop Orchestra: Jackie Gleason Orchestra, Nelson Riddle, Axel Strodahl, Les Baxter.

Murder Mystery Tea Dinner

Objective: Throw a late night murder mystery theme tea dinner.

MENU

Tea Sandwiches

Lady Mary's Blueberry Patch
Peruvian Chocolate and Avocado
Tarragon-Herb
Waldorf Astoria

Canapé

Mushroom and Caramelized Onion Polenta Bites

Scones

Krazy Boysenberry
Sir James Decadent Dark Chocolate-Pecan

Soups

Cherry and Dumplings
Golden Cream of Mushroom

Salads

Nicoise
Salade Tangiers

Desserts

Cherry Cobbler
Pistachio Matcha Torte

Vintage Tea Leaf: Teas

Platinum Earl Grey
Blueberry Vanilla
Chocolate Coconut
Oolong

Murder mystery dinners are exciting affairs. Usually guests will dress up as a suspect character and through the service of a 3 course dinner will try to discover which guest is the murderer. Usually and traditionally there are four male and four female guests acting as suspects. However murder parties have become so popular that there are now parties that have suspects up to 45 guests and more as well as all male or all female parties. The themes are fun and can include: English Victorian Manor, 1920s Speakeasy, 1940s World War II, Civil War, High School Reunions, Vampire Teas and much more. Murder parties work so well with tea because you can serve tea and sandwiches to guest when they arrive, then begin round 1 of the murder, serve scones —soup and salad, then round II, and finish with dessert and round three.

Dramatic lighting, music, dancing and costumes can all help to create the perfect atmosphere. Murder party kits can be purchased online. Here are a few of my favorite websites:

mymsyteryparty.com
nightofmystery.com
host-party.com
murdermysterygames.com

New Orleans Mardi Gras Tea Luncheon

Objective: Throw a festive Mardi Gras flavored tea luncheon.

MENU

Tea Sandwiches

King Charles (Black Bean, Guacamole and Mango Wrap)
Lady Anne's Lemon –Dill
Monte Cristo
Tarragon-Herb

Canapé

Dijon Potatoes

Scones

French Vanilla
Spencer Key Lime

Soups

Chilled Nectarine
French Onion

Salads

Blood Orange and Almond
Nicoise

Desserts

Chocolate Berry Parfait
Lavender Lemon Cheesecake

Tea Recommendations:

Pirate Tea (Black Ice Tea with Rum).
Veranda (fruit):
French Plum
Jasmine Green

Champagne Toast

Mardi Gras (often in mid to late February) is a most festive time in the Christian calendar before the start of Lent. Mardi Gras or Fat Tuesday is a huge festival of parties, parades and festivities. Often called Carnival it happens all over the world besides the most noted city of New Orleans. Most people have heard of the Carnival of Venice, or Carnivale in Rio. You can create any one of these festivities for an exotic and interesting tea ceremony. Here are some festive ideas:

Mardi Gras: Decorate your table with festive china, crystal and silver. New Orlean's French touches are appropriate such as Mardi Gras masks, beads, confetti, Dixieland jazz motifs, and colorful regal colors such as purples, royal blues, golds and silvers. Consider having a masquerade tea party where guests wear costumes or at least masks. For music try: Dixieland, Ragtime Piano, Jazz: especially Louis Armstrong and Sydney Bechet. Or most jazz standards would be appropriate.

Carnival of Venice: For a Carnival of Venice theme, think Baroque and elaborate. Gold and guilding, chandeliers, and dramatic lighting and decorating with porcelain harlequins and clowns. You could serve Italian dishes or desserts with your tea. (The Tiramisu recipe in this book is delicious). For music try Italian Baroque masters: Works by Antonio Vivaldi or harpsichord works by Domenico Scarlatti.

Carnival of Rio: For a Brazilian themed party consider having exotic tropicale touches such as birds in cages, tropical floral arrangements, and exotic tropical desserts such as the mango cheesecake recipe in this book. For music think bossa nova and samba: Sergio Mendes and Brasil 66, Astrud Gilberto and Jobim are all good choices.

Pretty In Pink Tea Party

Objective: *Throw an all pink girl's tea party, or an 80s theme "Pretty in Pink" movie party. Other ideas or pink shabby chic, or pink gay Drag tea ball.*

MENU

Tea Sandwiches

Artichoke
Lady Anne's Lemon-Dill
Lady Emily's Raspberry Rose
Watercress

Canapés

Beat-Nectarine
English Cucumber

Scones

French Vanilla
Razzle Dazzle Raspberry

Soups

Cherry and Dumplings
Irish Potato-Leek

Salads

Blood Orange and Almond
Watermelon

Desserts

Coconut Pineapple Cake
Lemon Bars

Tea Recommendations:

English Breakfast (selected)
Green with Lemongrass (green)
Vintage Rose (scented)
Rooibos (herbal)

Pink Lemonade

All little girls love the color pink and if you want to go for an ultra feminine tea, you could go all out with an all pink theme. You may also decide to pick a specific era to focus on to add drama to your pink party. Here are some suggestions:

Victorian: Pick pink china and pink glasses. Decorate with pink roses and other pink flowers. Be sure to serve Old-Fashioned Pink Lemonade in an attractive display.

French Shabby Chic: Oooh la la. Mix your pink with black and white. Eiffel Towers, Pink Poodles, Pink French Hat Boxes and Pink perfume bottles may give the right vintage touch of Paris of the 1920s-1950s.

Pink Barbie Dream Party: Little girls love to play with Barbie, and you could create a little girls' Barbie party with a pink theme.

Pretty in Pink 1980s Retro Party: You could recreate the classic 1980s movie with guests wearing retro 1980s clothes, showing the movie, and playing favorite 80s New Wave music. This might be a perfect idea for a 1980s high school reunion get together.

Music: Music can help create the appropriate feel.

Victorian: romantic and impressionist classical music selections, harp music

French Shabby Chic: French singers like: Edith Piaf, Francoise Hardy, Charles Aznavour, Juliette Greco, Serges Gainesbourg. Or choose Ultra Lounge: *A Bachelor in Paris.*

Pink Barbie Dream Party: Pick your child's fun music. Everything from Disney tunes to Lady Gaga might be appropriate.

Pretty in Pink 1980s retro: New Wave bands like: Culture Club, Duran Duran, Spandau Ballet, Tears For Fears, Eurhythmics. Or solo female artists like: Madonna, Stacey Q, Paula Abdul and Janet Jackson.

Russian Tea Room

Objective: Throw a Russian themed "Dr. Zhivago" or Csar themed Russian tea.

MENU

Tea Sandwiches

Curried Tofu Salad
Figgy Cheese
Sir James (Nutella, Cream Cheese, Preserves)
Watercress Tea

Canapé

Black Lentil

Scones

Cherry Almond
Grandma Sarah's Scottish

Soups

Creamy Zucchini Dill
Russian Borscht

Salads

Blood Orange and Almond
Caesar

Desserts

Cherry Cobbler
Holiday Date Squares

Tea Recommendations:

Russian Caravan
Brandy Apricot
Cherry Vanilla
Black Currant

Theme: *Russian Tea Room*

Recreating the winter world and exoticism of St. Petersburg and Moscow can be exciting and stimulating for a tea party. The Russians have their own traditions of partaking in tea that would take too long to give a full history on. However you may read about Russian Tea traditions by picking up the book *The Russian Tea Room Cookbook* by Faith Stewart-Gordon. Her book recreates famous Russian recipes from the famed New York Russian Tea Room.

Russian tea is often smoky and robust as the black tea leaves are roasted in leather satchels. Russians often sweeten their tea with dark cherries. Partaking of tea started as early as 1638 in Russia.

Russian Tea in the United States often refers to a spicy winter tea blend of blacks mixed with hot spices like ginger, cloves and cinnamon with oranges, lemons and even pineapple. Russian evokes a wintery world and thus in recreating a Russian Tea Room you might want to keep that in mind or look at photos of the famed NY Russian Tea Room for photos and ideas.

Decorations: If possible try to locate traditional Russian teacups and settings as well as a silver samovar (Silver canister Russians make tea in). Use wintery floral settings, and dark rich colors. Touches of Faberge eggs would also be appropriate.

Music is important for creating the right atmosphere. Favor classical Russian composers such as: Tchaikovsky, Borodin, Mussorgsky and Rachmaninoff.

Saint Patrick's Irish High Tea Luncheon

Objective: *Throw an Irish Saint Pattie's Day High Tea Luncheon.*

MENU

Tea Sandwiches

Cucumber
Matcha Mango
Lady Mary's Blueberry Patch
Tofu Eggless

Canapé

Dijon Potatoes

Scones

Irish Soda Bread
Lemon-Ginger

Soups

Cherry and Dumplings
Irish Potato Leek

Salads

Melon and Jicama
Spencer Potato

Desserts

Blueberry Cobbler
Lemon Bars

Tea Recommendations:

Irish Breakfast
Jasmine Cream
Black Currant
Sencha (green)

The Irish love their high tea just as much as the English, and Saint Patrick's Day is a perfect time to partake in traditional Irish tea cuisine with all it's elegance and of course your best greenery.

Irish tea is often not as fancy and elegant as the English equivalent due to the fact there was more working class in Ireland. The Irish still had their twist on foods and service. Irish often cooked scones with oats, raisins and black currants. Potato and Leeks would be a simple but hearty soup choice. Irish aristocrats would follow the English example and partake of cucumber or watercress sandwiches.

Table Settings: Obviously you will want to set your finest greenery. Green linens, green china or glassware can help create the holiday mood. I often cut tea sandwiches into the shape of shamrocks or clubs. I also have a recipe for Old Fashioned "mint" lemonade that adds a touch of green crème de menthe to create a brilliant vibrant green. In Savannah, Georgia they go all out on St. Paddie's and actually put green food coloring in public fountains. You may also decorate with Celtic Crosses and Celtic knot patterns.

Music: Music obviously helps to create the right ambiance, and I would opt for the Celtic Harp, Irish Folk ensembles or Celtic choral music to create a quiet but elegant Irish feel.

Costumes: Have guests where their finest greenery or go all out and dress up like leprechauns

Fortune Telling: Hiring a fortuneteller might be a fun addition. The Celts often liked to have their fortune told through runes, tealeaves or tarot cards. A fortuneteller might bring a little drama and excitement to your event.

Salon de Paris
Tea Luncheon

Objective: Create a Parisien themed tea luncheon.. ooo la la

MENU

Tea Sandwiches

AALT (Avocado, Alfalfa, Lettuce, Tomato)
Monte Cristo
Monsieur Poire Bleu
Tarragon Herb

Canapé

Dijon Potatoes

Scones

Fraises Lavande
French Vanilla

Soups

French Onion
Potage Saint Germain (French Split Pea)

Salads

Nicoise
Quebecois Pear and Arugula

Desserts

Chocolate Berry Parfait
Lavender Lemon Cheese Cake

Tea Recommendations:

Champagne Breakfast (select):
French Vanilla Bean (flavored)
Apricot Brandy
Springtime Plum and Pear (green)

Champagne

Believe it or not the French do high tea just as well as the English with great flair and festive flavors. There are so many fabulous "eras" of Paris to choose from when creating your perfect French tea luncheon: Here are a few favorites:

Baroque Versailles: Recreate the private salons of Louis XIV at Versailles. Powdered wigs, and all the fluff that goes with it.

Vive la France French Revolution: Recreate the time of Marie Antoinette and let and "Let them eat Cake!" minus of course the guillotine.

Belle Époque: Create the Paris of late 1800s with imagery from the Moulin Rouge, Parisien Salons with elegant waltzing and gaiety, or a masked opera ball a la Phantom of the Opera perhaps?

Lost Generation Era: Recreate the salons of Gertrude Stein and the art world of Picasso. Maybe some art deco. Paris of the 1920s with a little Josephine Baker playing in the background.

Paris Shabby Chic Retro 1950s: Ooooo la la, lots of pinks, whites and blacks, pink poodles, Eiffel Tours, and Coco Channel perfumerie.

Music Programming:

Baroque Versailles: Harpsichord music by Francois Couperin, Operas by Jean-Phillippe Rameau.

French Revolution: Mozart, Haydn or Beethoven Chamber Music

Belle Époque: Offenbach's Can Can

Lost Generation: James Spencer's *Piano Classics For Reflection.* Chanteuses: Edith Piaf, Josephine Baker, and Maurice Chevalier

Paris Shabby Chic 1950s: *Ultra Lounge's A Bachelor in Paris,* Serge Gainsbourg

Southern Plantation Tea Luncheon

Objective: Recreate the antebellum grandeur of *Gone With the Wind,* in this Southern inspired tea luncheon

MENU

Tea Sandwiches

Galician Apricot
Georgian Harvest Tea
Lady Anne's Lemon-Dill
Tofu Eggless

Canapé

Dijon Potatoes

Scones

Mary-Anne Blueberry Lemon
Savannah Peach

Soups

Chilled Georgian Peach
Creamy Wild Rice

Salads

Galician Gypsy Rice
Melon and Jicama

Desserts

Georgian Peach Cobbler
Lavender Lemon Cheesecake

Tea Recommendations:

English Breakfast
Ginger Peach Tea
Lemon Grass Green
Iced Southern Sweet Tea

My favorite area of the USA is the SOUTH. Growing up in Florida as a child, we often visited cousins and family in Georgia. When I was older my partner's family was from Savannah, Georgia which quickly became my favorite city in the US. I love lush gardens and sub tropical weather, antebellum homes, and Southern gentility and good manners. The South always feels homey, and people have been so loving and pleasant to me. I have spent a great deal of times in cities like: Savannah, Charleston, New Orleans, and Galveston. I plan to relocate back to the South hopefully within the next few years. The South has kept the elegant traditions of high tea alive, often with Southern flavors and traditions such as iced Sweet tea or Pirate tea with rum. I also love peach cobblers and other Southern flavors. A plantation style party is perfect for spring and summer season especially if you have a porch veranda or landscaped backyard to create ambiance.

Flowers: All types of flowers especially those you would find in the South are recommended: Honeysuckle, jasmine, hibiscus, orchids, lilies, tea roses, and anything that inspires your fancy. Check with your florist for other ideas.

Table Settings: fine Victorian china, crystal, silver. If serving your luncheon al fresco considering gazebos with hanging lanterns, tea lights or gas lanterns.

Consider having guest come in Southern "Gone With the Wind" attire. Or go for a more casual comfortable summer wear feel. My parents have a large pool. We often enjoy sipping ice tea and finger sandwiches and large salads by the pool.

Music: Ragtime Piano Parlor Music, Dixieland, or the Johnny Mercer soundtrack to *Midnight in The Garden of Good and Evil* are all great choices.

Parlor Games: Men especially enjoy playing games with their tea. Here are a few favorites: Chess, Chinese Checkers, Stratego (you could have a North against South tournament), Risk, Old Maid, Bridge or Poker.

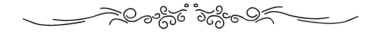

The Spencers of Althrop
High Tea

Objective: *To create a tea similar to tea presented at The Spencers' at Althrop. Paying homage to Princess Diana.*

MENU

Tea Sandwiches

Artichoke Tea
Cucumber Tea
Lady Emily's Raspberry-Rose
Sir James (Nutella, Cream Cheese, Preserves)

Canapé

Beet -Nectarine

Scones

Grandma Sarah's Scottish
Razzle Dazzle Raspberry

Soups

Spencer Cream of Asparagus
Spencer Sweet Pea

Salads

Melon and Jicama
Spencer Potato

Desserts

Blueberry Pie
Chocolate Raspberry Cheesecake

Tea Recommendations:

Royal English Breakfast
Prince of Wales Tea
Vintage Rose
Cherry Vanilla
White Diamond (white)

The Spencers are one of the most noted aristocratic families in England. I'm honored and fascinated by my family heritage. Charles Spencer, the current Earl, is the oldest brother of the late Princess Diana. The family estate is located in Northamptonshire called Althrop. The estate has been in the family for over four hundred years. Charles Spencer has written a wonderful documentary history about our family and the intriguing history of the estate.

At Althrop, they grow a lovely sweet pea "Spencer sweet pea" and there is local cuisine of Northampton I include in this book including vegan versions of sweet pea soup and cream of asparagus as well as the Lady Diana's favorite twist on traditional cucumber sandwiches with lemon and dill.

The Spencers are one of the only families in England that still own their estate. They are longtime allies and friends to the Washingtons (George Washington's family). The Spencers are also one of the few families in England that have a large gallery of rare art.

Flowers and Decorations: Consider any memorial to Lady Diana, Spencer's coat of arms, roses of all types (Spencer's family color is sweet pea or pastel green). I have created beautiful arrangements with ivory roses, sweet pea, wisteria, lilies, orchids etc.

Settings: If possible try soft green linens, and china with floral patterns.

Music: light classical especially English composers

Steampunk Tea Luncheon

Objective: *Host a steampunk explorer tea luncheon.*

MENU

Tea Sandwiches

Reuben Club
Sir James (Nutella, Cream Cheese, Preserves)
Tofu Eggless

Canapé

Mushroom and Caramelized Onion Polenta Bites

Scones

Savory Rosemary Tomato
Sir James Decadent Dark Chocolate-Pecan

Soups

Creamy Tomato
Ethiopian Peanut

Salads

Chinese Cole Slaw
Tahitian Tropical with Spicy Mango Dressing

Desserts

Mango Madness Cheesecake
Pistachio Matcha Torte

Tea Recommendations:

Black with White Lotus
Blackberry Sage
Black Currant
Gunpowder Green

Steampunk refers to a subgenre of science fiction and sometimes fantasy—also in recent years a fashion and lifestyle movement—that incorporates technology and aesthetic designs inspired by 19th-century industrial steam-powered machinery. Although its literary origins are sometimes associated with the cyberpunk genre, steampunk works are often set in an alternative history of the 19th century's British Victorian era or American "Wild West", in a post-apocalyptic future during which steam power has maintained mainstream usage, or in a fantasy world that similarly employs steam power. It may, therefore, be described as neo-Victorian. Steampunk is perhaps most recognizably features anachronistic technologies or retro-futuristic inventions as people in the 19th century might have envisioned them, and is likewise rooted in the era's perspective on fashion, culture, architectural style, and art. Such technology may include fictional machines like those found in the works of H. G. Wells and Jules Verne, or the modern authors Philip Pullman, Scott Westerfeld, Stephen Hunt and China Miéville. Other examples of steampunk contain alternative history-style presentations of such technology as lighter-than-air airships, analogue computers, or such digital mechanical computers as Charles Babbage's Analytic Engine.

I am a huge Steampunk fan, and I enjoy partaking in the culture which combines Victorian styles with science fiction and fantasy.

Flowers and Table Settings: If possible serve tea and food with either Victorian china settings or silver and copper. Find interesting gears, and industrial age imagery such as toy trains, hot air balloons, and model planes. Exotic world flowers and eccentric and unusual flower arrangements are suggested.

Costumes: Have guest come in their finest Steampunk attire.

Men: Wear Victorian colorful brocade vests, ascots, Victorian frock coats and capes, train engineer clothing, aviator wears with goggles, boots, knickers, paperboy caps, watches with gears, chocolate leather adventurer wear. Men can wear their hair in Victorian slicked back styles, or grow handlebar moustaches.

Women: sexy corsets, Victorian dresses, Victorian bonnets, spiked boots, broaches, Victorian jewelry, parasols, laced gloves. Women can wear their hair up or in ringlets.

Music: Victorian parlor piano music, light classical or ragtime

Victorian Afternoon High Tea

Objective: *Serve a late afternoon elegant Victorian style traditional high tea.*

MENU

Tea Sandwiches

AALT (Avocado, Alfalfa, Lettuce and Tomato)
Cucumber Tea
Lady Caroline's Strawberry Patch
Tofu Eggless

Canapé

Bavarian Apricot Flower

Scones

Apricot
Dried Very Berry

Soups

Chilled English Cucumber
Sweet Potato Curry

Salads

Spencer Potato
Tempeh Garden

Desserts

Chocolate Hazelnut Fudge
Lavender Lemon Cheesecake

Tea Recommendations:

Prince of Tales
Vintage Rose
Earl Grey
Rooibos Masala Chai
Sencha (green)

Afternoon tea served at 3 or 4 pm, is a tradition amongst the middle and upper classes in Victorian England. Since dinner was often served late at 8 or 9 pm, afternoon tea was a gathering to allow aristocrats to relax and have a little food, tea and sharing with friends. Often afternoon tea would include one or two teas, finger sandwiches or canapés and scones served with Devonshire Cream, lemon curd, preserves or orange marmalade. Occasionally a small desert like a fruit tart, petite cake or cookies/shortbread would be served.

Flowers: Tea roses in beautiful shades such as white, red, pink, yellow, lavender, peach, or mint green would be arrange in lovely crystal or porcelain vases. Feel free to throw in other flowers that compliment roses such as hydrangeas, gardenias, lilies, carnations etc.

Tea Settings: Serve tea and cuisine with Victorian china or silver. Consider soft linens, glass menagerie and other Victorian touches.

Candles: Long stemmed candles in candelabras, tea lights, Victorian oil lamps, chandeliers, and dimmed lighting adds ambiance.

Victorian Era Piano Music, Opera, Chamber Music

Victorian Christmas Holiday Tea

Objective: *Serve a festive holiday Christmas tea.*

MENU

Tea Sandwiches

Apple-Cashew
Lady Anne's Lemon-Dill
Pumpkin Harvest
Tarragon Herb

Canapé

Fig

Scones

Cranberry-Orange
Sir James Decadent Dark Chocolate-Pecan

Soups

Pumpkin Harvest
Vegetable Quinoa

Salads

Blood Orange and Almond
Salade Tangiers

Desserts

Cherry Cobbler
Winter Peppermint Patties

Tea Recommendations:

Snow Dragon Oolong (selected)
French Vanilla Plum (flavored fruit)
English Spiced Pudding (holiday)
Berries in the Snow (white)

Vegan Eggnog Hot Toddy
Hot Cocoa

A Victorian style Christmas brings to mind the world of Charles Dickens with cozy fireplaces, beautiful Victorian Christmas Tree and holly, mistletoe, elegant candlelit dining with fine china, and the smell of mulled cider and plum pudding.

In my family we would sit on Christmas Eve by a fireplace in our Victorian living room, opening gifts, and sipping hot tea with some scones, or better yet gingerbread. I always have fond memories of the coziness. My mother would usually put on some Elizabethan Renaissance Christmas albums, or maybe Handel's *Messiah*. We would often wear Victorian regalia and I would opt for a velvet dinner jacket, paisley silk ascot, and pressed black slacks. Dressing up was always part of the fun and I encourage you to have your guest dress in Dicken's apparel or at least favorite Christmas sweaters, scarves and Santa hats.

Here are a few ideas to make your Christmas tea elegant and spectacular.

Flowers: Holly and ivy, poinsettias, pinecones, red and white roses. Mistletoe.

Christmas Tree: Decorate a Christmas tree with Victorian ornaments and ribbons. There are kits you can buy online. If you have a fireplace, consider hanging stockings.

Candles: Consider holiday candles, candelabras, or floating candles

Decorations: Gingerbread houses, Victorian dolls, Nutcrackers, Santa dolls, Angels, Snow scenes.

Movies: *It's A Wonderful Life, A Christmas Carol, The Nightmare Before Christmas, The Grinch That Stole Christmas, A Charlie Brown Christmas, Frosty The Snowman, Rudolph The Red Nose Reindeer*

Music:

Victorian: Heavenly Angelic Light Orchestra: *Victorian Christmas;* Carlisle Ensemble: *Victorian Christmas;* Craig Duncan: *Victorian Christmas*

Lounge: *Ultra Lounge Series: Christmas Cocktails I and II,* The Carpenters' *Christmas Collection,* Frank Sinatra's *Christmas Collection, A Charlie Brown Christmas.* Perry Como's *Christmas Collection*

Baroque: G. F. Handel's *Messiah;* J. S. Bach's *Magnificat;* Antonio Vivaldi's *Gloria;* Charpentier *Messe de Noel.*

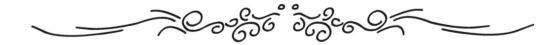

Victorian Valentine's Tea Luncheon

Objective: *Serve a romantic Victorian style Valentine's Day tea.*

MENU

Tea Sandwiches

Greek
Lady Emily's Raspberry-Rose
Sir James (Nutella, Cream Cheese and Preserves)
Watercress

Canapé

Edwardian English Cucumber

Scones

Razzle Dazzle Raspberry
Sir James Decadent Dark Chocolate-Pecan

Soups

Barcelona Roasted Red Pepper
Willy Wonka Chocolate

Salads

Ambrosia Tropicale
Quebecois Pear and Arugula

Desserts

Chocolate Raspberry Cheesecake
Coconut Pineapple Cake

Vintage Tea Leaf: Teas

Champagne Breakfast (selected)
Chocolate Raspberry Rum (dessert)
White Diamond (white)
Vintage Rose (floral scented)

Nothing says I love you more then intimate sharing with close friends or your significant other on *Valentine's Day*. Even in you are single, loving yourself with a cup of tea and some light cuisine indulgence can be replenishing to your soul. As an Aquarius man born on February 13, *Valentine's Day* is has not only been an extended birthday for myself but a time of sharing with the special someone in my life, good friends, family and my nephews and nieces. Victorian *Valentine's Day* celebrations are a perfect time to create a romantic, dreamy and intimate gathering. Here are a few suggestions in preparing for your gathering:

Flowers: Traditional Victorian indicates red, pink and white roses. Consider placing flowers in ruby red glass vases, or lovely porcelain or crystal settings. Pink and white tulips, carnations or tulips are also a good choice.

Decorations: Visit a stationery store to find vintage Victorian Valentine's Day postcards, table setting nametags, and other decorations. Hearts are the obvious. If possible consider white, red or pink table linens, and coordinating china, silver, or glass. A friend of mine served her tea with cranberry glass tea settings. It was stunning.

Sandwiches and Desserts: Consider cutting tea sandwiches into the shape of hearts. There are several delicious recipes in this book. Favor romantic flavors of chocolate, raspberries, strawberries and pair with a romantic tea like Vintage rose.

Music: light classical, harp and flute, jazz standards (romantic ballads), light easy-listening orchestral like Jackie Gleason's *For Lovers Only*.

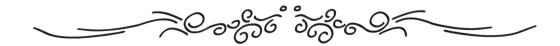

James Ross Spencer II

James is an internationally recognized concert pianist, harpsichordist and recording artist. His jazz and classical piano albums have been featured on radio stations internationally. Look for interviews with him as well as selected tracks on weekly jazz and lounge shows such as: *The Cocktail Nation, Evenings At The Penthouse, The Martini Hour* and *The Cool Jazz Collection.*

James currently resides oceanside in Belmont Shore, California where he is the founder of *Spencer Music and Artist Development.* He coaches students of all ages and levels in music and acting. As an artist developer and agent he develops new talent, specifically working with talented high school and college students.

A U.S. professor and preparer for The University of West London: London College of Music graded performance and theory exams and diploma programs, Mr. Spencer enjoys preparing artists for entrepreneurial careers in the arts.

A vegan activist for nearly 20 years, James has released vegan cook books and *Vegan Tea Time* is an expanded version of his limited edition release *The Vintage Vegan.* James is the founder of the Vintage Vegan movement: Vegans who enjoy a retro lifestyle that get together to partake in vegan tea ceremonies. The Vintage Vegans include members of the communities of: Victorians, Edwardians, Gothic Victorians, Steampunk, Retro 50s-70s Lounge, Urban Hipsters and Retro Roarin' 20s fans.

In addition to a Master of Music degree from California State University, Fullerton (1995), James holds a diploma in clinical hypnotherapy graduating with honors from Hypnosis Motivation Institute in Tarzana, California in 2006. There he studied in addition to several holistic modalities, nutrition.

James, a passionate vegan and high tea enthusiast, has studied the art of tea blending, reading of tealeaves, and vegan cuisine for nearly twenty years. James is passionate about the new movement towards vegan high tea, and hopes *The Vintage Vegan* will inspire others to choose a vegan plant-based diet and choose healthier alternatives for vegan tea ceremonies.

James Spencer would love to hear from you. Please feel free if you enjoyed this book to write him a positive review at Amazon. James plans to create more tea books in the future. Feel free to send photos of your tea gatherings, your favorite vegan recipes, and feedback on your favorite recipes in this book, or suggestions to **spencermusicschool@gmail.com.**

For information on upcoming book signing, workshops, album releases, recitals and tours, or private music/acting coaching at Spencer Music or via Skype, visit: **jamesrspencer.com.** You may also sign up there for his periodical newsletter, or you may read his monthly blogs.

Wishing you radiant health, veganism that promotes life and respect for Mother Earth, elegant and intimate tea gatherings, and enjoyment of the recipes in this book.

Signing off to enjoy a cup of Oolong tea and scone.

James Spencer

Web: **jamesrspencer.com**
Email: **spencermusicschool@gmail.com**

Made in the USA
Middletown, DE
20 July 2020